Sandino

The profound hypocrisy and inherent barbarism of bourgeois civilization lies unveiled before our eyes, turning from its home, where it assumes respectable forms, to the colonies, where it goes naked.

Karl Marx

Sandino

By Gregorio Selser

translated by Cedric Belfrage

Monthly Review Press
New York and London

972.85051
Se 4s
1195℔
oct 1981

Originally published as Sandino, general de hombres libres by Editorial
Diogenes, S.A., Mexico, D.F., copyright 1978 by Editorial Diogenes, S.A.

Library of Congress Cataloging in Publication Data

Selser, Gregorio.
    Sandino.

    Translation of: Sandino, general de hombres
libres.
    Includes bibliographical references and index.
    1. Sandino, Augusto César, 1895–1934.
2. Nicaragua—History—1909–1937.   3. Revolution-
ists—Nicaragua—Biography.   I. Title.
F1526.3.S24S4413   972.85'051'0924 [B]   80-8086
ISBN 0-85345-558-9   AACR2
ISBN 0-85345-559-7 (pbk.)

Monthly Review Press
62 West 14th Street, New York, N.Y. 10011
47 Red Lion Street, London WC1R 4PF

Manufactured in the United States of America

10 9 8 7 6 5 4 3 2 1

To Marta, my compañera

Contents

The Eagle Over His Quarry

Our Latin American neighbors have heard us proclaim the new faith, but they have also learned of
our new interest in naval and air bases which bring
United States marines and soldiers to their territory as permanent visitors. Their memory of our
dollar diplomacy has not yet been erased by our
current policy of restraint, and our professions of
noble intent are taken with several grains of salt.
. . . Our so-called painless imperialism has seemed
painless only to us. The Central American republics, who played host to our marines, custom directors, and bank supervisors, found the bayonet-
supported lessons in modern accounting very painful indeed. It looked at the time as if our respect for
frontiers and territorial integrity was merely the
outcome of our preference for custom houses and
central banks.

Nicholas J. Spykman[1]

From the year 1820, Europeans cascaded into the United States:
hunger and political and religious persecutions provided its growing
industry with the human material it needed. Six hundred thousand
immigrants in the 1830s, 1.7 million in the 1840s; in the 1850s, despite the imminence of civil war, nearly 2.5 million. Even that was not
enough proletarian brawn for the Northern nonslave states and for the
conquest of the legendary West by brutal conquistadors, barefaced
usurpers of lands, and greedy merchants as well as by rugged pioneers.

But something happened on January 24, 1843, which would
reverberate not only in the United States and Central America (one
of whose countries is the theme of this book) but in the economies of
the whole world. Just before the peace treaty was signed signaling
U.S. triumph over Mexico's disorganized forces, James W. Marshall,
a worker for sawmill owner John A. Sutter on the Sacramento
Valley's American River, discovered gold on Sutter's property.

A stampede resulted. No one wanted to lose the chance to get rich. What began as a trickle of intrepid prospectors to California became a furious race in which all forms of transport were too slow for the gold fever. By the end of 1849, San Francisco's few hundred inhabitants had swollen to 25,000. Few faced the dangers of crossing the immense virgin continent with its unconquered Indian tribes. Ships carried the gold-maddened horde around Cape Horn; parties were organized to defy the fevers of the Isthmus of Panama, or to cross the rivers and lakes of Nicaragua, a journey saving still more time but equally hazardous.

Capitalists formed companies to transport people between the oceans: in January 1849, five were registered in London alone, with capital of more than £1 million. The population of California zoomed from 92,000 in 1850 to 380,000 in 1858.

With time pressing hard to get at the gold, shortening the coast-to-coast distance became an obsession of shipping concerns. The solution of an interoceanic route, which had tortured the conquistadors ever since the discovery of America, became doubly enticing and urgent. Studies of what seemed to be the most logical penetration points were resumed: Mexico's Tehuantepec isthmus, the Panama isthmus which was part of Colombia, and Lake Nicaragua, a predominantly water route with little land to cross.

The Gadsden Treaty imposed on Mexico in 1853 had given U.S. President Pierce the right (never considered economically viable, hence never turned to account) to build a railroad across Mexico.[2] The Panama route was already in use, thanks to the gracious disposition of Colombia. Under the Nueva Granada Treaty of 1846, Colombia had conceded to the United States not only the right of passage for its citizens but the right to build an interocean rail link, which was finished and operating by 1855.

The Nicaraguan route involved clearing all the underbrush which cluttered U.S. and British policy and diplomacy throughout the Caribbean. The Clayton-Bulwer Treaty of 1850 included a temporary agreement between the two countries for construction of a canal across Nicaragua. This project, still today an unfulfilled dream for Nicaragua, had for more than half a century fueled the hopes of builders, financiers, politicians, and diplomats, arousing suspicions, hatreds, intrigues, and revolutions. But at a time when U.S. diplomacy remained indecisive about Panama, the fact that the Nicaraguan route was favored by the pilgrims seeking gold in California caused the first U.S. intervention in Nicaragua.

Up to the discovery of gold in the Sacramento Valley, contacts between Central and North Americans had been few and sporadic. The exceptions were occasional voyages by U.S. merchant ships or the presence of solitary diplomats. But the gold fever violently reversed the situation, to some extent rousing Central Americans from their colonial somnolence. The natives blinked with amazement at this strange, choleric, and vicious migration which, in general, left nothing useful behind it.

Thus, without any initiative from Central Americans, the time had come for them to get acquainted with their Northern "elder brothers," with that people whose illustrious figures—Paine, Franklin, Washington, Jefferson, and Madison—had had great impact on students and scholars in the isthmus.

But the visitors bore no resemblance to the image Central Americans had formed of their neighbors. Quarrelsome, drunken, and lustful, they treated their hosts stupidly and brutally. What the Hispanic tradition would have given them with goodwill and sympathy, they took with arrogant violence. The worst of the human conglomerate in the United States, pursuing the golden will-o'-the-wisp via the interocean crossing, was spewed out from the ships.

Most of these floating pigsties belonged to the famous Cornelius Vanderbilt, who had amassed a fortune from steamship lines, first on the Hudson River and Long Island Sound and then in the Atlantic. So ambitious were his schemes, according to Edward Kirkland, that they involved not only a canal across Nicaragua but financing revolutions in Central America.[3]

Apart from bringing the gold-seekers, Vanderbilt's ships symbolized a new aspect of the imperial ambition for interoceanic communication. It was no longer merely a means of satisfying European aspirations in Asia; it had become the potential instrument of penetration by the United States, a nation in full ascendancy. But in this, the aspirations of Vanderbilt, the "wise and fearless pioneer" who was studying Central America as a possible personal fiefdom, coincided with those of Britain and even of Louis Napoleon as much as with those of the U.S. establishment, which saw the isthmus as a territory it could dominate.

Thus it was no surprise that Vanderbilt got concessions for his ships, previously plying the Atlantic coast, to penetrate into the Caribbean and internally, with auxiliary lines of shallower draft, into Lake Nicaragua. He had been preceded in this business by George Law, who had founded the United States Mail Line together with Albert G. Sloo, Marshall O. Roberts, and others; and by "Mr. Harris and others" who organized the Pacific Mail Steamship Company. The former was known as the Sloo Line, the latter as the Harris Line. The Sloo Line brought passengers and cargo from New York to what is now the city of Colón on the Atlantic coast of Colombia's province of Panama: from Colón passengers and cargo proceeded overland to the city of Panama on the Pacific, whence the Harris Line completed the voyage to San Francisco. The trip cost $600 first-class, $125 in steerage: relatively dear considering that the U.S. government subsidized the transport of mail.

Vanderbilt envisaged fat profits and went to Britain for financing of a shorter competing line across Nicaragua. He didn't get it but arranged to charter eight big ships on both oceans and enter the lists against Sloo and Harris. His passengers went by sea to the San Juan River mouth, upriver to Lake Nicaragua and the Bay of Virgins, then covered by stagecoach the twelve miles to San Juan del Sur on the Pacific. The twenty-five coaches, painted with the white and blue of Nicaragua's flag, were an innovation; but of greater interest was the fact that passengers reached San Francisco two days earlier than by the Panama route, and paid only $300—half of what the other lines charged. The steerage fare was only $35 compared with the other lines' $125, yet without any subsidy Vanderbilt made money. He hauled two thousand passengers a month to California and most of the gold that came back with them, and pocketed $1 million a year. In 1853 he bragged to a friend of having made $11 million from the enterprise, which he called Accessory Transit Company.[4] He sold shares in the company, keeping only the 51 percent necessary to control it. With his interocean transit concession from the Nicaraguan government, he felt secure and carefree. He sent men down to build piers on both coasts, put gangs to work improving the San Juan River, and macadamized the twelve-mile road used by his coaches.

The North American invaders whom Nicaragua and Panama had to put up with were a very different lot from those who had appropriated half of Mexico's territory a few years earlier. They came in a torrent: neither colonists, nor merchants, nor missionaries, nor workers, nor even mercenary soldiers, merely a rabble inflamed by avarice and alcohol, always ready with or without pretext to whip out jackknives or to press triggers with total irresponsibility and cynicism.

Vanderbilt's influence grew in Nicaragua as it had grown in his own country. He had practically run off with his competitors' business and made a packet out of nothing but energy and imagination, not even having to resort to the methods used to dominate U.S. railroads. When he considered the business to be running smoothly he decided to take a well-earned rest. He set sail on May 20, 1853, on the *North Star,* a yacht built specially for him, leaving Accessory Transit in the care of his partners Charles Morgan and C. K. Garrison.

He returned after months of pleasure-voyaging to find Morgan and Garrison secretly buying up shares to gain control of Accessory Transit. The "Commodore" controlled his fury in a famous letter to them: "Gentlemen: You have decided to swindle me. I will not sue, for justice is slow. I will ruin you. Sincerely yours, C. Vanderbilt."

The resulting battle has much to do with subsequent events in Nicaragua, and foreshadows the tragic conflicts of which the nation would be the victim.

After the Central American countries' Pact of Federation broke up in 1838–1839 under the assaults of the Guatemalan Indian fanatic, Rafael Carrera, so-called Supreme Directors governed the Republic of Nicaragua—presidents of a sort with two-year terms. For physico-economic (today we would say geopolitical) reasons, two ideological tendencies became clearly defined. Apparent local rivalries, symbolized by the power pretensions of such cities as Granada, León, and Corinto, merely expressed commercial factors of the time. Granada represented the big coffee- and sugar-growing landowners; the Pacific port of Corinto, open to ideas as well as merchandise, represented with León the small proprietors, artisans, workers, and the budding class of retail merchants. The former were the Conservatives, the latter the Liberals.

Standing apart from these rivalries was the Caribbean coastal region dominated by the British fleet, producing fruit and precious woods, a territory traditionally lending itself to every kind of smuggling, with a mixed Indian-black population resenting white domination, ruled by British merchants who schemed as enthusiastically to stir up civil strife as to consolidate their own position in the area vis-à-vis the North Americans. One of the period's frequent civil wars brought the U.S. buccaneer William Walker on to the stage.

In August 1849, when Norberto Ramírez was Supreme Director, Nicaragua signed the first contract (modified in 1850) with a U.S. concern to undertake canalization work on the San Juan River. Among other notable events during Ramírez' term were the arrival in Nicaragua of the first U.S. minister, studious George Squier; the outbreak of a civil war on April 16, 1850; and pronouncement by the Legislative Assembly in Managua of the principle of "absolute exclusion of foreign interventions in the state's internal affairs, calling upon other Central American states to take the same position."

Ramírez (1849–1851) was succeeded in mid–civil war by Laureano Pineda (1851–1853) and then by Frutos Chamorro, last of the Supreme Directors who became Nicaragua's first president. This title was conferred on him by a constitution ratified in 1854, which provoked his adversaries to rebellion. Chamorro represented Granada (landlord class) and his enemies were led by General Máximo Jerez and Licenciado Francisco Castellón, top figures of the Liberal or democratic faction. Jerez and Castellón were exiled to Honduras, whose President Trinidad Cabañas gave the greenlight on an expedition to unseat Chamorro. They landed at El Realejo in May 1854 with a small army of Liberals, denounced Chamorro's constitution and presidency, proclaimed a return to the 1838 Charter, and named Castellón a chief of state.

Chamorro put himself at the head of "legitimist" (as his faction called itself) troops, leaving Senator José María Estrada in charge of the state. But fate willed that fever should strike down Chamorro after a few months, at which point (March 1855) Castellón offered to talk peace with Estrada. Estrada wouldn't play and the war went on.

An adventurer from the United States named Byron Cole now turned up in Nicaragua, offering Castellón the services of three hundred U.S. sharpshooters in return for cash on the barrelhead and a final payoff in state land after the Conservatives were beaten.

These mercenaries would be commanded by one William Walker, in whose name the proposal was made. To Nicaragua's misfortune, Castellón accepted the deal in a contract signed by Byron Cole and Máximo Jerez.

On June 13, 1855, Walker landed at El Realejo equipped with Nicaraguan citizenship, an ad hoc rank of colonel, and soldiers and guides of both U.S. and native extraction. Walker had won distinction in his country as a slaveholder; he had fought for the incorporation of Mexico's Alta California into the United States and, when that was achieved, had taken up arms against General Santa Anna in Mexico to carve off Baja California as well.

A detailed account of the performance of this character known as "Filibuster Walker," so fatal for Nicaragua, is beyond our present scope, but its general outlines and the reaction it produced need to be described. Walker turned defeat at Rivas in July 1855 into victory against General Santos Guardiola at La Virgen. On October 13 he took Granada by storm, having already imposed peace in September on the Conservatives' commander, General Ponciano Corral, who reluctantly signed the treaty in the name of "legitimist" President Estrada. By this time Walker had appointed himself a general.

As a consequence of the treaty, Patricio Rivas assumed the presidency on October 30. Confronted with evidence that Walker was really going to rule the country from the wings, Corral tried to conspire against the intruder. Walker discovered the plot and had Corral condemned to death before a firing squad by a war council composed of U.S. officers. On November 8 Corral became Walker's second important Nicaraguan victim. The first, shortly before, had been Estrada's foreign minister, Mateo Mayorga.

According to Stewart Holbrook, Walker's exploit had been encouraged by Morgan and Garrison, the two partner-swindlers of Cornelius Vanderbilt.[5] In apparent confirmation of this, on February 18, 1856, President Rivas, prompted by Walker, annulled Frutos Chamorro's concession permitting Accessory Transit to transport passengers and cargo across Nicaragua. On the very next day Rivas granted a new, similar concession to a concern formed by Walker and backed by Morgan and Garrison, after Treasury Secretary Fermín Ferrer (according to Isidro Fabela) had managed to get a first draft turned down on the ground that it meant selling out the country.

Walker's manipulations soon became so blatant that even his puppet Rivas tired of yes-ing him and determined—though it took him a long time—to remove all authority from the filibuster. Walker responded by repudiating the president and "provisionally" replacing him with Ferrer by decree of June 20, 1856. Rivas now summoned all Central America to arms in his defense since, as his appeal said, "the latest events in Nicaragua have shown this government the perfidy and evil with which Walker and his men attack the national interests."

So broke out a struggle that soon took on such dimensions as to be known in Central America as the National War. This indeed it was, for the filibuster brought all the Central American peoples together against Walker's attempt to become ruler not only of Nicaragua but of all five nations of the isthmus.

In a famous decree of June 26, 1856, Rivas accused Walker of having declared "in the presence of the Secretary of War and others, his determination to seize power by force." This had compelled Rivas to move his government to Chinandega, "to preserve at all costs the dignity and sovereignty of the Republic and the freedom necessary to confront the evil demands of said señor Walker for immense and inadmissible alienations of land to the foreigner, as a device to introduce political and religious innovations in Nicaragua; for annulment of popular elections of supreme authorities; and for comprehensive powers he required to be conferred on him to provide himself with resources, not excluding that of confiscating the property of private persons and selling them to foreigners. . . ."[6]

In the face of all this, Vanderbilt developed a plan to get rid of Walker, Morgan, and Garrison. As Holbrook tells it, he fell short of his vow to ruin Morgan and Garrison but "left them wounded and humiliated by recovering control of Accessory Transit." This he accomplished by converting the North Star into an elegant Panama Line passenger ship, putting two other ships into service between the Pacific Coast and California, and further slashing fares.

Simultaneously Rivas was denouncing Walker as "an enemy of Nicaragua with the brand of traitor" and summoning all Nicaraguans "without exception or privilege between the ages of fifteen and sixty to take up arms against said Walker and his henchmen, and serve the government in whatever way they may be called upon in defense of the liberty, independence, and sovereignty of the Republic."

Another Rivas proclamation spelled out the reasons for his fury against Walker. On July 12, disdainful of the opposition he had aroused, Walker had himself elected president of Nicaragua, frankly revealing his intention to emulate Sam Houston in Texas by making the whole isthmus a territory of the United States. For this feat he had in his favor not only a propitious political situation in the United States but the benevolent posture of President Pierce. Far from reproving Walker when he proclaimed that his "election" as Nicaragua's "president" had been supervised by U.S. troops from New Orleans and California, Pierce sent the U.S. minister in Nicaragua on an official visit to notify Walker that "the Department of State, and especially President Pierce, wished to establish relations with his Government which of course enjoys recognition."[7]

Walker's antics, in a performance so well attuned to the man's past, brought a positive result: all the Central American peoples, previously divided by hatreds and rivalries, were united without distinction of faction or creed. Volunteers flocked from every corner of the isthmus to throw out the foreigner. The institutions and laws which he so crudely and arrogantly mocked were far from perfect or even satisfactory, but at least they had not been imposed by an invader's jackboot. Yet learning that El Salvador was preparing to send a force against him, Walker simply declared himself president of that republic. And so he would have continued with the others, now deep in discussions about mutual defense, had it not been for the new move by Cornelius Vanderbilt.

The "Commodore" provided arms to some Central American governments and, by halting his ships on the Nicaraguan run, cut off the lines to the United States on which Walker depended for reinforcements and supplies. Costa Rica, Honduras, and Guatemala also got money from Vanderbilt and went into action against Walker, who now apparently enjoyed the support of the new U.S. president, Buchanan.

Expert in the political game between slavery and antislavery elements in the United States (which the Civil War would soon terminate), Walker went all-out for the goodwill and support of Dixie. He set the Central American clock running backward by declaring null and void all acts and decrees of the Federal Constituent Assembly and the Federal Congress, and finally ordered restoration of slavery in the isthmus with these "scientific" and "philosophical" propositions:

> When the Latin American countries won independence, they sought to establish republics without slavery, and the history of forty years of public disorder and crime abounds in lessons for anyone with eyes to see and ears to hear. . . . The decree re-establishing slavery, while showing how the North Americans propose to regenerate Nicaraguan society, places the country in the vanguard of the Southern states of the Union in the allegedly "insuperable" conflict between the work of slaves and of free men. The politics of this decree consists of indicating to the Southern states the only way, apart from revolution, in which it is possible to preserve the present organization of society. . . .[8]

There was another character in the melodrama with whom Walker had to clash and clumsily make enemies: Britain. In the rush of his conquistadorial zeal he tried to meddle in the Mosquito Coast—then a British colony, claimed by and later a part of Nicaragua—and exact tribute from its planters. He had his eye on the British port of San Juan del Norte (Greytown) dominating the Atlantic entrance to the San Juan River, where the interoceanic transit line started. By way of pricking the lion, he withdrew the credentials of the British resident vice-consul in Managua, Thomas Manning, on the pretext that Manning was interfering in Nicaraguan internal affairs.

But the British planned to take over the interoceanic route for themselves, just as Walker planned to take it for the North Americans. Unlike the designs of the Almighty, those of the United States' Manifest Destiny were not inscrutable. Walker symbolized the impatient and aggressive U.S. style of intervention, as distinct from the pacific and gradual style favored by businessmen and financiers. And leaving aside the picturesque aspects of his performance in Central America, there is no doubt that had he won the battle against the five nations jointly opposing him, their history would have been very different.

On September 12, 1856, six Nicaraguan generals signed an agreement on behalf of the traditional Liberal and Conservative parties. It committed them to bury all hatchets as long as foreign troops remained in the country, to back Rivas for as long as it took to crush the army, and to call presidential elections in accordance with the 1838 Constitution a week after the freebooting armies quit Nicaraguan soil.

Almost a year later this had still not been achieved. The little republics' armies under Costa Rican general José Joaquín Mora managed to corner Walker in Granada, but he got away after setting fire to the city and leaving on the smoking ruins a sign: "Here was Granada." Then a cholera epidemic swept through the allied—especially the Costa Rican—forces, and a back-and-forth struggle went on till May 1, 1857. By then Walker's supply lines were cut and, rather than let himself be taken alive, Walker surrendered—to the captain of a U.S. warship cruising off Nicaragua. The captain took him to Panama and put him aboard a homeward-bound vessel.

The United States gave him a triumphal reception of the kind (according to New York newspaper accounts) that is still vouchsafed by that city to national heroes. His political and military exploits were lauded to the skies, with special hosannas for his attempt to "reclaim" the Mosquito Coast for the United States. He was reported soon afterward to be seeking arms and money, and again gathering recruits in Dixie, for the "reconquest" of his "presidency." Before the end of 1857 he was back off the coast of Nicaragua trying to land his forces. He failed and made no further attempt for three years.

Meanwhile, however, the Northern antislavery states got sufficiently alarmed to try to block him. It was appreciated that if he succeeded in stealing the isthmus and annexing it to the United States as a slave state, it would break in the South's favor the precarious equilibrium between the components of the Union.

This thought coincided with Vanderbilt's determination to get Walker out of the isthmus once and for all, and likewise with the patriotic sentiments of Central Americans: they had learned the hard way that even without the direct menace of Walker, their own dissensions were a direct invitation to powerful countries to intervene in their affairs whether they liked it or not. Any similar adventurer, whether individual or nation, could at any moment come and try his luck, taking advantage of Nicaragua's internal disunity and consequent weakness.

There had been general confidence that, with the invading forces removed, elections for a successor to Rivas would be held in June 1857 according to the pact of September 1855 guaranteed by Guatemalan and Salvadorean generals. But instead of this, generals Martínez and Jerez proposed to Rivas that he resign in favor of a junta presided over by them. Rivas did so and on June 24 the generals took the reins.

Two years later the junta shrank down to one general, Martínez, who sent Jerez to Washington as minister.

All this seemed to have put Walker out of the picture; and as for Vanderbilt, turbulent Central America had ceased to preoccupy him. He had defeated Harris and Sloo in the fare-cutting war and made his traitorous associates bite some dust. But he did reflect tenderly on an interesting gambit that Harris and Sloo had brought off with their fellow shipowner Law. Ever since 1848 they had been pocketing $900,000 a year of U.S. taxpayers' money as subsidy for carrying mail, and Vanderbilt saw a device for getting a slice of the cake. He proposed to them that, for due consideration, he might withdraw from the California ship-line business. So Harris and Sloo bought his ships for a price that suited Vanderbilt, promising to pay him $40,000 a month as long as he stayed out of the business. Later Vanderbilt raised this to $56,000 a month, or $672,000 a year, by threatening to come back in. According to Flynn, he thus recouped the entire capital he had invested in the business. He drew his $672,000 a year—the lion's share of the government subsidy—without moving a finger, while Harris and Sloo bore the load of the work and the burden of obtaining the necessary capital.

What of the other character in the plot? "Filibuster" Walker never faltered in his determination to recover his former kingdom. With ever-vaulting amibition he challenged fate again with an expedition to Central America. It was his third try and all he got out of it was his own funeral. Turning up in 1860 at the Honduran island of Roatán, he took by surprise the coast town of Trujillo where the British cruiser *Icarus* lay at anchor. As we have stated, Britain never took a kindly view of Walker's antics, and the Honduran authorities, well aware of this, recruited the ship's commander into a get-Walker plan. Walker finally had to surrender, this time to the British, who were undisposed to play by his rules. They handed him over to the Hondurans who, on September 12, promptly put him up against a wall.

Filibusters in White Gloves

> The victory of the Union drew the United States
> and the sister republics of the western world into
> closer bonds of friendship.
>
> Henceforth the United States Government and
> the people of the country remained keenly sensi-
> tive to the possibility of a violation of the Monroe
> Doctrine, particularly in the Caribbean area. When-
> ever diplomatic despatches reported rumors of
> European powers planning to acquire naval bases
> in the Caribbean, whether Great Britain, or France,
> or the new kingdom of Italy, or the new Ger-
> man Empire, successive Secretaries of State were
> prompt to instruct the appropriate diplomatic rep-
> resentatives to protest any such possibility. These
> protests rested directly or indirectly on the Mon-
> roe Doctrine.
>
> Samuel Flagg Bemis[1]

When Walker was ousted the Department of State began to worry.
The famous "Transit Line" from sea to sea had no legal status
whatsoever. The British might have their eye on it for an interocean
canal of which they already possessed the entry port of San Juan del
Norte (Greytown).

Early in 1857 the forces of Costa Rican general Juan Rafael Mora,
which had gone to Nicaragua's aid, sought to retain possession of the
"Line." Since war now seemed likely between Nicaragua and Costa
Rica, Mora and Martínez reached an agreement which soon became
the Cañas-Jerez Treaty. Before it was signed, to avoid misunder-
standings, both generals issued a manifesto to the effect that "Nicaragua places the Interocean Canal Contract under the protection of
Britain, France, and Sardinia, to the end of containing the absorption
of Central America by [North] American filibusterism."

The United States naturally found this offensive and General
Máximo Jerez, as Nicaraguan minister to Washington, had to solve

the ensuing diplomatic problem. His solution produced a treaty signed in Washington by Dr. Irissari, his successor as minister, and General Lewis Cass, providing the United States with a legal instrument to oppose British ambitions and incidentally satisfy its own. Armed pirates gave place to filibusters in white gloves.

This "friendship, trade, and navigation" treaty of November 1858 was signed under the shadow of Walker's armed intervention and of the foreseeable consequences to U.S.-British relations. Its nearest antecedents were President Monroe's friendship treaty of October 3, 1824, between the United States and New Granada (Colombia), signed when the possibility of a canal across the isthmus was already foreseen, and the Mallarino-Bidlack Treaty of 1846 between the same two nations. The interest in the Nicaraguan route also had antecedents, one of them in 1831 when a Dutch concern had gotten a concession for a San Juan River–Lake Nicaragua–Nuevo León canal. Although this never materialized, Jackson's secretary of state Livingston asked his minister to the Central American states for details and the Central American Federal Congress offered the United States, in view of its interest, the right to build the canal. In March 1835 the U.S. Senate had asked President Jackson to view the idea favorably; he so viewed it and sent an agent down to Nicaragua, but in 1837 advised dropping it as impractical. As usual, businessmen had longer vision than politicians and persisted with the Congress. As a result, Jackson's successor Van Buren had sent down another agent to study the Panama and Nicaragua routes as to which was more convenient. The agent plumped for Nicaragua, calculating the construction cost at $25 million. The Nicaraguans themselves were interested in the plan, as witness Buitrago's letters to Secretary of State Buchanan in November 1847 and those of Sebastián Salinas to President Pierce.

But when in March 1848 Nicaragua made a pact with Britain, agreeing to end its disputes with the Mosquito Coast Indians who enjoyed British protection and guarded the outpost, an alarmed United States had signed the above-mentioned Mallarino-Bidlack Treaty with Colombia. The treaty implicitly confessed that Colombia was too weak to defend itself and needed protection by a power that in fact was less concerned to provide it than to achieve economic penetration. Scorning the rules of British diplomatic cricket, Colombia ogled the United States while Britain contented itself with nullifying the treaty's advantages by signing with Nicaragua the pact of protection of the King of Mosquitos—which not only seemed like, but was, a British joke. Under that pact, Britain, without firing a shot, won authority to occupy the entry to the probable Nicaraguan canal, San Juan del Norte.

Nevertheless, U.S. prudence and British realism had then blandly resumed the pursuit of their common aspirations, after the manner of well-educated cousins, with the Clayton-Bulwer Treaty of 1850,[2] which unintentionally saved the Central American republics' integrity by putting the first brake on Manifest Destiny.

The Pierce-Buchanan era of rising free trade immediately preceded the U.S. Civil War. This was the period during which the British had begun digesting their empire in Oceania, Africa, and Asia and thought it much more convenient not to quarrel with their cousins, with whom they were collaborating in the westward expansion of U.S. railroads. It was also the time when London's City was clamoring for someone to keep order in Central America (since the chaos there was "depressing for our investments") even though it might have to be the United States. But even without Walker's intervention, the "aggressive spirit" of the United States, to which Disraeli perspicaciously referred in a June 1856 speech to the Commons, was not to delay long in showing itself again.[3] When in May 1857 the United States expressed resentment at the joint Costa Rican–Nicaraguan declaration, it found solace in an incident on a ship plying the San Juan River, in the shape of a bottle hurled at a U.S. citizen. President Buchanan demanded that Nicaragua pay $24,000 indemnity. Whether because the Nicaraguans thought the price high for a single glass missile, or because they didn't have $24,000, the demand went unheeded.

A warship was then heading for San Juan del Norte; it subjected the town to a terrible bombardment, then landed marines who put everything to the torch. Thus Walker saw his defeat avenged. Nicaragua was still stanching the wounds of its civil war, and the governing junta could but submit to the implicit aim of the bombardment: a "friendship, trade, and navigation" treaty, sign here please. This was the basis of the Cass-Irisarri Treaty which would have such consequences for Nicaragua's later history, since it would open the door to U.S. imperial penetration.

In violation of the Constitution, the one-man presidency of Martínez that followed the Martínez-Jerez junta lasted eight years (1859–1867), then Fernando Guzmán was president till 1871. In Guzmán's first year a new pact was signed with Washington—which resumed its imperialist course after the U.S. Civil War—giving the United States the same substantial advantages it had obtained from its pact with Colombia in 1846. After Vicente Cuadra (1871–1875) and Pedro J. Chamorro (1875–1879) came President Joaquín Zavala, during whose term Indians installing the telegraph rebelled in Matagalpa against their bad treatment and were savagely put down. This led indirectly to the mass expulsion of Jesuits. The next three presidents, Adán Cárdenas (1883–1887), Evaristo Carazo (1887–1889) and Roberto Sacasa (1889–1893) were all Conservatives.

Sacasa was re-elected in 1893 but quickly overthrown in a revolution headed by General Francisco Gutiérrez. The United States decided to intervene, and its ambassador Baker imposed the Sabanagrande peace pact on July 6; five days later, when the civil war was supposed to be over, Liberal Party leader, General José Santos Zelaya rose in arms.

Cárdenas had exiled Zelaya to Guatemala, where he joined Justo Rufino Barrios in fighting for political reunification of the isthmus. Returning under an amnesty decreed by Carazo, Zelaya continued working to oust the Conservatives and succeeded in July 1893, when he entered Managua at the head of his army. The Constituent Assembly named him president in September, and he took his place in Nicaraguan history as the reconqueror of the Mosquito Coast. One of his government's first actions was military reinforcement of all territory that was considered part of Nicaragua. An army was landed at Bluefields in October and the Mosquito chief Henry Clarence was told to respect Nicaraguan sovereignty. Clarence declined, backed by the British government through the governor of Jamaica, but in February 1894 General Rigoberto Cabezas occupied Bluefields and decreed Nicaragua's annexation of the Mosquito Coast.

The imprisonment or exile of recalcitrant British subjects gave London its cue, early in 1895, to send troop-carrying warships to the Pacific port of Corinto. Zelaya declared a state of seige and called all compatriots to arms. But diplomatic intervention by the United States, Guatemala, El Salvador, Honduras, and Costa Rica cooled the situation, and it was finally agreed that Nicaragua would pay a £15 million indemnity to the British, who withdrew on May 4.

Zelaya continued governing in the face of constant revolutions, some organized by the Conservatives, some by Liberals who resented his constitutional reforms—first in 1897, then in 1905—designed to perpetuate his own rule. In 1905 he got the British to renounce all rights to intervene in the Mosquito Coast, under the Harrison-Altamirano Treaty which made Nicaragua master of all its territory. Zelaya was a typical enlightened despot of Latin America, equally anxious to promote public education and to remain president indefinitely. Under him, railroad projects begun in earlier administrations were completed and others initiated to link hitherto unexploited areas on both coasts. He produced a labor code and legalized civil marriage, which Conservatives and clergy had always resisted. Two Liberals, Francisco Baca and José Madriz, attempted a revolution against him in 1896 but failed.

It was the period of growing U.S. power, the war for Cuba, the conquest of the Panama Canal, the resented efforts by the Kaiser's Germany to gain a foothold in Hispanic America; of U.S. War Secretary Elihu Root's creation in 1903–1904 of a European-type army general staff and its academy at Fort Leavenworth; of the U.S. Navy's growth at the rate of two new first-line battleships every year. Mastery of Cuba was assured by the Platt Amendment, and the collection of debts and protection of investments provided Root with a legal formula for keeping European governments out of Central America. The device used by Root, now secretary of state, was a Central American Court of Justice with a judge for each of the five countries represented. Purportedly the first step toward a new federation, the court would settle all disputes between the countries and squelch any pretext for European intervention.

Despite his juristic passion for legal formulas, Root was clearly not going to neglect defense of the interests he represented. His appointment was designed to remove the bad taste which the Panama Canal affair had left in the world's mouth and to revive his country's damaged prestige. The Big Stick Diplomacy image needed softening, and Root provided the indispensable link with the Dollar Diplomacy of his successor, Philander Chase Knox.

There were different interpretations of Dollar Diplomacy. For

Isidro Fabela it meant extending loans to certain countries under more or less harsh conditions, with official guarantees to the lending bankers of reasonable U.S. State Department "protection"—guarantees based on control of the "favored" countries' railroads, telegraph systems, and customs. If an insolvent state declined to relinquish its sovereignty in this way, Washington would introduce its marines as a persuader. Countries allergic to such loans were induced to accept them by "wearing down their will through various means, the more effective the poorer and weaker the country which the United States sought to protect with its pecuniary support."[4]

For Harry Elmer Barnes, Dollar Diplomacy was a response not merely to mercantile interests but to eminently geopolitical ones.[5] Both were right, as exhaustively shown by Nearing and Freeman's book of that title,[6] but in Nicaragua's case only the strategic factor really counted. Events would have turned out differently but for Zelaya's persistent refusal to let the United States build a canal across his country. Zelaya's totalitarianism went hand in hand with his fervent nationalism. Despite Moore's opinion that Zelaya did not want foreign powers intervening "even as mediators" [7] in disputes with neighboring countries, there is evidence that he had no objection so long as they did not disturb his power;[8] yet Zelaya was proud of his renown as having no truck with North American subjection. Confirming this, when his deal with Porfirio Díaz for construction of a railroad from Mexico all across the Central American isthmus broke down, he sought German help to build a canal on the understanding that it was "for Nicaragua." That flirtation plus the U.S. need to assure its control of the Gulf of Fonseca prompted the State Department to promote Zelaya's downfall.

Before the hostilities ended during the Root era, Root had sent down an oil agent—Washington S. Valentine of the Rosario Mining Company, with offices in New York and Tegucigalpa—to try to convince Zelaya to be good. The agent landed at Corinto from a U.S. warship and immediately went into a huddle with the dictator. "We will give you, señor Zelaya, all you need to unite Central America—arms, money, whatever you want—on the sole condition that you negotiate with my government and guarantee us the San Juan canal route and a naval base in Fonseca Gulf."[9] Zelaya said no.

There was a brief pause before the newspaper chains of James

Gordon Bennett and William Randolph Hearst simultaneously revealed the presence of a terrible despot in Nicaragua, a peril to the cause of democracy and the peace of the isthmus. President Taft joined the game in his message to Congress in December 1909: "Since the Washington Conventions in 1907 were communicated to the U.S. government as a consulting and advising party, this government has been almost continuously called upon by one or another, and in turn by all of the five Central American Republics, to exert itself for the maintenance of the conventions. Nearly every complaint has been against the Zelaya government of Nicaragua which has kept Central America in constant tension and turmoil."[10]

The 1907 Peace and Friendship Treaty, one of the Washington Conventions, set forth that in the event of armed conflict in any of the signatory countries, the others would be neutral. But when the rising against Zelaya occurred in 1909, Zelaya felt compelled to pursue the rebels into Costa Rican territory. A month later Mr. Merry, the U.S. minister to Costa Rica, proposed to President Cleto González Víquez a joint attack on Zelaya with El Salvador and Guatemala. The report sent to his government in November 1909 by Costa Rica's minister to Washington, Joaquín Bernardo Calvo, is quite illuminating.[11]

U.S. Secretary of State Knox's activities were not solely on behalf of the state. He had been attorney general in the Teddy Roosevelt government, and as such intervened in Paris in the liquidation of the New Panama Canal Company and its subsequent sale to the United States. As a lawyer in 1900 he gave legal form to the organization of the Carnegie steel trust, which would then disburse $100,000 to build a Temple of Peace in Corinto. His open interference in Nicaragua's internal affairs derived from his being lawyer for the Fletcher family which owned big mineral properties there; one of these, the La Luz and Los Angeles Mining Company, had constant disputes with Zelaya about nonfulfillment of obligations prescribed in the concession. And despite British Ambassador Bryce's view that Knox neither "did, knew or thought anything about foreign policy till they made him Secretary," some of his speeches suggested otherwise.

3
The United States Invents Quisling

I am . . . troubled about the question whether the Nicaraguan government which has made the treaty is really representative of the people of Nicaragua and whether it will be regarded in Nicaragua and in Central America as having been a free agent in making the treaty. I have been looking over the report of the commanding officer of our marines in Nicaragua, and I find there the following:

"Their present government is not in power by the will of the people; the elections of the House of Congress were mostly fraudulent."

And a further statement that the Liberals, that is to say, the opposition, "constitute three-fourths of the country." It is apparent . . . that the present government . . . is really maintained in office by the presence of the U.S. Marines in Nicaragua. . . . Can we afford to make a treaty so serious for Nicaragua, granting us perpetual rights in that country, with a president who we have reason to believe does not represent more than a quarter of the people of the country and who is maintained in office by our military force, and to whom we would, as a result of the treaty, pay a large sum of money to be disposed of by him as president?

Elihu Root[1]

The means used by Knox was the same as Hay's in the case of Panama: a revolution. The motive was the purported disagreement of Juan J. Estrada, governor of Bluefields, with the negative policies of Zelaya; and the odd phenomenon of the U.S. consul knowing about it in advance was repeated. Mr. Moffat cabled Knox on October 7, 1909, that Estrada would be rebelling next day with the assistance of Conservative general Emiliano Chamorro, that foreign property would be respected, and that Zelaya would be unseated without a fight.[2]

On October 13 Moffat cabled that events had turned out as he said they would, with one variant: there was a fight. Despite the United Fruit Company's flagrant support with men, arms, and munitions, Zelaya put up such resistance that two cruisers, the *Paducah* and *Dubuque,* had to be sent into the fray. Nor was this the only aid given. According to the *New York Times* of September 9, 1912, Estrada admitted having received for the Bluefields revolution $1 million from "U.S. companies on Nicaragua's Atlantic coast," and about $200,000 and $150,000 respectively from the Joseph W. Beers and Samuel Weil concerns.

Caught *in flagrante* with the rebel forces were Edmond Couture, a Frenchman, and two North Americans, Lee Roy Cannon and Leonard Groce. On Chamorro's instructions they had placed mines in the San Juan River to blow up Zelaya's ships. The mines exploded without doing any damage, and the three culprits, apprehended near the scene, confessed and were sentenced to death by a war council. Cannon appealed to Zelaya on November 14, affirming his guilt but "imploring the extension to me of your well-known magnanimity." Groce, likewise admitting the deed, promised "never to mix again in the politics of your country" if Zelaya would spare him. When Zelaya was inflexible, the United States had grounds for breaking relations, which it did in an infamous note from Knox to Nicaragua's chargé d'affaires in Washington, Felipe Rodríguez:

Washington, December 1, 1909

Sir:

Since the Washington conventions of 1907, it is notorious that President Zelaya has almost continuously kept Central America in tension or turmoil; that he has repeatedly and flagrantly violated the provisions of the conventions, and, by a baleful influence upon Honduras, whose neutrality the conventions were to assure, has sought to discredit those sacred international obligations, to the great detriment of Costa Rica, El Salvador and Guatemala, whose governments meanwhile appear to have been able patiently to strive for the loyal support of the engagements so solemnly undertaken at Washington under the auspices of the United States and Mexico.

It is equally a matter of common knowledge that under the regime of President Zelaya republican institutions have ceased in Nicaragua to exist except in name, that public opinion and the press have been throttled, and that prison has been the reward of any tendency to real patriotism. My consideration for you personally impels me to abstain from unnecessary discussion of the painful details of a regime which, unfortunately, has been a blot upon the history of Nicaragua and a discouragement to a group of Republics whose aspirations need only the opportunity of free and honest government.

In view of the interests of the United States and of its relation to the Washington conventions, appeal against this situation has long since been made to this Government by a majority of the Central American Republics. There is now added the appeal, through the revolution, of a great body of the Nicaraguan people. Two Americans who, this Government is now convinced, were officers connected with the revolutionary forces, and therefore entitled to be dealt with according to enlightened practice of civilized nations, have been killed by direct order of President Zelaya. Their execution is said to have been preceded by barbarous cruelties. The consulate at Managua is now officially reported to have been menaced. There is thus a sinsiter culmination of an administration also characterized by a cruelty to its own citizens which has, until the recent outrage, found vent in the case of this country in a series of petty annoyances and indignities which many months ago made it impossible to ask an American minister longer to reside in Managua. From every point of view it has evidently become difficult for the United States further to delay more active response to the appeals so long made, to its duty to its citizens, to its dignity, to Central America, and to civilization.

The Government of the United States is convinced that the revolution represents the ideals and the will of a majority of the Nicaraguan people more faithfully than does the Government of President Zelaya, and that its peaceable control is well-nigh as extensive as that hitherto so sternly attempted by the Government at Managua.

There is now added the fact, as officially reported from more than one quarter, that there are already indications of a rising in the Western Provinces in favor of a presidential candidate intimately associated with the old regime. In this it is easy to see new elements tending toward a condition of anarchy which leaves, at a given time, no definite responsible source to which the Government of the United States could look for reparation for the killing of Messrs. Cannon and Groce, or, indeed, for the protection which must be assured American citizens and American interests in Nicaragua.

In these circumstances the President no longer feels for the Government of President Zelaya that respect and confidence which would make it appropriate hereafter to maintain with it regular diplomatic relations, implying the will and the ability to respect and assure what is due from one state to another.

The Government of Nicaragua which you have hitherto represented is hereby notified, as will be also the leaders of the revolution, that the Government of the United States will hold strictly accountable for the protection of American life and property the factions de facto in control of the eastern and western portions of the Republic of Nicaragua.

As for the reparation found due, after careful consideration, for the killing of Messrs. Cannon and Groce, the Government of the United States would be loath to impose upon the innocent people of Nicaragua a too heavy burden of expiating the acts of a regime forced upon them or to exact from a succeeding Government, if it have quite different policies, the imposition of such a burden. Into the question of ultimate reparation there must enter the question of the existence at Managua of a Government capable of responding to demands. There must enter also the question of how far it is possible to reach those actually responsible and those who perpetrated the tortures reported to have preceded the execution, if these be verified; and the question whether the Government be one entirely dissociated from the present intolerable conditions and worthy to be trusted to make impossible a recurrence of such acts, in which case the President, as a friend of your country, as he is also of the other Republics of Central America, might be disposed to have indemnity confined to what was reasonably due the relatives of the deceased and punitive only in so far as the punishment might fall where really due.

In pursuance of this policy the Government of the United States will temporarily withhold its demand for reparation, in the meanwhile taking such steps as it deems wise and proper to protect American interest.

To insure the future protection of legitimate American interest, in consideration of the interests of the majority of the Central American Republics, and in the hope of making more effective the friendly offices exerted under the Washington conventions, the Government of the United States reserves for further consideration at the proper time the question of stipulating also that the constitutional Government of Nicaragua obligate itself by convention, for the benefit of all the Governments concerned, as a guaranty for its future loyal support of the Washington conventions and their peaceful and progressive aims.

From the foregoing it will be apparent to you that your office of chargé d'affaires is at an end. I have the honor to enclose your passport, for use in case you desire to leave this country. I would add at the same time that, although your diplomatic quality is terminated, I shall be happy to receive you, as I shall be happy to receive the representatives of the revolution, each as the unofficial channel of communication between the Government of the United States and the de facto authorities to whom I look for the protection of American interests pending the establishment in Nicaragua of a Government with which the United States can maintain diplomatic relations.

Accept, etc.,

P. C. Knox[3]

For less serious offenses the United States had executed two Englishmen, Arbuthnot and Ambrister, during the Jackson administration, and it had not protested when the Hondurans put Walker before a firing squad. But as Zelaya pondered the matter in his memoirs, "when the *Maine* blew up, not so much as the smallest bit of wire was found which could prove a crime had been committed. But the mere fact that the ship was in Cuban waters sufficed for the U.S. government to declare war on Spain. . . ."[4] This time, when the crime and the guilty parties were clear, other pretexts were resorted to, such as that of torture, which the Belgian consul, Louis Layrac, certified to be unfounded. If Zelaya refused to commute the sentences, he was within his rights as head of a sovereign state and made Knox's justifications thin indeed.[5]

But since it was evident to Zelaya that the United States had decided to remove him, he resigned on December 16 to contribute, as he told the National Assembly, to "the good of Nicaragua . . . and above all to the suspension of the hostility shown by the U.S. government, to which I don't wish to give a pretext for continuing any sort of intervention in our country." Mexico put the ship *General Guerrero* at his disposition to go into exile. The assembly replaced him with José Madriz who, eager to continue the struggle, soon had Bluefields at his mercy by capturing the Bluff fortress dominating that city. But the commander of the *Paducah* warned the loyal troops to proceed no further, and landed marines to make the threat more forceful.

Equally barefaced was the *Paducah*'s and *Dubuque*'s intervention at the approaches to Bluefields, to prevent the loyal ship *Máximo Jerez* from detaining vessels bringing Estrada supplies from New Orleans. The marines set up an artifical customs station at Schooner

Key so that the rebels could collect duties properly payable at Bluff. To top this off, Estrada was authorized to fly the Stars and Stripes to protect his positions.

When Madriz protested to the ship commanders and to Knox, the former told him they would "use their guns to compel respect for U.S. commerce, even though it consisted of arms and munitions for the revolution, and that one shot fired against those ships would be a declaration of war against the United States." Knox's reply was that the U.S. government "merely demands that each side collect customs duties only in the territory under its de facto control, and will not permit collection of double duties."

Thus confronted with the fact that he was equally unacceptable to Washington, Madriz resigned on August 20, 1910. A week later the patriots' resistance collapsed and Estrada and Chamorro entered Managua in triumph. On October 11 the State Department named Thomas G. Dawson, then its minister to Panama, as special agent in Nicaragua. He had instructions to negotiate a loan, to be guaranteed by a percentage of customs duties.[6]

Madriz was replaced by a junta of three generals—Estrada, Mena, and Chamorro—and a civilian, Adolfo Díaz, to whom Dawson presented himself with five demands of his government: (1) election of a constituent assembly which would confirm Estrada as provisional president and name Díaz as vice-president, and which apart from approving a new constitution would abolish certain concessions Zelaya had granted to non-North Americans; (2) creation of a mixed commission of claims; (3) punishment of those responsible for the execution of Cannon and Groce; (4) request to U.S. bankers for a loan; (5) elimination of Zelaya partisans from the administration.

The new assembly was at first docile and obeyed the order to name Estrada and Díaz in November. In January Taft formally recognized the new government in which Mena was war minister and Chamorro president of the assembly. In February Northcott appeared as the new U.S. minister and promptly reported to Knox his impression that Estrada was unpopular, and that all of Central America resented its subjection to the United States. He added that a loan must be negotiated without delay since the president was only kept in office "by the moral effect of our support and by the belief that he will surely enjoy it in the event of any upset."

As if to confirm his impressions, publication of the hitherto secret "Dawson accords" exploded like a bomb. The Liberals got hold of a copy and spread it throughout Latin America. The National Assembly, compelled to echo the general indignation, included clauses in the Constitution to the effect that "only Congress may authorize loans and negotiate contracts by direct means" and that "taxes and public funds may not be alienated nor given as rent." U.S. Chargé d'Affaires Guenther asked Díaz and Mena in alarm to postpone approval of the Constitution "pending the arrival of the minister sent by the cabinet in Washington, who would want to make some amendments to that document."

The unheard-of request was accepted, causing a split between Mena and Estrada. At Northcott's suggestion, Estrada dissolved the assembly and jailed Mena, whom Northcott then proceeded to free. But Estrada had become so unpopular that he had to resign in favor of Vice-President Díaz.

While Chamorro was journeying to the United States and Mena was wondering what would happen next, Adolfo Díaz took the Nicaraguan stage—the most abject figure of the next two decades until the arrival of the no less sinister Somoza. Thirty years before the word "quisling" became synonymous with unconditional treason to one's own country, the United States created its symbol in Díaz. Through him it set up the system that would permit it to enjoy its Caribbean conquest without complications, and opened a new chapter in America's dismal history.

Díaz was a $1,000-a-year employee of the La Luz and Los Angeles Mining Company, property of the Fletcher family for whom Secretary Knox showed tender solicitude. As his first move he authorized his chargé d'affaires in Washington, Salvador Castrillo, to make a deal for a $15 million U.S. loan to Nicaragua at 5 percent interest and 1 percent for amortization. As security he offered the country's railroads and steamships. Since the proposal was in fact a State Department product, and there was no time (or no one wanted that there should be) to translate it, it was presented to the Nicaraguan Congress in English with strict instructions from U.S. plenipotentiary Weitzel that it be approved without the change of a single comma. Six deputies and two government secretaries who presumably knew English, and who "did not want to dirty themselves by selling their country out," refused to sign the treaty but could not prevent its approval. Yet what the deputies' scruples prevented, the U.S. Senators' legalistic itch could do: three times they declined, despite the special recommendation of President Taft, to ratify the Knox-Castrillo Treaty, and it remained a dead letter.

When the time came to hold elections, Díaz, knowing they would go against him, postponed them indefinitely—to the disgust of Mena who, on the basis of a hint from Knox after Mena voted in the assembly for the aborted loan, saw the throne within his grasp. Although patently no saint, Mena gathered about him a group of Conservative and Liberal adherents and volunteers from Honduras, El Salvador, Costa Rica, and Guatemala, with whom he raised the banner of revolt in July 1912. General Benjamin Zeledón, a popular figure among military liberals and students, joined the rebels and they quickly took over Managua, Granada, and Masaya. Unlike Castellón, Díaz did not expect some Walker to come to his aid, but he immediately brought the filibuster's compatriots onto the scene against his own brothers. U.S. marines landed, reached Managua and Masaya by express train, and subjected them to ferocious bombardment. Mena was captured and shipped out from Corinto to Panama, but Zeledón covered himself with glory resisting the U.S. assaults in Coyotepe.

The 412 marines commanded by Major Smedley Butler were the advance guard of a force comprising 2,600 soldiers, 125 officers, and eight warships which the secretary of the navy later admitted using for the operation.[7] Zeledón was called upon to surrender but did not bother to reply. The governments of the isthmus countries protested the intervention, and the protest by El Salvador's President Araujo was made public. But the most noteworthy document of the "Mena War" was a note from U.S. Minister to Nicaragua Weitzel to Nicaraguan Foreign Secretary Diego M. Chamorro, restating the U.S. motivations for invading Nicaragua:

> Excellency:
>   I have the honor to inform Your Excellency that the Department of State has instructed me by cable to transmit to Your Excellency's Government, and unofficially to the rebel chiefs, and to make public, the following authorized declaration of the policy of the United States in the present disturbances.

The policy of the Government of the United States in the present Nicaraguan disturbances is to take the necessary measures for an adequate legation guard at Managua, to keep open communications, and to protect American life and property.

In discountenancing Zelaya, whose regime of barbarity and corruption was ended by the Nicaraguan nation after a bloody war, the Government of the United States opposed not only the individual but the system, and this Government could not countenance any movement to restore the same destructive regime. The Government of the United States will, therefore, discountenance legally constituted good government for the benefit of the people of Nicaragua, whom it has long sought to aid in their just aspiration toward peace and prosperity under constitutional and orderly government.

A group of some 125 American planters residing in one region in Nicaragua have applied for protection. Some two dozen American firms doing business in that country have applied for protection. The American bankers who have made investments in relation to railroads and steamships in Nicaragua, in connection with a plan for the relief of the financial distress of that country, have applied for protection. The American citizens now in the service of the Government of Nicaragua and the Legation itself have been placed in actual jeopardy under fire. Two wounded American citizens are reported to have been ruthlessly slaughtered. Besides the Emery claim due American citizens and the indemnity for the killing of Groce and Cannon in the Zelaya war, there are various American claims and concessionary interests. Under the Washington conventions, the United States has a moral mandate to exert its influence for the preservation of the general peace of Central America, which is seriously menaced by the present uprising, and to this end in the strict enforcement of the Washington conventions and loyal support of their aims and purposes all the Central American Republics will find means of valuable cooperation. These are among the important moral, political, and material interests to be protected.

When the American Minister called upon the Government of Nicaragua to protect American life and property, the Minister for Foreign Affairs replied that the Government troops must be used to put down the rebellion, adding:

"In consequence, my Government desires that the Government of the United States guarantee with its forces security for the property of American citizens in Nicaragua, and that they extend this protection to all the inhabitants of the Republic."

In this situation the policy of the Government of the United States will be to protect the life and property of its citizens in the manner indicated and, meanwhile, to contribute its influence in all appropriate ways to the restoration of lawful and orderly government in order that Nicaragua may resume its program of reforms unhampered by the vicious elements who would restore the methods of Zelaya.

The revolt of General Mena in flagrant violation of his solemn promises to his own Government and to the American Minister, and of the Dawson agreement by which he was solemnly bound, and his attempt to overturn the Government of his country for purely selfish purposes and without even the pretense of contending for a principle, make the present rebellion in origin the most inexcusable in the annals of Central America. The nature and methods of the present disturbances, indeed, place them in the category of anarchy rather than ordinary revolution. . . .

Accept, Your Excellency, etc.,

George F. Weitzel
American Minister
9/13/1912[8]

Rarely in the history of diplomacy have clumsiness, stupidity, and arrogance been so combined in a single document; but when that has occurred, the authors were almost invariably North Americans who confused the negotiating tables of sovereign states with the counters of stores or banks. The weird missive of this State Department official, and Knox's earlier note, are the best proofs of our assertion.

Yet absurdity had still not reached its height. Instead of running to hide his shame in his country's most Stygian well, instead of joining the patriots to throw the invaders out, Chamorro had this insulting note printed and distributed among military leaders and rank and file and civilian authorities, as proof that Díaz was really supported by U.S. troops!

Zeledón, the heroic defender of Coyotepe, was killed on October 4, 1912, at El Arroyo when attempting to break the U.S. encirclement. With his death and the imprisonment of Mena the revolution was deprived of leaders. Of no avail the defense of Masaya, later pillaged and put to the torch; nor the resonant protest from the authorities of León to Admiral Sutherland; nor the valiant denunciation by the government's delegate, Leonardo Argüello, to which the boss of the occupation of León, Charles S. Long, replied with threats "in the event of nonsurrender of the rolling stock."[9]

By the end of October, technical superiority had overwhelmed the patriots, and on November 12 Managua newspapers announced: "Only 400 marines remain. On Friday of this week Admiral Sutherland and the U.S. forces will depart for Panama, leaving 300 marines in Campo de Marte and 100 in León." On November 13 they reported: "At 7 A.M. today the three-car presidential train left for Corinto with President Adolfo Díaz, General Emiliano Chamorro, Secretary Diego M. Chamorro, don Carlos Cuadra Pasos, and other friends in the central car. In the forward and rear cars rode 100 U.S. marines. . . ."

The bankers were left in tranquil possession of their loot. In March 1912, just before Mena's rebellion and in defiance of the Constitution, they had arranged a supplementary $725,000 loan to Díaz, of which $500,000 was earmarked for use by monetary experts to stabilize the exchange rate and $225,000 for government expenses. The loan was for six months at 6 percent plus a 1 percent bankers' commission, with customs duties, railroads, ships, and Nicaragua's claims against the London Ethelburga Syndicate as security.

Zelaya had contracted a £1.25 million loan from Ethelburga, and this is said to have precipitated the U.S. intervention on the basis that it was a new British pretext to infiltrate Nicaragua. But the March 1912 agreement between Nicaragua and U.S. bankers authorized the latter to negotiate in London in the name of Nicaragua. The consequence was that the balance in London, amounting to £1.195 million, was transferred to the bankers as payment for their loan, after payment of interest and amortization. The most serious aspect of the contract was the stipulation that Nicaragua must transfer its rail lines and ships to a corporation to be organized in the United States, which would enjoy exemption and a one-year option to acquire 51 percent of the shares for $1 million, and also, through an extraordinary $500,000 loan to the corporation, an option on the 49 percent of remaining shares. And as the U.S. documents show, Nicaragua could not sell its share to anyone except the bankers until the loans were repaid.[10] Furthermore "all negotiations must be carried out with participation of the State Department," in effect converting that department into the "manager" of Brown Brothers and J. and W. Seligman.

Díaz' achievement was the zooming economic crisis of his country: the exchange rate rose to an astronomical 1,500 and 1,485 respectively on U.S. and British drafts. The contract he signed in September 1912, when the "Mena War" was still raging, became known as the "Treasury Note Agreement" and was thus summed up by Nearing and Freeman:

> (1) $100,000 of the loan was to be used as initial capital for the proposed bank. (2) The balance was to be used for reforming the currency of Nicaragua. (3) The bankers were to hire monetary experts to reform the currency, but Nicaragua was to pay for them. (4) The bankers were to deposit the sum used for reforming the currency— $1,400,000—with the United States Mortgage and Trust Company. (5) The loan was to be secured by a lien on the customs. (6) The customs were to be collected by an American nominated by the bankers, approved by the Secretary of State, and "appointed" by Nicaragua. (7) The customs were not to be charged without the bankers' consent. The contract also gave the bankers a lien on the liquor tax, and reserved to the bankers the right "to solicit of the United States of America protection against violation of the present contract, and aid in enforcing its execution." The bankers and Nicaragua were to submit disputes to arbitration by the Secretary of State of the United States.[11]

Mr. Taft, for his part, was staunch in his unconditional support of Díaz. The "Mena War" had filled Central American governments with alarm, and one of them, El Salvador, complained about Washington's open intervention. Taft's reply was par for the long and agonizing course.[12]

What were the results of the defeated revolution and the U.S. armed intervention? First, as the historian Charles P. Howland writes, a force of a hundred soldiers that remained (along with various warships) to guard the legation was "stationed in one of the forts of the capital as a sort of fire brigade; they were successful during the next thirteen years of Conservative control in preventing smoldering Liberal aspirations from breaking into flame."[13] Second, another loan was organized in November 1912 to defray the costs originated by the revolution. This time it was for $500,000 with alcohol and tobacco taxes as security, these being in any case collected by the Bank of Nicaragua which the U.S. bankers controlled. But when the Nicaraguan Congress declined to approve it, after $350,000 of it had already been received, the bankers suspended payment and waited for new winds to blow—a development considered probable since Woodrow Wilson had been elected U.S. president.

On the heels of Wilson's election, in February 1913, the U.S. minister in Managua announced that the bankers would not advance another dollar nor consider any other proposal "until there is assurance that the next administration will follow the same policy. This will greatly perturb President Díaz who wishes to reach a definite arrangement of the financial question while the present administration remains in power in Washington, since it knows the problem intimately. However, President Díaz assures me that he will make no definite loan contract without previously consulting the Department. . . ."

Knox replied that "there was no basis for the rumor that the next Administration would change U.S. policy toward Central America," and recommended the minister to have a chat with Mr. Bundy Cole, manager of the National Bank of Nicaragua and agent of Brown Brothers. Knox's guarantee and the resulting chat flowered into a new agreement dated October 8, 1913, under which (1) the bankers would pay $1 million to take up the option for purchase of 51 percent of the railroad shares; (2) they would lend Nicaragua $1 million; (3) they would lend the railroads $500,000 for improvements and extensions; (4) they would buy 51 percent of the shares in the National Bank for $153,000, retaining first refusal of the remaining 49 percent; (5) they had the right to transfer the shares in the event of Nicaragua reneging; (6) the bank and the railroads would both get new directors, six to be named by the bankers, one by the U.S. secretary of state and two by Nicaraguans.

What did Nicaragua get out of all this? Precisely nothing. According to Nearing and Freeman, of the $2 million advanced to Nicaragua for the railroad shares and as a loan, the Republic received just $772,424. This was used to pay up previous debts, to renew the exchange stabilization fund, to buy National Bank shares, and to pay assorted profits to the bankers, as a result of which "not only had the American bankers collected all previous loans, but Nicaragua owed them $1,000,000, her Ethelburga balance was gone, and the bankers controlled and managed her railroads and bank."[14]

The third consequence of U.S. intervention—actually the pivot of all the others—was still to come: signing of the canal treaty. With the civil war in full eruption, Secretary Chamorro and U.S. Minister Weitzel signed a treaty conceding to the United States the rights to build, service, and maintain an interocean canal via the San Juan River to Lake Nicaragua, in addition to the territory for a Pacific naval base on the Gulf of Fonseca and in various east coast islands.

The Chamorro-Weitzel pact drew furious protests from Costa Rica and El Salvador which also had rights over the Gulf of Fonseca. Even the U.S. Senate found its stipulations unsatisfactory and refused to ratify it. To such an extent did the interests of Brown Brothers and J. and W. Seligman coincide with State Department policy that the bankers sent the department this note in anticipation of the signing of the canal treaty: "If the Senate . . . ratifies the treaty . . . the proposed $3 million payment in compensation to Nicaragua will put that government in a position to liquidate the greater part of its internal debt and claims."

It looked as if the senatorial negative had put an end to the matter, since Wilson, who was expected to modify his predecessor's policy, was to assume the presidency in March 1913. Just the reverse occurred.[15] Latin American–style elections which the Liberal Party boycotted put Díaz back in the presidency with 15,000 votes, a figure suggesting the enthusiasm of the populace. Before the end of 1913 Nicaragua had a new constitution (which continued in force till 1939) and the *córdoba* became the national currency. All seemed to be going smoothly.

But on August 5, 1914, General Emiliano Chamorro and Secretary of State William Jennings Bryan signed the treaty ceding to the United States the right to build a transocean canal across Nicaragua, plus some other concessions contained in the previous aborted agreement. Mr. Knox knew just what he was saying when he maintained that the change of administration in the United States would not modify his country's imperial policy. President Wilson, in defiance of his proud title as the "Apostle of Democracy," approved the infamous treaty, which the Senate finally ratified, with an addendum, on February 18, 1916. It stipulated:

> 1. The Government of Nicaragua grants in perpetuity to the Government of the United States, forever free from all taxation or other public charge, the exclusive proprietary rights necessary and con-

venient for the construction, operation and maintenance of an inter-oceanic canal by way of the San Juan River and the great Lake of Nicaragua, or by way of any route over Nicaraguan territory, the details of the terms of which such canal shall be constructed, operated and maintained to be agreed to by the two governments whenever the Government of the United States shall notify the Government of Nicaragua of its desire or intention to construct such canal.

2. To enable the Government of the United States to protect the Panama Canal and the proprietary rights granted to the Government of the United States by the preceding article, and also to enable the Government of the United States to take any measure necessary to the ends contemplated herein, the Government of Nicaragua hereby leases for a term of 99 years to the Government of the United States the islands in the Caribbean Sea known as Great Corn Island and Little Corn Island; and the Government of Nicaragua further grants to the Government of the United States for a like period of 99 years, the right to establish, operate and maintain a naval base at such place on the territory of Nicaragua bordering upon the Gulf of Fonseca as the Government of the United States may select. The Government of the United States shall have the option of renewing, for a further term of 99 years, the above leases and grants upon the expiration of their respective terms, it being expressly agreed that the territory hereby leased and the naval base which may be maintained under the grant aforesaid shall be subject exclusively to the laws and sovereign authority of the United States during the terms of such lease and grant and any renewal or renewals thereof.

3. In consideration of the foregoing stipulation and for the purposes contemplated by this convention and for the purpose of reducing the present indebtedness of Nicaragua, the Government of the United States shall, upon the date of the exchange of ratification of this convention, pay for the benefit of the Republic of Nicaragua the sum of $3,000,000 United States coin of the present weight and fineness, to be deposited to the order of the Government of Nicaragua in such bank or banks, or with such banking corporation as the Government of the United States may determine, to be applied by Nicaragua upon its indebtedness or other public purposes for the advancement of the welfare of Nicaragua in a manner to be determined by the two high contracting parties, all such disbursements to be made by orders drawn by the minister of finance of the Republic of Nicaragua and approved by the Secretary of State of the United States or by such person as he may designate.

The view of Elihu Root (at the head of this chapter) reflected not only North American misgivings—vigorously expressed in many newspapers and magazines—but the indignation of all Latin America at this iniquity. Yet Washington, impervious as ever to its neighbors' opinions, was well satisfied with an agreement enabling it to complete the defense system for the approaches to the Panama Canal: not only because the Gulf of Fonseca was ample enough to hold all the squadrons on earth and easily defensible, but because Lake Nicaragua with its numerous islands could serve as shipyards, sanitary and coaling stations, etc. Not to mention that geography made Nicaragua a potential fire station to put out any possible conflagration in Central America.

El Salvador, Honduras, and Costa Rica protested in vain against the alienation of Nicaragua's sovereignty: after this, what price their own? Under the Washington Conventions of 1907, the work of Secretary Root, any dispute had to be submitted to the Central American Court of Justice. Previous treaties barred Nicaragua from unilaterally modifying the status of the area. Of this the court found it guilty in September 1916: it said that Nicaragua had violated the 1858 Border Treaty with Costa Rica, the arbitration decision of President Cleveland in 1888, and the Peace and Friendship Treaty of December 1907. The court also rejected Nicaragua's plea that the Bryan-Chamorro Treaty only gave the United States the right of option. In view of this, Nicaragua refused to accept the court's decision, and the United States likewise rejected it on the poor excuse that not having signed the Washington Convention agreements it was not bound by them.

The sophism proved mortal to the Central American Court which, due to renew its authority in 1917, expired in March 1918. As historian David Moore relates it: "Nicaragua, looked upon as the protégé of the United States, refused to renew the convention, and so the final sessions of the Court closed in March, 1918. It must be recalled that it was largely owing to the United States that the Court had come into being. It ceased to exist when the United States disregarded its judgments."[16]

Another American, Senator Borah, thus described what had happened:

> The treaty which we made with Nicaragua did not in any sense represent the expression of view or wishes of the Nicarguan people.

So far as Nicaragua was concerned it was made by a government which we set up, which by force we maintained, and which did not represent the views of the Nicaraguan people at any time. We made an important treaty with a helpless people, a people under our military domination.

The American admiral who had charge of the affairs in Nicaragua stated in the hearings that if the Nicaraguan people were permitted to express themselves, 80 percent of them, in his opinion, would be opposed to the government as it then existed and would be opposed to the treaty as submitted.

I have never regarded the Nicaragua treaty as binding on the Nicaraguan people. We were making a treaty with ourselves. We were making a treaty with a government which was our puppet. We were making a treaty with a government which represented us at the other end of the treaty-making negotiations. It is one of the most indefensible transactions of which I have knowledge in international affairs.[17]

Some years later a Spanish journalist would express this opinion: "It is said that Chamorro has more than once regretted the consequences of the famous agreement, and that he has good reason to do so. For unlike Adolfo Díaz, Chamorro is not an employee rising in the service of a foreign company that uses him as a straw man. Chamorro comes from an old landowning family. . . . How then can we explain his name being placed among the blackest in history? . . . But in the United States they have got what they wanted: a state of law achieved by pressure or political rewards where the leaders, as we see, have not hesitated to sell their souls to the devil to satisfy their ambitions and crush their enemies."[18]

4
"A Short-lived Benevolent Imperialism"

Amidst the new order of sea power and world politics that appeared at the end of the nineteenth century, a concern for the security of the Continental Republic and naval communications between its two populous seacoasts led to a series of interventions by the United States itself within the sovereignties of the independent republics of the Caribbean and in certain states of Central America. These interventions led to a short-lived benevolent imperialism that disappeared as soon as the European danger seemed to vanish after Versailles.

Samuel Flagg Bemis[1]

You, my fellow countrymen of the United States, know full well how sincerely we desire the independence, the unimpaired sovereignty and political integrity, the constantly increasing prosperity of the peoples of Latin America. We have our domestic problems incident to the expanding life of a free people, but there is no imperialist sentiment among us to cast even a shadow across the pathway of our progress. We covet no territory; we seek no conquest; the liberty we cherish for ourselves we desire for others; and we assert no rights for ourselves that we do not accord to others. We sincerely desire to see throughout this hemisphere an abiding peace, the reign of justice and the diffusion of the blessings of a beneficent cooperation.

Charles Evans Hughes[2]

The later history of this and other Chamorros compels us to doubt that Emiliano was all that sensitive. He was not in the least embarrassed to become Díaz' successor through elections "supervised" by the U.S. Marine fire brigade, under the paternal eye of the *Chatanooga's* and *San Diego's* guns. The action in the electoral wings, as Salvatierra describes it, was a new demonstration of what "Apostle of Democracy" Wilson understood by free elections.

It turned out that U.S. Minister Jefferson summoned Julián Irías, the Liberal candidate,

> to an interview in the Legation on the morning of 17 September 1916, in the presence of Admiral Caperton and the interpreter Dr. Francisco Brown Webber . . . and the US minister, dispensing with the ambiguous verbiage of diplomatic amiability, made these statements to Irías in the Secretary of State's name:
>
> That no one could be President of Nicaragua who did not prove to the satisfaction of U.S. secretaries of state (1) that he accepts without modification the agreements made with the United States by the present Nicaraguan government, (2) that in all that concerned its economic system the Nicaraguan government must proceed in total agreement with the State Department, (3) that the candidate accept U.S. policy for maintenance of order and peace in the republic, and the United States' right to withdraw or not withdraw its forces stationed in Nicaragua, or bring them back, as it sees fit, (4) that the candidate show he did not participate in any way in Zelaya's administration, (5) that he prove to the Secretary of State that he never directly or indirectly participated in revolutionary movements against the Nicaraguan government since the fall of Zelaya.[3]

Elemental dignity and decency prevented the Liberals from accepting this imposition and hence from competing in elections. Thus Emiliano Chamorro became president in January 1917, describing as a "sacrifice" his acceptance of an office which less perceptive souls called a prize for treason. During his term he introduced the Lansing Plan, a financial system controlling all state income, albeit not necessarily to the state's benefit.[4] Attentively counseled by the bankers and sustained by the U.S. Marine Corps, in 1918 he appointed a Supreme Commission of the Republic to control the nation's expenses, consisting naturally enough of two State Department nominees and one Nicaraguan named by Chamorro.

Wilson responded to all this with his proverbial idealism: "The United States will never again acquire a foot of territory by conquest. . . . The small states of the world have the right to enjoy the same respect for their sovereignty and territorial integrity as the great and powerful nations."

Latin Americans might have greeted his words with emotion had not events in Nicaragua, Panama, Mexico, Haiti, Cuba, and Santo Domingo shown them what U.S. bankers understood by Pan-Americanism: the Big Stick subjugating sovereignties, corrupting consciences, establishing bestial dictatorships, and resorting to blackmail and coercion, while idealistic and puritanical presidents devoted themselves to fomenting democracy—on paper. Or we might have taken seriously Wilson's famous speech at Mobile (October 27, 1913) and his promise that states that were weighed down by debt would be freed from the intolerable situation of capitalist control of their internal affairs.

As for Central America, one way of avoiding that domination was through a united front of its people against avarice and hegemony. This was what the republics had in mind when in December 1920 they began conferring in San José, Costa Rica, on "a definitive pact of perpetual and indissoluble union between the peoples of Central America." The discussions proceeded swimmingly until someone mentioned the subject of international treaties. Then all hell broke loose. Chamorro's delegates asked for recognition of the Bryan-Chamorro Treaty and the agreements with the bankers, and for Nicaragua's right to make its own arrangements with the United States concerning those agreements. Yes, certainly they wanted unification, but at the same time that the United States should continue governing Nicaragua. Or more concretely, they didn't want the Federal Republic of Central America.[5]

This being the situation, Guatemala, El Salvador, and Honduras formed a Tripartite Republic on December 1, 1921, with its capital in Comayagua, Honduras. All three held elections for federal deputies and only the election of senators in Guatemala was lacking for the Federal Congress to meet on January 15. But on December 5 General Orellana rebelled against Guatemalan President Herrera, and on January 14 the Guatemalan assembly voted to quit the Tripartite Pact, which in consequence fell apart.

Significantly, on December 23, just after Orellana's putsch, U.S. Secretary of State Charles Evans Hughes sent a cable impugning the tripartite federation, citing stipulations of the 1907 Peace and Friendship Treaty to the effect that "the High Contracting Parties will not recognize any regime arising from a coup d'état or revolution against a recognized government, until such time as freely elected representatives of the people shall have reorganized the country in constitutional form." In his cable Hughes exhorted El Salvador and Honduras to strict observance of the convention, which also imposed nonintervention by any contracting party in another's internal affairs. He was saying in effect that if El Salvador and Honduras tried to aid Herrera against Orellana in conformity with the Tripartite Pact, they would be guilty of intervention, since the organism resulting from the pact had not yet begun functioning nor had been recognized by the United States.

Hughes' casuistry tended to favor Orellana, the dictator who was to distinguish himself by his gracious concessions to the United Fruit Company. The pact as conceived did not suit the interests of the United States, which needed rather to update the 1907 stipulations in line with its material concerns. With this in mind, Hughes and Sumner Welles produced a pact, signed on February 7, 1923, which besides limiting armaments and shoring up "peace and friendship," provided in Article 2:

> Desiring to make secure in the Republics of Central America the benefits which are derived from the maintenance of free institutions and to contribute at the same time toward strengthening their stability and the prestige with which they should be surrounded, they declare that every act, disposition or measure which alters the constitutional organization in any one of them is to be deemed a menace to the peace of said Republics, whether it proceed from any public power or from the private citizens.
>
> Consequently, the Governments of the Contracting Parties will not recognize any other Government which may come into power in any of the five Republics through a *coup d'état* or a revolution against a recognized Government so long as the freely elected representatives of the people thereof have not constitutionally reorganized the country. And even in such case they obligate themselves not to acknowledge the recognition in any of the persons elected as President, Vice-President or Chief of State Designate should fall under any of the following heads:
>
> 1) If he should be the leader or one of the leaders of a *coup d'état* or revolution, or through blood relationship or marriage be an ascendant or descendant or brother of such a leader or leaders.
>
> 2) If he should have been a Secretary of State or should have held

some high military command during the accomplishment of the *coup d'état,* the revolution, or the election.

Furthermore, in no case shall recognition be accorded to a government which arises from election to power of a citizen expressly and unquestionably disqualified by the Constitution of his country as eligible to election as President, Vice-President or Chief of State Designate.[6]

Another stipulation of the pact was formation of a National Guard in Nicaragua to replace the U.S. fire brigade stationed in Managua's Campo de Marte since 1912. In token of the goodwill of the new U.S. president, Coolidge (successor to Harding, who succeeded Wilson), it was from the U.S. minister that Vice-President Bartolomé Martínez learned this happy news. Martínez was occupying the throne due to the death in 1923—in bed, though it seems hard to believe—of President Diego Manuel Chamorro. This Chamorro had inherited the scepter from his nephew Emiliano in January 1921.

Martínez had broken the chain so laboriously woven by the Díazes and Chamorros. He was neither one of the Granada Conservatives nor one of the León Liberals, nor a pro-Yanqui from Bluefields, but a northerner from Segovia. This was not only a novelty but an enigma. The enigma was solved when Martínez decided in July 1924 to repay Nicaragua's debts to Brown Brothers and Seligman, thus recovering the Pacific railroad. He also bought out the National Bank creditors for $300,000. He crowned these actions with efforts to unify Liberals and Conservatives in a joint crusade for national recuperation. To that end he put forward a reconciliation ticket of Conservative Solórzano and Liberal Sacasa which won the elections in 1924 in a landslide.

In January 1925 Martínez handed the reins to Solórzano and on August 3 the U.S. marines finally departed, leaving Nicaragua's flag over the Campo de Marte for the first time in fourteen years. As might have been expected, the military rose in arms on August 28 under *chamorrista* General Alfredo Rivas. But Mr. Hughes, invoking the pact of February 7, 1923, sent two warships as a decisive persuader and Rivas failed.

Not so our old friend Emiliano Chamorro, who seized the Tiscapa fortress in October. Solórzano made no effort whatever to resist. After a huddle with Díaz and the U.S. minister, he handed over power to Chamorro—instead of delegating it to Sacasa—and sent this message to all political and military leaders:

After the taking of the Tiscapa fortress and surrender of the penitentiary, we have come to a politico-military understanding with General Emiliano Chamorro by which he remains commander in chief of the army of the Republic for as long as is necessary to restore constitutional order. I trust that you and the friends in your department will realize how difficult the situation is through which the Republic is passing, and will be equal to the duty that a well-understood patriotism imposes on us. Comandante General, Solórzano.

This curious sample of "well-understood patriotism," which asks collaboration "to restore order" in favor of the man mainly perturbing it, is not the only pearl in the legalistic necklace with which Latin American governments have adorned their betrayals of their peoples for the benefit of spurious interests. And for those in Our America who really believed Coolidge was different from Wilson, the hour of their conviction to the contrary soon arrived. On the one hand, it was certified by the U.S. historian James Truslow Adams:

> His interests were narrow, and he apparently knew and cared little about international affairs or the larger problems of the postwar world. His comment on the debts when there was a question of their reduction—"they hired the money, didn't they?"—gives us a fair measure of the man.
>
> Silent, without culture or intellectual tastes, a mind that in many respects was singularly ordinary and commonplace, he [Coolidge] nevertheless had a certain hard-bitten Yankee shrewdness and common sense which made him appear to many as a wise and safe leader.[7]

And on the other hand, the words of our compatriot Palacios:

> . . . any reader of his book *The Price of Liberty* will have pronounced him a paladin of human rights, morality and justice . . . that such a man should be destined to bring about a basic change in U.S. political procedure, to become the agent and champion of continental solidarity. But here we find this fervent apostle . . . using his position as president of the world's strongest nation to perform the most arbitrary and unjust act conceivable, moved by material interests, against a defenseless people of America—to the point of finding no valid excuses even for the benefit of his own countrymen, who openly reproved him. And with this act he brings upon his nation the derision of history and the anathema and hatred of all free men.[8]

The ones who really felt the sting of Mr. Coolidge's altruism were as usual the Nicaraguans, but this time the silent rebellion was going to explode. The explosion was sparked by an obscure but passionate worker with no access to culture or wealth, who drew worldwide admiration for holding U.S. money and firepower in check and reclaiming for Our America the right to rule itself without foreign tutelage or interference.

Yet at no time did the Nicaraguans stop their resistance to U.S. oppression and exploitation and to the shameless sellout by Chamorro and Díaz. So much so that in February 1921 some marines were goaded into attacking the editorial office of *La Tribuna,* which had rebuked their outrage; they were not court-martialed but given two years in jail. At the end of that year and the beginning of the next more clashes occurred between patriots and invaders in which five Nicaraguans were killed and five wounded. This time there were indemnities and excuses and ten-year sentences for the marines responsible, but the sentences were soon commuted; the deaths remained incommutable.

The U.S.-guaranteed pact of 1923 with Central American countries was an attempt to cool the climate of protest and hatred that the excesses of U.S. Pan-Americanism created throughout the continent. Within the United States there was steadily growing protest by well-known liberals such as Samuel Guy Inman, Waldo Frank, and senators Borah and Ladd, supporting a movement in which trade unions and university people were involved.[9] Borah was hopefully pointing out that the works of the president and secretary of state suggested repugnance for the policy of violence, but any illusions arising from this were empty ones. Chamorro, representing the U.S. bankers, took power using Sacasa as intermediary. Bartolomé Martínez' measures of national recuperation had made the bankers uneasy. Chamorro's coup dissipated their worries and even when Washington—cornered by its own guarantee—denied recognition to its own puppet, that did not prevent Congress from accepting Solórzano's resignation and naming Chamorro as successor instead of Sacasa as the Constitution demanded. But since Washington couldn't untangle itself from its guarantee, Chamorro decided to resign in favor of Senator Sebastián Uriza, who went through a legalistic pantomime to transfer the presidency to the known traitor Díaz.

As was to be expected, the State Department now extended recognition on the spot. Through the early months of 1926 the defrauded Sacasa, who had been educated in the United States, tried vainly to regain power. Finding it hopeless, he began preparing his revenge, and in May an insurrection broke out in Bluefields under General José María Moncada. Sacasa, who was then in Washington hoping to convince the State Department, took off for Guatemala where he conferred with Moncada and named him commander in chief of the army which was to install Sacasa as president.

Moncada, the man responsible for the jailing of General Mena, was noted for his constant switching from Liberal to Conservative and back. Now a Liberal, he was ready to fight "to restore constitutional order." On August 6 he and Luis Beltrán Sandoval landed from the *Foam* at Prinzapolka on the Atlantic. After winning battles at La Barra and La Cruz they decided to dig in at Puerto Cabezas to protect the government of Sacasa, who arrived there in short order. The struggle then spread across the country. Samuel Sediles, Julián Venegas, and Roberto Bone led a Pacific landing force but were defeated by General Roberto Hurtado, who executed every prisoner he took.

By then the United States was alarmed and decided on quick action. Lawrence Dennis was sent as an envoy to mediate the conflict. He succeeded in bringing together on the warship *Denver* at Corinto delegates of Sacasa and Díaz. Nothing resulted except a sensational news item published by the *New York World*.[10]

Could the charge be valid? As occurred twenty-seven years later with his colleague Mr. Peurifoy in Guatemala, U.S. envoy Dennis achieved world fame by his doings in Nicaragua and statements such as the following: "You mustn't think we're going to bring the vice-president on a warship; but if he lands at some point in Nicaragua, that is something else;" "Here people often think we come to serve the interests of one lot against the other, but they're wrong. We only serve our own interests." All in all, a cascade of brazen impertinences and botcheries which was far from flattering to the State Department's criteria for selecting emissaries. Dennis never took the trouble to deny the public and formal accusations that pictured him as pushing Díaz for president with offers of cash. Apart from the serious statement by Solórzano's former minister Salvador

Mendieta,[11] a mass of rumors and legends accumulated about Mr. Dennis' mission.

Since the huddle on the *Denver* led to nothing, Dennis suggested to Díaz that he should seek U.S. protection. Well trained as he was in such procedures, the quisling had no trouble doing so, stressing the defeat of his forces by Moncada at Las Perlas lagoon and accusing Mexico of having supplied "three hundred Mexican bolsheviks" to Sacasa's army. An Associated Press cable from Managua indicated how worried Díaz was:

> President Díaz betrays great anxiety over the situation and said: "A few days ago I informed the U.S. ambassador that Mexico, if it so desires, can easily defeat all of the Central American republics and that I would not be able to hold out long against it. Another Mexican gunboat, the *Temporal,* sailed some days ago from Mexico with more ammunition from the Mexican government and also light and heavy artillery. We have a few old guns which cannot be compared with modern ones. Reports from Puerto Cabezas and Rio Grande say that naval forces are disarming indigenous troops and that many weapons bearing the Mexican government mark have been found. . . ." President Díaz said his government is without funds or munitions.[12]

The new intervention began on December 24, 1926, when, after an unsuccessful attempt had been made on the quisling's life, Admiral Julian Latimer ordered marines to land at Puerto Cabezas to disarm Sacasa's forces or force them out of the position. Latimer then ordered mahogany exporters to pay their taxes only to the Conservative government. The *Cleveland* and the *Denver* guaranteed the success of the landing which, according to the State Department's official explanation, was "to protect U.S. interests and foreigners resident there." Carter Field, the *New York Herald Tribune*'s man in Washington, who favored the intervention, noted that "the State Department has made no direct reply to the charge published by the Liberal Nicaraguan agent in Mexico that there had been no request for protection by U.S. citizens and companies in Puerto Cabezas; the department limited itself to repeating that it had received requests from there that marines be sent in, without giving names of those who made them."[13]

At all costs the patriotic revolution had to be linked with the conflict then developing between President Calles of Mexico and the U.S. oil companies.[14] The quisling lost no opportunity to stress the help his opponents were getting from Mexico, and the State Department acted as if it really believed and was concerned about this. Latin Americans were not alone in taking such pretexts with a grain of salt. In the United States itself, senators, correspondents, newspapers, and trade unions loudly denounced the real promoters of the intervention. For example, on December 28 the *Evening World* editorialized under the heading "Foreign Policy at 'The Admiral's Discretion'":

> American marines have landed in Nicaragua, assumed political power despite honeyed denials, and the State Department, "without further advices," complacently announces that it has confidence in Admiral Latimer's "discretion." Senator Borah, Chairman of the Foreign Relations Committee, is not so complacent and proposes to demand an explanation, and, in the absence of one that is satisfactory, to order an investigation. There ought to be an investigation to the end that the American people and the Latin-American world may know what these strange happenings mean.
>
> The vague excuse that the marines were landed and the Admiral given discretionary power for the protection of American property would be more impressive but for our well-known partiality for President Díaz. The latter would be more impressive as the "constitutional" Executive but for his admission, by his action, that he must depend on American bayonets to keep him in office. Our ally is not an inspiring figure.
>
> If "constitutional government" means the same in Nicaragua as in the United States, the constitutional ruler would have been Sacasa, who, as Vice-President, had the right to succeed the President who resigned.
>
> There is so much to explain that Senator Borah will act wisely in insisting on an explanation or an investigation. It does not satisfy any right-thinking American to have the announcement from the State Department that marines have been landed in a foreign country to interfere in a domestic controversy and that, the Admiral having been given "discretionary powers," the Washington Government is merely waiting to see how it comes out. It is impossible to believe that the Government at Washington is not thoroughly informed. The alleged denial to the Nicaraguan Minister of Foreign Affairs by the American authorities of the right to use of the code in radiograms to the official representatives in foreign lands does not make the picture any brighter.

Meanwhile in Mexico *El Universal* was ironically editorializing on December 28 that "the United States has built a navy equal to that of the world's strongest sea power for the sole purpose of using this prodigious instrument to invade the coasts of Nicaragua." The newspaper added that "the indignation of Latin American republics has been made all the greater by the web of spurious interpretations behind which the State Department conceals its aims, from the undersecretary's propaganda about Mexico spreading bolshevism into Central America to the most recent pretext that Nicaragua has been invaded to protect the property and rights of U.S. residents in Puerto Cabezas."

Dr. Vaca, Sacasa's representative in Washington, noted the significance of the intervention having been launched just as the U.S. Congress was going into recess. For his part, Nicaraguan Federation of Labor Secretary de la Selva said publicly: "We have organized and developed under the patronage of the [North] American Federation of Labor, and only in the event that this great bulwark of democracy is bolshevik could we also be bolsheviks. The Nicaraguan Federation of Labor expects a movement among U.S. workers to exert influence against the landing. . . ." One of the frankest condemnations of Kellogg's policy came on December 28 from Henry Suydam, veteran correspondent of the *Brooklyn Eagle* (who later became State Department press chief):

KELLOGG KILLING HUGHES'
FINE WORK IN LATIN-AMERICA

BLUNDER AT NICARAGUA PLAYS INTO MEXICO'S HANDS.
FEAR LAMENTABLE RESULTS

The foreign intervention of the United States in Nicaraguan politics, under the pretext of protecting American property, is a singular example of the ineptitude of Frank B. Kellogg, Secretary of State. There is not a single Latin-American diplomatist in Washington who is not in despair over the present incumbent of our State Department. Moreover, Mr. Kellogg's diplomacy is calculated to produce the very result that he is most anxious to avoid, for Mexico more and more is being placed, through his clumsiness, in the position of banner-bearer for the other Republics of this hemisphere.

This is all the more lamentable in view of the fact that Charles Evans Hughes, during his four years as Foreign Minister, sought to remove causes of irritation and to demonstrate that this Government, while possessed of giant power, intended to use it temperately. Under the Hughes clear-headed and strong administration, there was a growing light in the darkness, a definite development of good will.

Distrust Spreads Under Kellogg

Under Mr. Kellogg, fear, suspicion and distrust are spreading in the Caribbean and throughout Latin-America. It is not without significance that *La Nación,* the largest newspaper in The Argentine, always a strong supporter of the idea behind the Pan-American Union, came out in a recent editorial to inquire how the precepts of that union could be reconciled with the practices of the State Department.

Playing into Mexico's Hands

American intervention in a Nicaraguan political situation, undertaken for the purpose of thwarting Mexico in that country can have no other effect than to increase Mexican influence and Mexican opportunity there. Although it may, for the moment, eliminate Dr. Sacasa and his Liberal Cabinet, it is bound to create sympathy and support for him among Nicaraguans, otherwise indifferent or even hostile. . . .

Other Countries Suspicious

It is not mere speculation to say that Mr. Hughes would have gone to extreme lengths to avoid the use of force in Latin-America. Intrinsically, the landing of a few marines is no great matter, but its repercussions will be heard throughout the other American Republics, already suspicious of the United States as a result of recent American performances.

Mr. Kellogg is already embroiled in an unhappy dilemma respecting Mexico. He is interfering in Nicaragua. His technique in the Tacna-Arica dispute is anything but pleasing to those involved.

Further Sources of Irritation

Several of the greater countries in South America find pseudo-scientific embargoes erected against their products—a device to raise, through an administrative act, the protective barriers still higher than the existing high tariff rates, which have failed to satisfy some lines of American business. The recent Treaty with Panama is another source of irritation. The State Department's desire to negotiate unconditional "most favored nation" treaties with Latin-America, rather than to grant reciprocal special treatment, is still another.

Economic Independence

Behind all these developments is the vast pressure of the outward thrust of American business, what is sometimes called "economic imperialism." This outward thrust is legitimate enough in itself, but it will never be carried on with any lasting success in an atmosphere of irritation and suspicion. The elements working for conciliation in Latin-America realize that our Northern markets can never be expanded to their full possibilities if a blundering diplomacy is permitted to antagonize our Southern neighbors.

Destroying Hughes' Good Work

A broad development is now in progress under Mr. Kellogg which, if allowed to continue, will destroy the last trace of Mr. Hughes' work, will envelop this country's American relations in an evil atmosphere from which it will take years to recover and will thrust Mexico forward as the protector and standard bearer of all the republics in this hemisphere.

The hands of Latin-American diplomats in Washington are tied, but it will not be long before the U.S. Senate will take a hand to find out just where Mr. Kellogg is heading his country.

None of this had any effect. Having declared Puerto Cabezas, Bluefields, and other key Atlantic points to be a neutral zone, Latimer learned that the rebels were winning on the Pacific; he extended his fire brigade operation and decided to occupy the whole of Nicaragua. The big landing began on January 6, 1927, with such grandiose convoys of troops that they took all night and part of the morning of the next day to march from the railroad station to the Campo de Marte. Latimer's forces consisted of sixteen warships, 215 officers, 3,900 soldiers, and 865 marines.

On January 9 quisling Díaz cabled his justification of the unjustifiable to the *New York Times*:

For us, as for the United States, the question of constitutionality has been satisfactorily settled. . . .

Obviously, if the Mexican Government elects, and is permitted, to pour money, arms and men into a small country like mine to enable an unsuccessful minority to make war on the Constitutional Government, that Government cannot answer for the consequences of foreign lives in its territory. . . .

So penetrated with the logic of this situation were the British and Italian, as well as other foreign representatives in Managua, that after learning from me the limit of our means for assuring order against Mexican invasion they went to the American Ministry, forthwith, to make representations on behalf of their menaced nationals. . . .

The Conservatives realize that Nicaragua is small and weak. In difficult situations such as that of the moment we solicit frankly the aid of the United States in an open and legal manner, while our Liberal adversaries seek the sinister help of Mexico. . . .

On January 10 Secretary of State Kellogg announced: "We have extended our recognition to Adolfo Díaz, for which reason anyone stating that he is not Constitutional President of Nicaragua is mistaken," and President Coolidge told the Congress:

> The United States cannot . . . fail to view with deep concern any serious threat to stability and consitutional government in Nicaragua tending toward anarchy and jeopardizing American interests. . . . It has alway been and remains the policy of the United States in such circumstances to take the steps that may be necessary for the preservation and protection of the lives, the property, and the interests of its citizens and of this government itself. In this respect I propose to follow the path of my predecessors.[15]

On January 12, in reply to the criticisms aimed at him, Kellogg presented a memorandum to the Senate Foreign Relations Committee chaired by Mr. Borah, alleging communist activities against the United States in "Mexico and other Latin American countries."

Quisling Díaz put his case in an Associated Press dispatch published in *La Prensa*, New York, on February 9: "Should the United States think it better that I resign my post to any other person, I would do it immediately. . . . I always opposed the withdrawal of marines from Nicaragua, and welcome them on their return in aid of our nation. . . . As long as I am president, and in the governments that follow me, the U.S. marines should remain in my country." If this were not in itself a sufficient sample of the infamy of Díaz, here is a cabled story published in the principal New York papers on February 24, as for example in the *New York Times*:

> MANAGUA, NICARAGUA, FEB. 23 (AP)—President Díaz' proposals for a treaty with the United States, by which protection of the interests of Nicaragua for 100 years would be assured, will be placed before the Nicaraguan Congress Thursday, and he announced last night his assurance that they will be approved.

In addition to the right that would be granted the United States to intervene when necessary to maintain an adequate Government and assure free elections, to guarantee the sovereignty and independence of Nicaragua and retain the agreements of the Bryan-Chamorro Treaty, now in force, including the right to build a canal through Nicaraguan territory, Nicaragua would concede rights to develop the country so as to assure financial rehabilitation and security and the public health.

Under the financial rehabilitation provision, the President of the United States would recommend a financial adviser to be appointed by the Nicaraguan President. This adviser would be an American and have supreme power over financial dispensations and the power to veto expenditures. There would also be an American Collector General of all revenue.

These two offices would exist only for the duration of the refunding and consolidation of the present internal and external debt of $7,000,000, revolutionary claims of $4,000,000 and a debt of $4,000,000 for proposed railway construction. A loan is expected to be floated for this construction, virtually under American guarantees.

The United States would work out plans for the Nicaraguan constabulary, sanitation, financial and economic rehabilitation, a credit system and fiscal administration. It is stipulated that collections of revenues shall first go to the expenses of the office of the Collector General, then to the national debt, the National Guard and the budget.

Nicaragua would not have a standing army, but would have a trained, armed constabulary, which would include municipal and rural police and be the only armed organization of the country. The constabulary would be officered by United States Marine officers.

The constabulary would be non-political, and if after a ten-year period it became necessary to prevent a coup d'état of a political uprising, American officers would automatically be given the privilege to take control of the constabulary.

The treaty terms provide that Nicaragua is not to enter a treaty with, or lease or sell territory to a foreign power other than the United States without the consent of the United States.

It seemed that the object of the marines, to whom the supreme traitor had not only opened the doors of his country but handed it over tied hand and foot, was more than a long stay in Nicaragua: they expected to take it over. As Salvatierra tells it: "Shortly afterward they took Nicaragua's principal fortress, the Tiscapa, and on February 23 the Stars and Stripes flew over it. But within a few days the flag was no longer there. It was said that the British chargé d'affaires, musing on the situation, had put in an official request to know whether the Republic of Nicaragua had ceased to exist."[16]

The bankers did not remain idle. With White House approval, Guaranty Trust Company and J. and W. Seligman Company made a contract on March 21, 1927, with Joaquín Cuadra Zavala, the quisling's agent in Washington, extending to Nicaragua a $1 million credit to be used for maintenance and equipment of an Indian army, for purchase of provisions, or for whatever might be decided by a committee consisting of U.S. High Commissioner Roscoe Hill, National Bank chief Louis Rosenthal, and a Nicaraguan who might be the treasury secretary.

The cost of arms shipped in ran to $217,718 at 6 percent, a transaction engineered this time by Alejandro César after telegraphic consultation between the White House and Minister to Managua Charles E. Eberhart. On the previous day Kellogg had told the *New York Herald Tribune* correspondent: "These are the same terms under which the War Department sold to Nicaragua in November 1921 10,000 rifles, 50 machine guns, and 7 million rounds of ammunition, at a cost at the time of $170,585 with the same 6 percent interest." The price had gone up: this time there were 200 machine guns, 3,000 rifles, and 3 million rounds of ammunition.

On February 25 the press published the view of Senator Borah: "This dishonest action by the U.S. government is so objectionable that I have no words to comment on it. What I would like to say could not be printed in the papers."[17]

For the $1 million they "loaned," these were the "compensation" to the bankers: a charge on dividends, supplies, and properties of the Nicaraguan National Bank, the total value of which exceeded $600,000; a concession to collect income created by the Nicaraguan Congress in January 1927 to aid small farmers; transfer of all the railroad and National Bank stocks prior to any use of the credit extended, with authorization to the bankers to transfer or sell them in the event that Nicaragua did not cancel the debt.

The bankers' first step was to transfer to Guaranty Trust and Seligman the funds and reserves of the National Bank and the railroad securities in cash, a transfer required by previous cancellation of a deposit contract with the Royal Bank of Canada.

Truly a delightful operation! The last word in political-financial brazenness! Before the puppet could make use of the credit, the lenders already had for their million $3.5 million in cash, in the form of the railroad and National Bank securities and the paper money reserve fund. Candidly stated, the bankers were lending Nicaragua its own money at 6 percent interest, while the $3.5 million withdrawn as security by the bankers would pay 2 percent.

The sequel to this odious transaction, in which as usual the State Department intervened without a blush, was a news item published on June 4, 1927, by the *New York Times* and *Herald Tribune*: Lawrence Dennis, ex-plenipotentiary extraordinary of the U.S. government to the government in Managua and noted agent of Wall Street, entered the service of J. and W. Seligman Company.

To such plenipotentiaries, such potentialities. None could doubt that Dennis had performed his mission satisfactorily.

5
Sandino, Hero of Las Segovias

Conquest did not threaten from any quarter in
1927, although Secretary of State Kellogg feared
that Nicaragua was in danger of falling into the
control of Bolshevists inspired and assisted from
Mexico. Instead of more drastic action, President
Coolidge followed the suggestion of Secretary
of State Kellogg, and sent to Nicaragua Colonel
Henry L. Stimson, formerly Secretary of War in
the Taft Administration, as a wise man to study the
trouble and recommend a solution. "I want you to
go down there and if you can see a way to clean up
that mess, I want you to do it."

Samuel Flagg Bemis[1]

Shall we be delivered up to the wild beasts?
So many millions of us speak English?
Where are the noble hidalgos and brave knights?
Will we be silent now, to weep later?

Rubén Darío

Augusto Nicolás Calderón Sandino[2] was born in the humble village
of Niquihomo, Department of Masaya, on May 19, 1895. His father,
Gregorio, was a small farmer. His mother, Margarita Calderón, was a
campesina with white and Indian blood in her veins.

He finished elementary school in the times of Zelaya, and while
his brothers enjoyed higher education he went on to the study of
business amid the horrors of the "Mena War." With his own eyes he
saw the body of Zeledón being brought in. No kinsmen of the hero
or weeping multitude constituted the funeral cortege, but the soldiers who had killed him. They paraded the body placed feet fore-
most on a horse, to strike fear into any who would follow him in
rebellion. How could Sandino know that a similar fate awaited him?

Of his adolescence and early youth little is known. He was by
nature mild and circumspect, characteristics that only disappeared in

the thick of the struggle he was to undertake. A fragment or two emerges to reconstruct the years when he combined his studies with the tasks of a peasant, with administering his father's farms and carting farm products to Granada, Masaya, and Managua.

There was a moment in his youth when he was impelled to kill a man—some say because of an insult to his mother, some for political reasons. In any case he had to leave Nicaragua in 1921, and took a job in the northern Honduras port of La Ceiba, guarding machinery in the Montecristo sugar mill. In 1922 he was working as a mechanic for the United Fruit Company in Quiriguá, Guatemala; in 1923 for the Huasteca Petroleum Company in Tampico, Mexico, also as mechanic.

It is in Tampico that a biographer's search must begin for the origins of his later struggle. At the time, all of Mexico was shaken by the revolutionary and patriotic spirit. The great U.S. oil concerns—Sinclair, Doheny, Mellon—had launched a worldwide media campaign to force President Alvaro Obregón into line with their pretensions.[3] As Bemis tells it, a senatorial committee headed by Albert B. Fall of New Mexico, spokesman for the Doheny interests which made a big fuss about outrages against U.S. citizens, "merely" recommended diplomatic pressure on and nonrecognition of the constitutionally elected Obregón government to get all claims settled—and intervention only if the response was negative.

Secretary of State Hughes, a noted jurist fervently advocating that his country's imperialist policy should be conducted without violence, worked on Obregón to recognize by solemn treaty the existence and legality of the absurd multibillion-dollar U.S. and British claims. Obregón perceived what Hughes was really after: not only to compromise the whole nation by such a treaty, but to deprive Mexico of any juridical possibility of discussing the legitimacy of the claims. Backed by workers and students and the public opinion of all Latin America, Obregón refused to sign.

U.S. threats of intervention intensified. In Mexico the ancient custom of a people in arms was strengthened by the Russian people's victory over the combined forces of the world's great powers. A climate was maintained of readiness for possible resistance within which the Left parties' ideological and revolutionary activity was able to develop.

This was the climate in which Sandino had his first anti-imperialist experiences. In the heart of the Doheny interests—the Huasteca Petroleum Company—he made contact with a Mexican labor movement agitated by a dispute that bore the seeds of possible war, and there his innate spirit of patriotic rebellion began to mature.

Facing the determined resistance of Obregón and of workers and democratic elements in the United States itself, Hughes had to make do with agreements of an executive type known later as the Bucareli treaties. Only then did Obregón win the United States' reluctant recognition. He was followed as president by Plutarco Elías Calles who, anxious for popular prestige, promulgated oil laws violating the Bucareli agreements and denied that he was bound to them. Then the Cristero rebellion broke out and Calles' violent suppression of it fueled the media campaign against him.

Hughes' successor Kellogg was determined to finish with Calles as he had done with Sacasa in Nicaragua. The general climate seemed propitious for crushing the "Mexican bolsheviks;" but the U.S. Senate had had enough of the reaction produced by the Nicaraguan intervention, and voted unanimously on January 25, 1927, to resolve the differences with Mexico by arbitration. President Coolidge, now persuaded to proceed pacifically, took Kellogg's suggestion of naming as ambassador to Mexico Kellogg's old college chum Dwight W. Morrow, banker and Morgan partner. It is possible that Mr. Morrow was persuasive enough to make Calles revise his whole oil policy overnight, but we incline to suspect that the reason for his change of course was the open blackmail of the oil companies, which simply stopped all operations. Thousands of workers became idle in this colossal lockout, which more efficiently brought about the same results as armed intervention would have done.[4]

The misery of his work comrades, decreed by the Huasteca Company, must have been among the deciding factors in Sandino's resolve, apart from the ideological discussions in the Masonic societies he joined. He would tell it in his own words.

> . . . This intervention caused the peoples of Central America and Mexico to despise us Nicaraguans, and I had opportunities to confirm this contempt in my journeyings through those countries. I felt wounded to the heart when they said things like "traitor, betrayer of your country." Not being a statesman, I didn't think I deserved such

names, and at first I answered back; then I thought about it and saw they were right, because as a Nicaraguan I had the right to protest. Then I heard that a revolutionary movement had broken out in Nicaragua. I was working at the time for the Huasteca Petroleum Company at Tampico; it was May 25, 1926. I had some savings amounting to about $5,000, so I took $3,000 of it and went to Managua. I heard what was going on, went to the San Albino mines, and got into active political life.

Thus Sandino curtly describes how the freedom crusade that shook the world began. He omits such details as his meeting with a group of workers who came from Léon looking for jobs in those mines—U.S.-owned, of course. San Albino was where he grasped for the first time the full wretchedness to which the workers of his country had been reduced. Ill-paid in coupons without value outside the company stores, working up to fifteen hours a day, housed in hovels where they had to sleep on the floor, under constant vigilance, despised, plundered—these workers were the first soldiers of Sandino's struggle against intervention.

Sandino emerged more as guide than as chief to those who followed him, taking leadership because of his fervent anti-imperialism, of knowledge that was somewhat greater than theirs—above all because of the fire that burned in him, seeming to endow his lean body with the proportions of a giant. Political conviction led to military decision: $300 of his savings went for the few weapons, obtained across the Honduran border, with which he and a handful of miners launched their first mountain skirmishes.

North Americans, strutting like feudal lords to the exasperation of Sandino's democratic countrymen, now occupied all of Nicaragua, and he had resolved to throw them out.[5] As a starter, on learning that Sacasa had received 700 tons of war materials at Puerto Cabezas, he set off to request some for his forces. It took him nine days to float down the Coco River from Las Segovias in one of the primitive canoes known to the Mosquito Indians as *pipantes*. Sacasa told him to put himself under the orders of Moncada, who had known Sandino from childhood and was a personal and political friend of his father. Moncada gave him a chilly reception, wanting to know what Sandino expected to do with the arms. Sandino argued that his knowledge of the Las Segovias region would enable him to defend it effectively, and this would permit the Constitutionalists to march on the capital with their rear protected. It made sense but Moncada refused any arms and pooh-poohed Sandino's military potential. Sandino saw what was behind the refusal:

> Sacasa, his cabinet members, and especially War Secretary Moncada had personal ambitions, and I had a real problem to get what I wanted. I met people willing to go to Las Segovias but personal glory was what they were all after. Since these egotistical types were many and varied, I always had trouble making out with the politicians. My good faith, working-class simplicity and patriotic spirit got their first political shock. . . . Moncada flatly turned down my request for arms. I hung around the Atlantic coast for some forty days and got a real bellyful of the ambition and disorganization in Sacasa's circle. And I discovered something else, that they were trying to organize an expedition to Las Segovias shoulder to shoulder with the North American interventionists. They even proposed that I should accompany Espinosa, if I would only agree to make propaganda for their presidential candidate.

Guileless Sandino was amazed at the reaction to his will to fight. The good faith to which he himself referred prevented him from understanding that behind the politicians' tortuous game lurked a readiness to throw in the towel which soon became evident. Moncada was in fact playing his own game, trying to make himself important in North American eyes. When Latimer landed at and neutralized Puerto Cabezas, he rounded out the operation by proposing that Sacasa hand over all the arms in his possession. Sacasa did not need to be told twice. Concerned only about himself and his entourage, he accepted the offer of a U.S. concern, the Bragmans Bluff Lumber Company, to occupy one of its properties in Puerto Cabezas while his honor guard left in disorder for Prinzapolka.

With Sacasa under Latimer's amiable umbrella, Latimer dumped the arms in the ocean—but not all of them, as Sandino relates:

> I took off with six of my men, and a group of girls came along to help us grab rifles and ammunition—thirty rifles and 6,000 cartridges. The politicos were so soft it was ridiculous, and I finally got the point that we sons of the people were without leaders and needed new men. I found Moncada in Prinzapolka and he received me contemptuously, ordering me to surrender the arms to a certain General Eliseo Duarte. . . . The minister Sandoval and Undersecretary Vaca turned up at that point and had us keep the rifles and the matching cartridges.

By early February 1927 Sandino was back in Las Segovias. Soldiers serving in the quisling's ranks were so moved by the action of the "group of girls"—actually port prostitutes—that defections mounted rapidly. The initial Sandinista army of twenty-nine men swelled to 300 officers, soldiers, and boys—for now boys were begging a place in the liberation struggle, the *palmazones*[6] who became famous for the part they played. So from village to village the little force spread the fervor of resistance, welcoming one and all into the fight against the "gringo invader." Small barracks fell after short skirmishes, and the defeated soldiers were invited to swell Sandino's ranks with their arms and accouterments. Moved by shadowy libertarian intuition which the leader made contagious, they became heralds of the national dignity of the great Nicaraguan poet Rubén Darío's country, and indeed of all the Latin American peoples' dream of freedom. Through the mouths of their rifles and of their distinguished leader, Augusto C. Sandino, the gagged and fettered race spoke.

The rebels established their base of operations in San Rafael del Norte, a day's journey from Jinotega, capital of the province of the same name. While General Moncada moved up the Rio Grande with his eye on Managua, reaching Matiguás in the Matagalpa region, Sandino dug in at Yacapuca on a ridge between San Rafael and Jinotega, where word came that Liberal General Francisco Parajón had been routed at Chinandega and his army had fled toward El Salvador. Sandino set off in that direction, won his first victory at San Juan de las Segovias, and proceeded on to El Ocotal, which the army had abandoned. Of his meeting there with *moncadista* General Camilo López Irías, Sandino writes:

> I agreed with López Irías that he would move on to occupy Estelí—also abandoned by the enemy—and I and my men would storm Jinotega. We left military forces and civil authorities in El Ocotal. López Irías added new men to his column and some days later took the enemy by surprise in Chagüitillo. A valuable armored train fell into his hands there, but the enemy recaptured it with such force that he had to flee in disarray to Honduras. The enemy occuped Estelí and Jinotega, and neither in the west nor in the north was there any Liberal force to confront them—only my column in San Rafael del Norte, which was raring to go although one of the defeated López Irías generals, Carlos Vargas, advised me that we were surrounded by the enemy and had

better clear out. Vargas had become as defeatist and cowardly as his chief, although he saw the heroism of my lads, who had just given the enemy hell on one flank and taken supplies and ammunition from him.

But nothing could prevent the invaders from occupying the rest of Nicaragua and aiding the Díaz-Chamorro forces which were about to surround Moncada. Seeing himself in a tough spot, Moncada took the course he had so recently disdained. He ordered Sandino to concentrate his forces in Tierra Azul (where Moncada was), threatening to hold him responsible "for impending disaster" if he didn't. The best historian of what ensued is Sandino himself:

> For my part, I would have flown to save the Liberal army, but my column was quite small and we were having to fight almost every day. However, I assigned 150 men—almost unarmed, with only eight rifles in bad condition—to the command of colonels Simón Cantarero and Pompilio Reyes. The instructions I gave them were to put themselves under General Moncada's orders and await my arrival to rejoin them. They took off and that same night I marched to Yacapuca and Saraguazca, to storm the Jinotega plaza.
>
> At 5 A.M. next day we had the plaza surrounded and minutes later the fight started. It lasted till 5 P.M. when we won the day. We took all the arms and supplies that the enemy had in the plaza. You could tell that our column was beginning to cause panic. The plateaus of Yacapuca and Saraguazca were strewn with bodies from the battle fought en route.
>
> The Segovias column now numbered 800 men, mounted and with good equipment, and our red and black flag flew majestically over those wild, cold hills. I learned later that the 150 men I detached had rescued Moncada's armored train which the enemy was about to capture. By this time "General" López Irías had completely vanished from Las Segovias, and in those same days we heard that Parajón, returning from his junket to El Salvador, was trying to regroup in the west. With the idea of helping out, I sent a note inviting him to come to Jinotega, so that we might join forces to save Moncada. Parajón got the note, and in the first half of April 1927 he arrived in Jinotega with his forces. . . Next day, leaving in Jinotega this man who is now Moncada's satellite, I took off with my 800 mounted troops to free Moncada from his encirclement by the Díaz government forces. Moncada had given the enemy a tremendous boost by abandoning even his guns.

Sandino goes on to relate how he extricated Moncada's forces, who then had the road open to take Managua:

On our way from Jinotega to Las Mercedes where Moncada was, we had two light engagements, one in San Ramón and one in Samulatí. After I left, "generals" Parajón, Castro Wasmer, and López Irías—who if you put them all together wouldn't make one man—got together in Jinotega to form a single column which followed close behind me. One afternoon late in April we reached El Bejuco, where we reined up in face of positive signs that the enemy was nearby. In fact he was right in front of us. Our horsemen quickly took positions and I ordered Colonel Porfirio Sánchez to take fifty of them and make contact with the enemy. At the same time I suggested to Parajón, Castro Wasmer, and López Irías that their men should string out in a line, which they immediately did.

After ten minutes a thunderous battle was on between our horsemen and the enemy, who was making liberal use of his machine guns. I ordered Colonel Ignacio Talavera, commander of our first cavalry company, to get cracking with his men for the protection of Colonel Sánchez. I was waiting for Parajón, Castro Wasmer, and López Irías to put in an appearance, but when they did only their aides accompanied them. I told them what I thought and proposed to take personal command of my own 150 lads who were with them. The "generals" stayed at the place where we met and I took off. In the foothills not far off I found my lads in a state of excitement because they had captured the headquarters of the enemy that had been harassing Moncada. We advanced toward the field hospital and found many wounded. . . . We took some splendid war booty consisting of thousands of rifles and millions of cartridges. With this Castro Wasmer's men generously fitted themselves out.[7]

The defeat of the enemy was greeted with outbursts of enthusiasm by the Constitutionalist troops, a great number of whom wanted to leave Moncada's ranks and asked Sandino to accept them into his. When Sandino got to talk to Moncada, Castro Wasmer had done so ahead of him, expatiating to the Constitutionalist generalissimo on "the trouble it had taken to get Parajón, López Irías, and Sandino here. . . ." In the face of the unrest among his troops, Moncada had an order of the day read out prohibiting the transfer of men from one column to another, to stop the drain of Liberal soldiers into Sandino's ranks.

Not content with this, Moncada ordered Sandino to occupy Boaco, which Moncada said was occupied by his own troops—a fact which Sandino found to be false, for as he wrote later, Moncada's "sole and spiteful intention was that I should be assassinated by Colonel Jóse Campos' forces whom Moncada had posted along the road I would have to take that night. When I later contacted Colonel Campos he told me Moncada had never mentioned I would be passing that way, and that was why he had set up his machine guns to be fired, as he thought, at the enemy." Sandino adds:

> When I reached the outskirts of Boaco where I expected to meet Moncada's forces, the enemy received us with bullets and I had to dig in; from there I sent word to Moncada that all the Conservative forces I had defeated at las Mercedes were assembled in Boaco, and I awaited further orders, since his statement that Boaco was occupied by his forces was not true. The word came back that Moncada had cleared out of Las Mercedes heading for Boaquito. So I turned my men around and followed him till I caught up, and it was then that Colonel Campos told me the above. At Boaquito, Moncada ordered me to occupy El Común hill. There I waited till the day Moncada committed the Nicaraguan Liberal Party to the hangman at Espino Negro de Tipitapa.

This is a reference to the denouement of Moncada's turbid machinations: when Sandino's victory at Las Mercedes had left the road open to the capital and plunged the traitors into panic, Moncada suspiciously kept his forces busy in diversionary operations until he could play his decisive card with the only key person he knew from the "Mena War" period, a man representing for Moncada the guarantee of his own ambitions: Colonel Henry L. Stimson, appointed by Coolidge to stop the war in Nicaragua.

According to Bemis—who likes to assume an air of naiveté or superficiality in his book when referring to his country's imperialism— "Stimson very quickly perceived that the cause of Nicaragua's political calamities was the impossibility under existing conditions of free-and-fair elections," and with this in mind brought together the contending leaders, Díaz and Moncada, "and arranged a truce. So convulsed and torn was the almost expiring republic that both leaders showed a high-minded disposition to stop the deadly strife and let the United States police a settlement." This version differs from that of the Nicaraguan Salvatierra, later a member of Sacasa's cabinet, who has Stimson beginning his intervention by ordering the leaders to appear and summoning a destroyer, "which flew rather than scudded over the Atlantic billows, plunged through the Panama Canal and reached Corinto with a speed never before known in those waters."

The concern was manifest to keep Managua from falling to Moncada, who has yet another variant of Bemis' high-minded disposition version.[8] The meeting with Stimson took place at Tipitapa, beneath a blackthorn tree, on the morning of May 4, 1927. Sacasa sent Rodolfo Espinosa, Leonardo Argüello, and Manuel Cordero Reyes as his delegates. The other participants were Stimson, representing not only President Coolidge but also President Díaz, who had vested him with full authority; Admiral Latimer; U.S. Minister Eberhard; and General Moncada, who was "specially invited."

Stimson told the distinguished gathering that not only the peace of the isthmus was at stake, but also the prestige of his country as guarantor of the 1923 Peace and Friendship Treaty; hence he "demanded" total disarming of the republic, with Díaz completing his quisling term until new U.S.-supervised elections would anoint his successor. If these conditions were not accepted, they would be imposed by force. Bemis noted that "the revolutionaries were to give up their arms, each man turning in a rifle to the custody of the United States to get ten dollars from the Díaz government; and a Nicaraguan constabulary was to be established under the instruction and *command* [Bemis' italics] of United States officers (as had been done in the Dominican Republic and as was being done in Haiti). . . ."[9] Stimson's confirmatory letter to Moncada is quite clear:

Tipitapa, May 4, 1927

Señor General José María Moncada

Esteemed General:

Confirming our conversation of this morning, I have the honor to inform you that I am authorized to say that the President of the United States intends to accept the request of the Nicaraguan Government to supervise the election of 1928; that the retention of President Díaz during the remainder of his term is regarded as essential to that plan and will be insisted upon; that all general disarmament of the country is also regarded as necessary for the proper and successful conduct of elections; and that the forces of the United States will be authorized to accept the custody of the arms of those willing to surrender them, including the government, and to disarm forcibly those who will not do so.

Very respectfully,
Henry L. Stimson[10]

Sacasa's delegates replied at the meeting that they had no instructions either to accept or reject the proposed conditions. On May 5 they wrote to Moncada that "with respect to the new and unjustifiable crime that is proposed against the honor of our government and the dignity of our Republic . . . and with due respect to yourself, we hereby repeat that we have full authorization and instructions from President Sacasa to accept no solution that is based on the continuance in power of Sr. Díaz."

But Moncada, who remained Sacasa's war secretary and visible head of the resistance, betrayed not only his chief but the cause of Nicaragua, as subsequent events showed. Salvatierra writes: "Colonel Stimson and General Moncada, detaching themselves from the other three, had a private talk which resulted—without consultation with the delegates—in all going to Managua, including Moncada. Everything pointed to Moncada having made peace with Stimson with the implications that Moncada would be the next president." He had decided to sell out his own people in exchange for Washington's green light for his ambitions. The journalist Belausteguigoitia, who knew Moncada later as president, wrote that "the word for him is Cynic; . . . with his air of an old Bacchic faun, lover of good wine and bad women . . . his life has a bit of everything, something of the fox if certainly nothing of the lion . . . and although now in the twilight of his years he builds some school or hospital for the poor of his town, the people say under their breath that first he made them poor. . . ."

By way of further enriching the saga of surrender, we note that quisling Díaz had already begun to disarm his men before Moncada agreed on it with Stimson. Even more curious—as *Time* correspondent William Krehm wrote—"Moncada, without the knowledge of his staff, allowed the U.S. marines to occupy the heights dominating Tipitapa . . . to convince those in his ranks who might consider the pact a betrayal." Moncada persuaded the Constitutionalist leaders to lay down arms, for a reward to each man who did so of $10, ownership of the horse he was riding, and a pair of overalls. (Moncada said the overalls were a calumny.)

On the day when Sacasa's delegates conveyed to Moncada their rejection of Stimson's terms, Sacasa sent the State Department a memorandum disclaiming all responsibility for bloodshed "which may result from execution of peace by the U.S. authorities." He added:

> I undertook to defend the Constitution, the law, and the outraged rights of the Nicaraguan people against the armed violence of the Chamorro-Díaz clique, due to the State Department's neutral attitude toward the Nicaraguan conflict. If the defenders of constitutional authority had known that the protestations of neutrality, many times repeated by Washington from the time of Chamorro's coup d'état till the constitutional government was set up in Puerto Cabezas, were not serious and to be taken in good faith, they would have felt obligated to continue their political labors by the civic and patient methods that have guided them since the first armed intervention in favor of Díaz in 1912.
>
> Contrary to semiofficial reports in Managua, I have not given my consent to Mr. Stimson's peace conditions. Consequently, and despite the actions of U.S. naval forces, I will only feel obligated to suspend military operations when I am convinced that this will best serve the interests of the Nicaraguan people who are now helpless prey in the claws of a foreign power.

This odd document, a mixture of submission and pleading garbed in civic courage, is Sacasa's last decorous attempt to regain power. From then on *faits accomplis* "convinced" him that he must cooperate with Moncada. Thus it was no surprise that one of his reluctant emissaries to the Blackthorn Peace, Manuel Cordero Reyes, became Moncada's foreign secretary when Moncada assumed the presidency on January 1, 1929.

For as was to be expected, Moncada was a candidate in the November 1928 elections, held under electoral rules prescribed by General Franklin A. McCoy and typical of the conquered-nation status accorded to Nicaragua.[11] And as was also to be expected, U.S. concern had its equivalent in dollars: Moncada "had to arrange" a loan of more than $1.5 million, "which was largely spent on paying for the Electoral Mission sent from the north and on 'leftovers' from the Adolfo Díaz government."

6
The Ant Confronts the Elephant

For five years, with practically no outside assistance, fighting with guns torn from the enemy's
hands, hand grenades made out of sardine tins
filled with stones, they withstood the aviation and
modern equipment of the Marines and the Nicaraguan National Guard. His bitterest opponents
have paid tribute to his fantastically well-organized
espionage—a sure sign that he enjoyed the warm
sympathy of the population amongst which he
operated. In the lowland cities, Managua, León and
Granada, he had much less of a following, because
the presence of the open-handed Marines there
had brought on a business boom.

American old-timers in Nicaragua will assure
you that the Marines were not really eager to crush
Sandino; he offered too good a pretext for using
the country as a training ground. But there was
little that resembled feinting. . . . Throughout
Latin America Sandino became a legendary David,
who while he could scarcely hope to chop off
Goliath's big blond head, did administer a resounding tweak to his nose. For the American press, with
the exception of the liberal fringe, he was a vulgar
bandit. Never before or since had the two Americas been so widely at variance. Sandino, more than
any one man, dramatized the impasse into which
the Big Stick policy had led Washington's diplomacy. And by doing so, he cleared the boards for
the Good Neighbor Era.

William Krehm[1]

Let us go back for a moment to the time when this legendary David
was beginning his battle with Goliath—the last months of 1926. The
former mechanic for Huasteca, now a former San Albino miner, is
putting his 150-odd men through their first lessons in handling

weapons and guerrilla tactics. He teaches them the importance of the angle of the sun, the speed and direction of winds, the art of camouflaging a position—how to take advantage of every tree, every gully, every fold of the ground for entrenchment, every swamp for trapping the enemy.

No military school had taught Sandino any of this. It came from his profound knowledge of the land that bore him, from games he played as a child, from his acquaintance with the ways of the Niquirano Indians who had their special methods of communication, perfected over centuries, in mountainous terrain. While towns of Las Segovias were linked by telegraph, the indigenous telegraph system functioned in the mountains; smoke and mirror signals, the swift feet of couriers, apparently fortuitous groupings of rocks on the road or the odd position of a tree, whistlings or cries that seemed to come from some bird or animal. All very simple, but very efficient.

Men were few, weapons fewer: technique had to be replaced by ingenuity, military strategy by primitive tactics. A slingshot may not kill but it can take out an eye, and a pliant tree branch can take its toll, throwing a column of soldiers into sufficient confusion for hidden sharpshooters to take aim. A mattress of fallen leaves can perfectly conceal a well; dikes made of tree trunks and rocks can alter the courses of streams marked on maps, diverting enemy soldiers to where the guerrillas await their prey.

So it was not by chance that Sandino chose as headquarters one of Las Segovias' most inaccessible places, the Chipote heights—that El Chipotón which would soon appear with Sandino's name on the world's front pages, and would be on the awed and eager lips of every Latin American. The first word that reached him there from the outside was a proclamation from Admiral Sellers, announcing occupation of the country by U.S. troops and calling upon Sandino to lay down his arms as a contribution to peace. In the tradition he had learned from Mexican labor unions, he had the note read to his men and asked their democratic opinion, stressing the dangers involved in sticking with him. Since he "hadn't found many who would risk their hides," he invited those who would to take a pace forward.

Twenty-nine men stepped from the ranks—with himself that made thirty. A fine army, writes Belausteguigoitia, to take on the Yanquis! Yet those thirty were the nucleus of Nicaragua's liberating army. They fought their first battle at Jícaro on November 2, 1926: thirty wretchedly armed men confronting a 200-strong column of Chamorro's soldiers. Trying to compensate with courage for their lack of arms and training, they fared badly. A defeat, but Sandino's men inflicted losses without any on their side.

Then came the actions already described in Puerto Cabezas and Prinzapolka, and finally those in which he was under Moncada's command. After the Tipitapa betrayal, when Moncada got from Stimson (apart from the presidential leg-up) restoration of the dismissed Supreme Court judges and concession to the Liberal Party of five top political plums in the provinces, Moncada summoned all of his satraps and generals for briefing on his peace moves and the return of former Liberal privileges in which all would share. Everybody was there: Beltrán Sandoval, Escamilla, Parajón, López Irías, Pasos, Téllez, Caldera, Plata, Heberto Correa, Daniel Mena, Castro Wasmer.

Everybody except Sandino. He got the invitation but when he turned up at the stated hour, the party was already over. When he protested at the time of the meeting being put forward, Moncada said that as his subordinate Sandino must accept the decision to disarm. Sandino's reply to Moncada's ironic question, "And who made you a general?" became famous. "My comrades in arms, señor," he said; "I owe my rank neither to traitors nor to invaders." He ended by saying he would reach a decision in consultation with his guerrillas, requesting and being granted a reasonable time for his answer. This enabled him to leave Moncada's camp to prepare for resistance without any flare-up. As he himself tells it:

> Thus Moncada surrendered his arms. I knew he was betraying the revolution, since Dr. Sacasa himself had said so. I also realized with bitterness that the Nicaraguan people had been swindled. I was unable to remain indifferent to the position taken by a traitor. In those moments the contemptuous names that foreigners called us buzzed in my head. I spent three wretched, depressed days in the Común heights, wondering what attitude I should take, whether to join in the surrender or keep fighting for my country which begged its sons to defend it. I didn't want my soldiers to see me weeping, and went off to be on my own. I thought a lot and seemed to hear a voice crying "Traitor!" Finally I broke the chain of doubt and resolved to fight, feeling that I was the one called to raise Nicaragua's protest against the

sellout and that bullets were the only defense of our sovereignty. What right had the United States to meddle in our family affairs? So then I put out my first manifesto.

That first manifesto said: "Seeing that the United States of North America, lacking any right except that with which brute force endows it, would deprive us of our country and our liberty, I have accepted its unjust challenge, leaving to History the responsibility for my actions. To remain inactive or indifferent, like most of my fellow citizens, would be to subject myself to this vulgar multitude of parricide merchants."[2]

From that moment on, the Sandino story began to be known through a press that was happy to denigrate, mock, and belittle it.[3] Until the Honduran Froylán Turcios became his spokesman and propagandist outside Nicaragua, nothing was known of Sandino's movements. Later, his own statements in Mexico, and accounts he gave to journalists and writers who dared to interview him, enabled that part of his past to be reconstructed: the only part he was proud to talk about, the beginnings of his fight against intervention. Over the earlier parts he drew a veil, as having no biographical value. "My life," he said once, "has public value since my return to Mexico." He explained in one of his early manifestos:

We have been robbed of our rights over the canal. Theoretically they paid us $3 million. Nicaragua, or rather the bandits who then controlled the government with the aid of Washington, received a few thousand pesos which, spread among Nicaraguan citizens, would not have bought each one a sardine on a cracker. This contract signed by four traitors lost us our canal rights. The debates on this sale took place in a spurious Congress, behind closed doors guarded by Conservative soldiers with a backing of Yanqui bayonets.

As for his last interview with Moncada, Sandino later revealed details showing how well Moncada had learned the lessons imparted by the greaser of palms, Lawrence Dennis:

Moncada offered me the top political plum in Jinotega and told me the Díaz government would pay for everything: any mules I might have taken would be legally mine, and I would get $10 cash down for every day that I had been in rebellion. I asked for time to decide, and meanwhile I went to Jinotega where I was received cordially with flowers and bands. There I spoke of my plans to fight the Yankees, primed up my people, let the scared ones go, and with 300 men headed for San Rafael del Norte in the Segovias mountains. I left behind in Jinotega an organized city government to avoid abuses, and with an eye to future events sent forty machine guns and a lot of supplies to be hidden in the mountains for use when needed.

As soon as he knew about Sandino's rebellion, Moncada marched off to liquidate it. On May 21 he occupied barely defended Jinotega with the help of U.S. troops and wired Sandino to give up. The answer was in the negative: Sandino moved his force into the mountains, where at a place called Yalí his father Gregorio turned up with an olive branch from Moncada. Belausteguigoitia thus describes this strange father-son encounter, so painful for both:

> Don Gregorio told me that, convinced of the madness of the rebellion, he repeated the message he had got from Moncada: in this world saviors end up on crosses, and the people are never grateful. This was right out in the country, and the two talked it over in the presence of Sandino's handful of soldiers. When the soldiers saw that their leader remained adamant and insisted he had cast the die, they erupted in clamorous *Vivas!* for him. Then don Gregorio did something remarkable: he wrote to his other son, Sócrates, to come and join his brother's cause.

On May 28, with machine gun salvos for pealing bridal bells, Sandino married Blanquita Aráuz. She was the San Rafael telegraph operator thanks to whom his men had learned Morse communication, using percussion or whistles.

May, June, and early July were months of recruiting, spreading the rebel gospel, and training. Sandino's intentions were known throughout the country through his manifestos, and had galvanized all Latin America, whose sons saw the possibility of fighting their countries' unloved invaders. Young folk and old found countless ways to join an army of liberation that created local guerrilla-aid committees, sparked protest demonstrations outside embassies, and spread the indictment of imperialism.

On July 12, 1927, a U.S. marine officer announced in a letter to Sandino that the chips were down:

> General A. C. Sandino, San Fernando, Nicaragua:
>
> It does not seem possible that you still remain deaf to reasonable proposals, and despite your insolent replies to my suggestions in the

past, I hereby offer you one more opportunity to surrender with honor.

As you must undoubtedly know, we are prepared to attack your positions and make an end, once and for all, of your forces and yourself if you persist. Furthermore, should you succeed in escaping to Honduras or anywhere else, a price will be put on your head and you will never be able to return to your country in peace, only as a bandit in flight from your own countrymen. If you come to El Ocotal with all or part of your forces and peacefully surrender your arms, you and your soldiers will enjoy the guarantees I offer you as representative of a great and powerful nation that does not win battles by betrayal. In this way you will have the possibility of living a useful and honorable life in your own country, and will be able to help your countrymen tomorrow, setting an example of uprightness and leadership for the future.

Otherwise you will be proscribed and placed outside the law, hunted wherever you go and repudiated everywhere, awaiting an infamous death: not that of the soldier who falls in battle but that of the criminal who deserves to be shot in the back by his own followers. No one has ever prospered or died happily outside the law; and as an example of one who was in the same case twenty-five years ago, and who changed his ways in time, I would remind you of Aguinaldo in the Philippines who, after being the greatest of rebel leaders, came to be a splendid friend of the United States.

In conclusion I wish to inform you that Nicaragua has had its last revolution, and that soldiers of fortune will have no more opportunities to display their talents in the future. You have two days to give me an answer that will save many of your followers' lives, and if you are the patriot you claim to be, I will expect you at El Ocotal at 8 A.M. on July 14, 1927. Kindly inform me of your decision, yes or no, and I sincerely hope, for your soldiers' and your own sake, that it will be yes.

G. D. Hatfield
U.S. Marine Corps
Commanding Officer
Ocotal, Las Segovias

Moncada's carrot had been followed by a $100,000 bribe; now a man who had betrayed his country, the Philippines, was brought in to perfume the "reasonable proposals." This was Sandino's reply:

Camp El Chipote, Via San Fernando
Captain G. D. Hatfield, Ocotal:

I received your communication yesterday and fully understand it. I will not surrender, and await you here. I want a free country or death. I am not afraid of you; I rely on the patriotic ardor of those who accompany me.

A. C. Sandino

Sandino immediately called together the *campesinos* of the neighborhood and invited them to join his ranks. "On July 16," he records, "two days after receiving the note from the little Yankee captain, 800 men were ready for the assault on Ocotal. The force there consisted of 400 pirates and 200 Nicaraguan renegades at their service." Sandino was going to move to the attack a step ahead of the invaders.

The *campesinos* had no military training whatsoever, and only some 60 of the 800 could handle a gun. The others just contributed their presence and goodwill. The onslaught began on the morning of July 16. Sandino's eight machine guns opened the way into the town and by next day it was taken. Captain (later General) Colindres confirmed that all the enemy casualties were fellow countrymen: the North Americans had withdrawn behind the cover of a single block, to which Sandino's men promptly laid siege.

This set the *campesinos,* with their stored-up resentments from lives of misery and privation, on a rampage of plunder, emptying stores of food and clothing and wreaking their own justice on the persons of the high and mighty. Barracks and houses were dynamited. Finally Colindres suggested putting the town center to the torch to smoke out the North Americans. Sandino, moved by citizens' pleas, was against this and ordered withdrawal, considering the assault on the enemy's stronghold impracticable.

The members of his small army obeyed, but not the *campesinos.* In the midst of their looting spree, the invaders emerged from cover and took them by surprise; when they tried to flee, seven airplanes summoned by telegraph rained death upon them and destruction upon the town. After emptying their bomb racks, the unopposed airmen swooped low and nonchalantly machine-gunned the people in flight. Thus what was known as the Battle of Ocotal became the first fruit of Brigadier General Feland's order to "gun the bandits down mericlessly where they are encountered." The toll of this "battle" was one U.S. soldier and 300 Nicaraguans—men, women, and children—dead, and over 100 Nicaraguans wounded.

This "heroic action," as Coolidge called it, inspired quisling Díaz to request decorations for the airmen involved in the slaughter; and not satisfied with medals, he threw a banquet for them attended by General Moncada, among other chieftains. The reaction was much stronger in the United States than in Latin America. In an open letter to Coolidge insisting it was not a battle but a carnage, Governor Edward Dunne of Illinois wrote:

> In all of U.S. history there has been no action of such indecency as we now see in Nicaragua. According to press reports, in an affray between two Nicaraguan factions a detachment of marines joined with one of the conflicting sides and opened fire under the U.S. flag. An air squadron was also ordered out to bombard the so-called enemy, and this in a country with which we are at peace and where we know that no airplanes or antiaircraft guns exist. The slaughter of 300 Nicaraguans by the Americans is a blot on the United States, and for this reason I request the demotion and punishment of General Feland who ordered the bombardment.

H. H. Knowles, former minister to Nicaragua and to the Dominican Republic, said in a speech at Williamstown:

> I know of no inhuman actions and crimes greater than those committed by the United States against the defenseless peoples of Latin America through its legally authorized agents and representatives. The brutalities of the marines gave rise to a Senate committee investigation of the occupation of the Dominican Republic in 1924, and proofs were offered. The committee was to have sat for ten days, but after three days such atrocious evidence had been presented against the marines that the committee members decided to suspend the hearing *sine die*. We have imposed our force upon weak, defenseless, and completely powerless countries, murdering thousands of their subjects, and we have attacked them when they expected us to defend them. We have used the Monroe Doctrine to prevent European countries sympathetic to those republics from coming to their aid. Instead of sending them teachers, instructors, and elements of civilization, we send them hunters of usurious banking concessions, avaricious capitalists, corrupters, soldiers to shoot them down, and degenerates to infest them with every disease.[4]

Senator Borah expressed his condemnation in customarily trenchant terms. It so happened that on the same day that Hatfield sent his note to Sandino, *La Prensa* of Buenos Aires ran a seemingly prophetic article by Borah.[5] Another prominent North American, Thomas Moffat, said:

> Some of the reasons for sending U.S. forces to Nicaragua could be described as boners. The lives and property of Americans were never in danger. . . . The references to protection of our canal rights were ridiculous since that project only exists on paper. Its construction, if and when undertaken, will be welcomed by any faction that may be in power. . . . I am persuaded that we have dirtied our hands by plunging them in the contaminated waters of capitalist diplomacy. Most sane Nicaraguans take an extremely dim view of us.

While Admiral Sellers confirmed that his losses were one dead and one seriously wounded, General Feland, in the teeth of Governor Dunne's holy wrath, was decorated and specially congratulated for his part in the "heroic action." Meanwhile, Sandino's ill-used army headed for the village of Jícaro from which, with hard marching, it could reach the Chipote heights. And so began the undeclared war between U.S. troops and Nicaraguan patriots.

Eleven days after the attack on Ocotal a U.S. squadron made contact with Sandino in San Fernando and again defeated him: "They almost had us! We had to run like hares," Sandino would write. The invaders were now also in hot pursuit of the *campesinos,* in whose ranks they suspected that tacit or potential sympathizers of the patriot leader were lurking. This indiscriminate hounding became the best ally of Sandino's cause, since even the indifferent joined his forces after the marines burned their huts or destroyed their fields without pausing to determine whose side anyone was on. As Salvatierra tells it:

> The invading forces, applying the conventional yardstick that all who didn't submit were "bandits," adopted the tactics of terror, that is, they spread death among the inhabitants of villages, valleys, and hamlets. They slaughtered the poor and defenseless *campesino* without mercy, here machine-gunning cottages, there taking a prisoner and shooting him "while trying to escape" or making him climb a tree and laughingly shooting him down; sometimes they cut throats, often they also killed the domestic animals and burned all the buildings. The marines' contempt for life and the unhappy *campesino*'s desperation were equally complete.[6]

The presence of the gringo in Las Segovias was odious enough to its people; but if one adds to that his scorched earth policy, one can appreciate why Sandino could keep his campaign going so long without major food-supply problems for a force which, originally only thirty, rose at times to 3,000. Nor did his troops consist solely of Nicaraguans. Latin Americans, Europeans, and even Asians turned up at Las Segovias via Honduras to offer their services. Romain Rolland was one of those who reflected the worldwide reaction of sympathy, publicly calling for support to the Chipote forces. Others were Gabriela Mistral, who proclaimed that Rubén Darío and Sandino were the glory of Nicaragua; Vasconcelos, who stood up to defend Sandino in Paris; Manuel Ugarte; Alfredo L. Palacios[7]; etc. In China, many of Chiang Kaishek's revolutionary units marching victoriously into Peking [in 1927] carried banners with the image of Sandino.

From the enemy side came an indirect tribute when Colonel Fagan, commander of the invading forces in León, was asked to speak on Moncada's behalf at the Poneloya spa and said in front of the startled general: "I am an Irishman at the service of the United States, and I say as an Irishman that General Sandino is a patriot, but one without much sense, because if, for example, he demanded that they should build him a cathedral in some part of Las Segovias, he'd be asking for something possible; if he demanded that they give him $10 million, he'd be asking for something possible; but to think he's going to lick the United States—that's where he's short of sense."

In fact Sandino had no thought of licking the United States: he was asking it to get its troops out of his country. He had the sense to admit frankly it was "a war we're destined to lose," and no illusions as to what would happen to him if he fell into Yanqui hands. But taking all the defeats and failures, he continued to fight.

For at the outset there was nothing but defeat. San Fernando was followed by the disaster at Las Flores where he lost seventy men and a treasure in weapons. His raw troops could do little against the tactics of a regular army commanded by World War I veterans. When he tried implementing what he had read about the trench system in that war, the invaders easily outflanked him and forced him out with the aid of their planes.

The lesson needed little repetition to be understood. He saw that so long as the enemy had superiority in weapons, chose the terrain and the moment for engagements, and applied their academic military lore, playing the same game would get him nowhere. It followed that he must adopt guerrilla tactics, using his superior knowledge of the terrain to seek maximum results from his skimpy forces and armament. El Ocotal was a reminder of the decisive advantage of the surprise factor in battles of the sort he was engaging in, which required use of the ambush and of immediate retreat after gaining an intended objective.

Ten days after the Las Flores disaster he tried it out. The invaders having made their way into Las Segovias heading for the Chipote heights, he moved into their rear and on September 19 attacked the town of Telpaneca. By nightfall it was in his hands except for the barbwired communicating trench network after the European war model. Sandino wrote later:

> What idiots! Of course this enabled them to circulate through most of the town without exposing their hides; but I had taken the higher ground from which my machine guns could knock off any gringo head surfacing from the trenches, so that while they kept under cover below ground I let the populace take anything in town they had a fancy to. . . . The situation lasted all night. In the morning the Yankee airmen began dropping their bombs on the high ground we occupied, and then I began an orderly retreat into the woods."

To understand this change in Sandino's military thinking—all of it instinctive—one must know the geography of Las Segovias. Its four departments cover 30,000 sqaure kilometers stretching north from the center of Nicaragua to the whole of the Honduran border. From the Pacific coastal plain containing the cities of León and Chinandega, it rises gradually to the Nueva Segovia heights, where vast unexplored forests achieve their greatest density. The Atlantic region to the east is low but equally wooded, ending in uninhabitable swamplands. The Coco River, flowing down through the whole area from the Nueva Segovia heights to the sea hundreds of kilometers away, is only navigable for short stretches by shallow-draft vessels.

All the towns were of course in the invaders' hands from the start. Their access roads and perimeters were under the constant vigilance of machine-gun posts. The overt attitude of their inhabitants was a curious but understandable neutrality. They knew that collaboration with the gringos could cost their lives when the fortunes of war favored the patriots, whose occupation of a town might be brief but whose justice was swift against obsequiousness, cowardice, and servility.

But Sandino was master of the forests, mountains, and river. He knew every inch of Las Segovias, and his men were no less expert. Each tree, thicket, and rock was potential cover for a sharpshooter or a patriot spy. The invaders knew it and only ventured to enter by known roads or previously explored ground, with rifle or revolver primed to fire on the instant. At that, it was a strain on the stoutest nerves, for at any moment, without the slightest warning, the plod of invaders' boots could evoke a furious volley from several different directions. The ambushers had plenty of time to draw a bead and to avoid useless waste of ammunition; and when the enemy reacted for a counterattack, all he found were fresh tracks losing themselves in thickets where the unseen eyes of *sandinistas* were all the more dangerous. Their arms once discharged, their task of polishing off gringos done, the *sandinistas* melted silently away.

Not that it always worked out so neatly. "We beat them, they beat us," Sandino would recall later; "but the enemy couldn't figure out our tactics. Furthermore, our espionage always was and still is better than that of the mercenaries. So we kept on collecting North American arms and ammunition, because when we captured men we captured booty. Too bad the pirates are so tall—their uniforms just don't fit our fellows."

Thus Sandino's phantom army became undestroyable. Large numbers were not only not needed but a damper on its actions. Nor did it need costly preparations or arms and troop concentrations. Its smallness made it slippery, a problem to locate, able to disperse to predetermined points, hard to pursue.[8] And when the invaders heard over their rifle bursts and their Thompsons' impotent stutter the cry of "*Viva* Sandino!" or "Death to the gringos!" or "Fatherland and liberty!" they got the point that something more than a "bandit" was confronting, defying, humiliating, infuriating, and annihilating them.[9]

Those warcries in the Nicaraguan forests were the something more that was taken up by oppressed people all over the world, consoling and ennobling them; that flowered into songs and poems dedicated to Sandino by the anonymous masses. In Mexico years earlier, when Villa, Carranza, Obregón, and Zapata—that other great victim of betrayal—fought analogous battles against armies of reaction, each battle produced its song that spread over the land. They were simple songs set to the music of "Riego's Hymn,"[10] which early twentieth-century anarchists deliberately modified, or to Mexican folktunes, *corridos,* or songs like "La Adelita." And this sort of music served the *sandinistas* for verses such as these:

Compañeros, brother patriots!
Never falter in your courage,
If we die defending our land
History will say we died with honor.

Everyone who feels for his country
Come and swell in our ranks
So that tomorrow you won't be sorry
With Yankee boots on your chest.

Our leader Sandino has risen up
To come and free us;
But many a traitor confronts him
Who would come and disarm us.

Their time has passed
And they weren't able to disarm
These four Segovianos
Who came together to fight.

We've been able to chop
Moncadistas into bits,
And we just go on being
Enchanted with life.

Belausteguigoitia tells how after the Sandino battalion's guitarist Cabrerita sang the "Internationale"—"which sounded a bit odd up there in the mountains"—he heard Cabrerita sing this:

I will sing you, señores,
A song about life,
A song in honor
Of a brave general.

Fill up your glasses,
Let's have some more wine,
And here goes a toast
To our valiant Sandino.

Sandino has fought
With a handful of men,
And they say he'll die
But never sell out.

Sacasa said to Sandino
"I'm taking off
For the USA,
We aren't going to win"

And then said Sandino,
Clenching his fists,
"For a dime apiece
I sell North American heads."

Viva our country, señores!
Vivan all our brave ones
Who have spilled their blood
To win independence!

Viva the patriot, señores,
Who fights and is happy
And proudly has faced
The covetous gringo!

Stanzas with a feeling and sincerity that more than compensate for
their poetic and literary shortcomings; of no school, created by no
genius but by patriotism—courage their genius, death their poetry.
Improvised music also served to make this song:

On the road of our destiny
Augusto César Sandino
Forged powerful weapons
And taught us to defend ourselves.

And we must go forward
Like brave soldiers:

How much better to die
Than to accept humiliation.

On land and water
And through the air
He has proudly defended
His country Nicaragua.

And singing this *corrido*
Has kept us too long;
In Nicaragua, señores,
The mouse catches the cat.

"In Nicaragua, Señores, the Mouse Catches the Cat"

We have long had a Jehovah complex about Latin America. Mostly, however, we have emphasized kosher dietary laws rather than the spiritual attributes of our divinity. We have been less concerned with literature, art, social justice, liberty—whatever those vague terms may mean—than with Singer sewing machines and how many bolts of calico can be loaded on a llama's back. . . .

Our pro-consuls and marine officers, who have at times descended on Latin America for purely righteous causes, such as collecting debts, forcing ratification of concessions and payment of claims and to dispense quinine, have all been ardent defenders of democracy. . . . How often in one breath our worthy pro-consuls thus engaged in armed intervention used to tell me how they were saving the country by teaching the local uneducated hordes to vote honestly; then in the next breath, how the only solution for those countries is the strong man on horseback.

But the great justification for these and sundry activities on our part in Latin America in those days was that of sanitation, long the eighteenth amendment of the Monroe Doctrine. No matter how many marines and Nicaraguans or Haitians or Cubans might be killed, no matter what might be done, we had, at any rate, cut down the percentage of mortality for the rest of the population. Jehovah Uncle Sam was conceived of eternally in those palmy days of fabulous loans and marine invasions as a sort of glorified sewer-digger for the tropics.

Carleton Beals[1]

When the figures for *sandinistas* and invader forces are compared—3,000 and 12,000 respectively at maximum—one can only marvel that the struggle lasted the seven years that it did. That will to resist was not bolstered by any defined political or social convictions. Nor was there even a close identity of views among those who came to join the *sandinista* army: adventurers and smugglers, communists and syndicalists and anarchists and socialists, Latin Americans, Europeans, and Asians.

Only one thing held them together: the simple decision to throw the North Americans out of Nicaragua. Any other explanation is false, as can be seen from Sandino's hundreds of documents and public statements and the testimony of those who were at his side, either for a time or to the end. And if to Latin Americans this seems incomprehensible or a flight of fancy, we must realize that such a state of mind cannot be grasped by people whose soil has not, at least for a number of generations, borne the weight of foreign military incursion.

The other kind of intervention—pacific, sinuous, and persistent economic penetration by the great world empires—is so well understood, accepted, and even requested that within a few dozen years it has shaped the typical colonial mentality: the heaviest ballast that our people's struggle for liberation has to bear. The education of the masses along the lines of diminished sovereignty is propped by the psychological apparatus of the big press and news agencies which stoutly defend "liberty" so long as that word remains within the abstract limits the defenders have drawn around it.

Sandino did not only have military invaders to fight. Throughout the world United Press and Associated Press twisted the facts, baring frightful crimes committed by the patriots while ignoring those of the intervention. They attributed to Sandino intentions he never had, and were unfailingly liberal with references to "bandits," "hordes," or "seditious gangs," according to the propagandists' caprice. Photos of U.S. chieftains and Nicaraguan quislings were scattered with prodigal hand while the faces of *sandinistas* were rarely or never seen.

Short of becoming his own press agent, the resistance leader could not break into the press, and even when his side of the story was sent out, only left-wing publications would print it. Whatever he did send out was without pomposities, reflecting his modest reaction to the far-flung interest he aroused.

When the writer Froylán Turcios, his intermediary in Tegucigalpa, wanted data about him for the magazine *Ariel,* Sandino replied:

"Since you ask, I send this photo to use in any way you see fit. It was taken on May 1, 1926, the day I left Mexico. Should you publish it, make it clear in any caption that I'm not a professional politician, just a plain artisan. My profession is that of mechanic, and up to my present age of thirty-three I have earned my bread, tools in hand."

The mud thrown at him by the Hearst papers, and by those (the great majority) in Central America which followed the Washington line, drew this reply:

A man who doesn't even ask his country for a yard of ground to be buried in deserves to be heard, and not only heard but believed. I am a Nicaraguan and proud that Indian-American blood, more than any other, flows in my veins—blood that contains the mystery of loyal and sincere patriotism. The bond of nationality gives me the right to assume responsibility for my actions with respect to Nicaragua—and indeed to Central America and the whole continent that speaks our language—without caring what names the prophets of doom, cowards, and eunuchs may choose to call me. I am a city worker, an artisan as they say in my country, but my ideal is a wide horizon of internationalism, the right to be free and to demand justice, even if to win this state of perfection it be necessary to shed one's own and other's blood. The oligarchs, that is, the geese that paddle in the muck, will say I'm plebeian. Good enough: my highest honor is having come from the oppressed masses who are the soul and nerve-system of the race. We have been pushed aside and have lived at the mercy of those shameless hired assassins who helped incubate the crime of high treason. I refer to the Conservatives of Nicaragua who have wounded the free heart of our fatherland and who ruthlessly persecute us as if we were not sons of the same nation.

Seventeen years ago Adolfo Díaz and Emiliano Chamorro ceased to be Nicaraguans: ambition killed their right of nationality, for they tore the star from the flag that covered all Nicaraguans. Today that flag waves sluggishly, humiliated by the ingratitude and indifference of its sons. A superhuman effort is necessary, but they do not make it, to free our flag from the talons of that monstrous eagle who feeds on our people's blood—while over the Campo de Marte in Managua waves the flag representing the massacre of weak peoples and enmity toward our race.

Who was it who bound my country to the stake of ignominy? Díaz,

Chamorro, and their lickspittles, who still seek the right to govern our unhappy land, backed by the invaders' bayonets and Springfields. No, a thousand times! The liberal revolution is on the march. Some of us haven't betrayed or yielded or sold our rifles to satisfy Moncada's ambitions. We're on the march and stronger now than ever, because only the brave and the self-renouncing remain in our ranks.

Moncada, the traitor, naturally failed in his duty as soldier and patriot. Those who followed him were not illiterates, nor was he an emperor to impose his boundless ambition on us. Before his contemporaries and before history, I indict this deserter who went over to the enemy with gun, bullets, and everything. Unforgivable crime that demands vengeance!

The big frogs will say I'm a very small one for the job I've taken on; but as against my insignificance I offer the proud heart of a patriot, and I swear before country and history that my sword will defend our nation's dignity, that it will be a sword for the oppressed. I accept the invitation to fight, and will personally provoke it. My battle cry is my answer to the challenge of the cowardly invader and the traitors of my country, and my body and those of my soldiers will form ramparts against which the legions of Nicaragua's enemies will shatter. The last of my soldiers, the soldiers of freedom for Nicaragua, may die; but before that, more than a battalion of your blond invaders will have bitten the dust of my wild mountains.

I will be no supplicant for the mercy of my enemies, who are the enemies of Nicaragua, for I don't believe anyone has the right to be a demigod. I want to convince indifferent Nicaraguans and Central Americans and the Indo-Hispanic race that, up here in the Andean heights, there is a group of patriots who will know how to fight and die like men.

Come, all you morphine addicts, come and murder us in our own land; I am here on my two feet, at the head of my patriot soldiers, awaiting you no matter how many you are. But know that when this happens, the destruction of your grandeur will shake the Capitol in Washington; and the White House, the den where you plot your crimes, will be stained with our blood.

And you, my brothers: I have put before you my ardent desire for the defense of our land, and now I welcome you to my ranks without distinction of political color, only asking that you come in the right spirit. For remember that while all people can be fooled most of the time, all cannot be fooled all the time.

There is ingenuousness in many of the documents emanating from

Sandino, but it is the ingenuousness of a pure soul devoid of malice, a candor that burns for his self-appointed mission of freeing his land from the invaders. And the always implied premise was that true independence would come to Nicaragua through spiritual, economic, and political integration within a Central American peoples' confederation seeking a common socialist solution. Meanwhile Sandino pointed the way to the peoples' defense:

> The army defending Nicaragua's sovereignty has no commitments to anyone. It is bound by the sacred principle of loyalty and honor and, politically, recognizes only the legitimacy of Dr. Juan B. Sacasa's election by the sovereign will of the people. It doesn't yield to conventionalities nor accept outside interference, because it defines its image by its actions. If the Constitutional President of my country were ousted by Yanqui force, and villainously betrayed by the man to whom he confided command of the army, the brave handful who uphold the legality of his election with their blood would still hold in one hand the symbol of the nation and in the other a rifle, to defend the nation's derided and humiliated rights.

So the struggle went on without quarter. In those October days of 1927, while compatriots shed their blood for or against the North Americans, generals Emiliano Chamorro and Moncada arrived in Washington. Each on his own hook strove for a White House blessing on the sacrifice he offered to his country—acceptance of himself as favored candidate for the presidency. In addition to bankers, both paid calls on high-flying financiers and military men and on Coolidge and Kellogg. As is the sad custom in Our America, the elections were being held in advance in the White House and on Wall Street.

Of course neither Nicaragua's Constitution nor the Washington pacts of 1923, which we mentioned earlier, permitted either to have the job. But this—again according to sad custom—was a detail, a pseudolegal triviality which no "true patriot" should bother his head about. A year before the elections, due in November 1928, here were Moncada and Chamorro hovering eagerly over the banquet table, invoking their titles and merits for the tasty repast.

Here we should note that the Sixth Pan-American Conference was set to be held in January 1928 in Cuba, where another lusty trencherman, the tyrant Machado, ruled at the time. The stench that

Machado exuded throughout the continent, and the growing reaction inside and outside the country, prompted Coolidge, as the date approached, to give the tiller a sharp turn. Connected with this were the appointment of Stimson and the subsequent Peace of Tipitapa.

As we will see later, the conference was a noisy fiasco—thanks to Sandino's struggle and its repercussions throughout the Americas. But meanwhile Stimson declared with all solemnity: "From reports from other sources and those I have had from Moncada, I have reached the conclusion that Augusto César Sandino is a man who always lived by pillage." Five months earlier, when he received Admiral Sellers' note, the man who "always lived by pillage" had said to his soldiers:

> We are alone. The cause of Nicaragua has been abandoned. From today on, our enemies won't be the tyrant Díaz' forces but the marines of the most powerful empire in history. It's against them that we'll be fighting. We will be foully done to death by bombs their planes will drop on us, pierced by foreign bayonets, riddled by the most up-to-date machine guns. Those with wives or other family responsibilities should return to their homes.

From that ragtag army of twenty-nine men, who may or may not have had "wives and other family responsibilities," a force had arisen to harass the world's most powerful country to the point of making it lose its diplomatic style (always its Achilles' heel) and the most primitive standards of wisdom. In this unique "phantom army" were Hondurans like General Porfirio Sánchez; Guatemalans like General María Manuel Girón Ruano; Mexicans like General Manuel Chávarri; Venezuelans, like one of its doctors; an Englishman from Belice, Mr. Hodson, who converted Moncada's pet gun "La Chula" into an antiaircraft weapon manned by the Honduran José de la Rosa Tejada; Germans like the one who challenged his *compañero* Colonel Padilla to a submachine gun duel and who, seeing the colonel fall, besought Sandino to shoot him so he could "rest by the side of my friend Padilla." Others, such as Colonel Francisco Estrada, Major Carlos Barahona, Colonel Raudales and generals Colindres, Gómez, Umanzor, and Pedro Altamirano—the fearsome "Pedrón" who never forgave a collaborationist—were men of Las Segovias.

Sandino had said: "Nicaragua must not be the patrimony of imperialists and traitors; for that I will fight while my heart beats. . . .

And if fate should lose me my whole army, I have 100 kilos of dynamite which I'll set off with my own hand. Sandino will die without letting the criminal hands of traitors and invaders profane their spoils. And only God Almighty and the hearts of patriots will know how to judge my work."

And how much he needed to keep fighting! A ship had sunk near the south of the Coco River. The *Concón* carried some hundreds of rifles used in 1899 (almost thirty years earlier) during the war in Cuba. These antique weapons, Springfield rifles which his men christened *concones,*[2] constituted his whole arsenal along with those taken with the aid of the Puerto Cabezas prostitutes. There were a few Browning rifles captured from dead or wounded invaders. Later came the famous "Sandino bombs," hand grenades made of empty sardine cans filled with dynamite and stones, whose use produced victims among the *sandinistas* themselves; then some Thompson machine guns, likewise taken from the enemy. The gun "La Chula" was obtained much later.

Yet meanwhile and always, Sandino had the most efficient of all guerrilla-war weapons: a perfect information and espionage system which penetrated into the incipient National Constabulary, combined with a primitive communications system which alerted the *sandinistas* to any troop movement in the direction of Las Segovias. We have already described how this worked, based on natural phenomena in the mountains that were full of esoteric significance for the patriot troops. The small peasant communities took note of every suspicious movement, and within less than an hour the Chipote headquarters was apprised of it. Each Indian working in the fields or taking his merchandise from one village to another was a potential spy for Sandino, using not only his dialect but a special argot and the ancestral signs of his race, known only in the Segovias region. Belausteguigoitia, who visited the camp for some weeks, writes of Sandino's army:

A weird motley of types, of whom refinement of dress and person was hardly the salient characteristic. People of all ages, many kids. Some were fully enough dressed, but the general costume consisted of ragged pants of white cotton cloth, cheap peasant style. They all had a hard look about them, and one may imagine how tough men would get, forced to live in the jungle for years on end. The common denominator was the red and black ribbon adorning their sombreros. Many had a big kerchief of the same colors around their necks. Their weapons were a rifle and a machete hung from the belt. Some had two pistols and many had hand bombs. . . . [I saw] the typical Sandino saddle with a circle and the legend "Patria y Libertad" and, in the camp center, a *sandinista* guerrilla wielding a machete to decapitate a [North] American soldier whom he held by the hair with the other hand, with his foot on the man's belly to hold him down.

Belausteguigoitia saw Colonel Raudales returning with his men from a mission:

There must have been some 200 men of the most varied aspects, dried and hardened by weather and privations; some, the fewest, white-skinned and even blond; others with the light brown complexion of the local mestizo; many Indians of the mountain region with their air of abstraction; and even a black man, corpulent and with tight curly hair. Many of them wore virtual rags, their bronze skin showing through their tattered shirts or pants. Their sombreros, some of felt and others of straw, all bore the classic red and black ribbon. Less than half of them had Springfield rifles of the sort taken from the North Americans; the rest had pistol and machete or just a machete. In the footwear department I will say that shoes were scarce. Most wore huaraches tied with leather thongs, the peasant shoe typical of nearly all South America. Behind came the mounted men, comprising about a third of the whole, riding the small tough mules of the region and a few wretched horses past their time for the slaughterhouse which strove painfully to keep up with the column. . . . The cavalrymen ranged from graying oldsters with bent backs to boys who were really infants, twelve- and fourteen-year-olds who followed the column like seasoned veterans.

. . . Sandino's force moved in Indian file with their flag at the head, a rustic flag whose pole was a tree trunk with the bark still on it.

. . . The men filed by with a somber and weary air, their feet churning the mud, but soon broke the monotony of the march with rousing *vivas* in which all joined: 'Viva General Sandino! *Viva* the army of independence!'

Another journalist who was with Sandino, the North American Carleton Beals, wrote with respect about the man who confronted his compatriots "with a slingshot." In *Banana Gold* he told of a talk with General Feland, the hero-laureate of Ocotal. The general asked

Beals, "What do you think of Sandino?" Beals replied, "He is not a bandit, call him a fool, a fanatic, an idealist, a patriot—according to your point of view; but certainly he is not a bandit." To which the general drawled, "Of course, in the army, we use the word 'bandit' in a technical sense, meaning the member of a band." And Beals shot back, "Then Sousa"—referring to bandmaster John Philip—"is also a bandit?"

A famous visitor who for a time fought with Sandino and acted as his secretary was the Salvadoran communist leader Agustín Farabundo Martí, who later lost his life in the popular revolution against dictator Maximiliano Hernández Martínez. Martí had differences with Sandino which resulted in their estrangement. About this Sandino wrote:

> This movement is national and anti-imperialist. We fly the flag of freedom for Nicaragua and for all Latin America. And on the social level it's a people's movement, we stand for the advancement of social aspirations. People have come here to try to influence us from the International Labor Federation, from the League against Imperialism, from the Quakers. . . . We've always upheld against them our definite criterion that it's essentially a national thing."

He often returned to this stress on the nationalist and purely patriotic guidelines of his struggle. U.S. and interventionist Latin American publications branded him now as a bandit, now as a "bolshevik agent." Despite his meager political background, Sandino was well aware of the identity between sociological and political problems and how politics affected the peoples' lives. But he had only a dim perception of the relations between those factors and U.S. imperialism which retarded their solution. For him—as he never tired of repeating—the solution to Nicaragua's problems would appear once the invaders cleared out. The facts at the time of his death would show how wrong he was.

When in Mexico the theory was advanced that his movement was basically agrarian in the same way as Zapata's, he hastened to deny it, arguing how few latifundia and how many small farms Nicaragua had in contrast with Mexico. "Agrarianism," he wrote, "has quite a limited field of action here; the few who have no land don't die of hunger. . . . Near Granada there's a fine avenue of mango trees stretching all the way to the lake. There's a Cerberus-type who has a contract for the fruit and gathers it as he can, but meanwhile various ragged characters wait for the fruit to fall for their daily dinner. They don't choose to work on coffee estates because all they get is fifteen cents, so they prefer this modest idling way of life."

This simplistic view of a complex problem would not prevent him from choosing socialist solutions when, later on, it was proposed that idle Las Segovias lands be colonized:

"So they think I'm going to become a latifundist! No, nothing of the sort. A man of property, that I'll never be. I have nothing. This house I live in belongs to my wife. Some say that makes me a fool, but I've no reason to be different. . . . My idea is rather that the land should belong to the state. As far as our colonization of the Coco is concerned, I would go for cooperatives. . . ."

Yet he was always open to new ideas and knowledge. He boasted of no extraordinary insights nor revealed doctrines, nor did he believe that the "eagle with larcenous claws," as he called the United States, would ever fall at his feet. He did believe with utter sincerity that fate had called him to turn the North Americans out of his country. And this messianic sense of mission he retained until his death which, when it came, neither surprised nor frightened him.

While the presidential aspirants listed their merits in Washington, Sandino kept the banner of freedom afloat over Nicaragua. The first of five engagements between November 1927 and January 1928 was at Las Cruces, a crossroads on the way to El Chipote: "Opportunity advised of the North American advance," he wrote, "we prepared an ambush and trenches in appropriate spots and set up our machine guns. The enemy came along and we opened fire. A frightful carnage: the pirates fell like leaves from trees and we, well protected, hardly had a casualty. And after the first encounter we ambushed the columns that came to reinforce them."

No better chronicler of these battles than Sandino himself:

At Trincheras, so-called by the Spaniards at the time of the conquest; at Varillal, a brutal encounter; at Plan Grande; three more times at Las Cruces, where the last battle lasted four days—then back to El Chipote. The enemy had heavy losses, we some thirty. At Las Cruces we captured in battle a North American flag, and from Captain Livingstone, commander of their column who died there, we took orders of the day, documents, and maps. The pirate chief was shot by a bullet from Major Fernando Madariaga's pistol.

Another pirate who died at Las Cruces was Captain Bruce, who on December 24 had cabled to his mother in the United States that the campaign was drawing to an end: he believed that by the first of January Sandino would be obliterated. By then, said his message, "we will have cut the bandit's head off." On precisely that date Bruce lay dead, his own head sunk on his belly. I now use his field glasses. They're magnificent, a standard U.S. army issue, with fitted case and a compass attachment.

After those battles, the bloodiest that have been fought in Nicaragua, we returned to El Chipote, which was the pirates' objective. But the situation was getting tricky. They were encircling us to prevent supplies coming in, and the circle was constantly tightening. We had no shortage of arms and ammunition, having taken from the enemy in the last battles quantities of cartridges and splendid, brand-new weapons. During the sixteen days when we were under siege, the pirates' air squadrons paid us daily visits. The first four planes would come in at 6 A.M. and start dropping bombs. Naturally we shot back at them, and several of their steel birds were mortally wounded. After four hours of bombing, another squadron would appear, bomb for four hours, and then be replaced by another—they kept this up till nightfall.

The bombs did little damage to our men because we were well protected, but we lost some 200 cavalry mounts and cattle for our table. The situation was serious because the animals' decaying bodies made the camp insupportable. The air was full of vultures for days. They did us a service in wrecking visibility for the planes—which we often confused with them—but life there was getting tough and we decided to clear out.

So we started making straw dummies which, topped with the kind of hats we use, we stuck up at all the visible points in El Chipote; then we took off under cover of night. The planes went on bombing the camp, which was already struck and empty, for two days till they realized nobody was there. When they arrived there looking for us, we were far away. They had plenty to learn about how we operate. . . . So the struggle, more and more bitter and intense, goes on. But with North American dollars continuing to do their work, silence continues to prevail about it in the outside world.[3]

A stratagem similar to the straw dummies was behind the news of Sandino's death, published worldwide in January 1928. Sandino staged the comedy of his own funeral, and brought it to the attention of the marine commander at Ocotal, in so lifelike a way that the Department of Marines itself issued a description of the "bandit's" last rites—"removed from this world by the bullets of our great airmen." After leaving El Chipote, Sandino headed for San Rafael del Norte in the department of Jinotega, where he was promptly located and the harassment was resumed:

> The Yankee marines and their renegade allies really had us surrounded. When they charged, it was terrific. Thousands of men coming at us, the way you would hunt down a tiger, and the circle kept tightening. I finally managed to get out of it by obscure tracks and trails, only to fall into a broader ring of Yankees determined to get the bandit's head. My only choice was to march to the nearest village. The tactic saved our lives, for while the enemy was looking for us in the mountains we got through to La Luz mine.
>
> This was a North American mine belonging partly to ex-Secretary of State Knox, an insolent gentleman to whom we taught a lesson on his property. When I got there I gave the order to sack the place. The mine was totally destroyed and blown up with dynamite, and the Yankee settlement sacked house to house. I wrote receipts for everything taken there for the army, although the people were the beneficiary. The receipts made out to the U.S. Treasury amounted to $50,000. It was necessary to demonstrate that the Yankees can't give guarantees to Nicaragua.

Sandino took the mine manager prisoner, a Mr. Marshall who was brought along into the mountains. The death of this man was not a result of mistreatment but of the effects of a climate to which he was unaccustomed, but the newspapers exploited it as a demonstration of *sandinista* barbarity. At the same time they were silent about the famous "waistcoat cuts" invented by the North Americans and later emulated by Pedro Altamirano's troops—cutting off the arms of wounded *sandinistas* as a punishment for bearing rifles. And equally silent about the *cumbo* system of cutting throats with a saber as "propaganda material for the bandit in the other world."

Oddly enough, it was the sixty hundredweights of dynamite placed in the mine by Juan Romano that unleashed against Sandino the greatest campaign of vilifications and inventions, on a scale previously unprecedented. The punishment inflicted on collaborationists by the shooting of Dr. Juan Carlos Mendieta, Cayetano Castellón, Julio Prado, and other inhabitants of San Marcos was denounced as not an act of war but "brutal assassination." Mr. Marshall was said to have been given poison and then killed with machetes, children to have been burned alive, women raped, etc., etc. The charges tumbled over one another in the public prints to blacken Sandino's name in the eyes of those who had faith in him and his mission—and to stop him from becoming the star turn at the Havana Conference.

8
Interventions to Insure Investments

MANAGUA, OCTOBER 16 (AP)—The president of
Nicaragua, General José María Moncada, today
decorated thirty-seven officers and men of the U.S.
fleet with the Nicaraguan Medal of Merit and
Medal of Honor, in recognition of their aid to the
country in restoring law and order during the elections. Medals were awarded posthumously to seven
officers and thirty-two men of the U.S. Marines
who died in combat against the Nicaraguan revolutionaries. The president conferred the Medal of
Merit on rear admirals Sellers and Latimer.[1]

The Sixth Pan-American Conference opened on January 16, 1928,
in Havana, the Cuba of "butcher" Machado. (Twenty-six years later
it would open in Caracas, the Venezuela of Machado's brother
butcher, Pérez Jiménez, as tragicomic prelude to the U.S. intervention against Arbenz' revolutionary government in Guatemala.) The
chair was taken by the internationalist Antonio Sánchez de Busta-
mante, consultant to the biggest U.S. sugar concerns in Cuba, thus
described by Vicente Sáenz: "Legitimate father of the American
code of international law which facilitates foreign capitalist penetration of Latin America, and guiding brain of the assembly which
prolonged the presidential term of tyrant Machado, known to students as 'the political beast of Cuba.'"

The shadow of Sandino hovered over the deliberations, which
began in the presence of Charles Evans Hughes, eminent juriscon-
sult of imperialism, Charles Lindbergh, and of President Coolidge.
The conference bestowed juridical status devoid of political func-
tion upon the booby-trap organization, the Pan-American Union.
When the debates were in full cry, a sudden, deep hush fell over the
chamber: the Nicaraguan delegation had just arrived—the Nicaragua of Moncada. This alone sufficed to bring Sandino's phantom presence suddenly into the room, silencing voices and troubling spirits.[2]

The Salvadoran J. Gustavo Guerrero, most fervent defender of the dissolved Central American Court of Justice, gets booed and shuts up amid ostentatious applause. Kellogg and Coolidge act like stars of the show, as does Hughes. Machado's amanuensis, Orestes Ferrara, heaps panegyrics upon the man who pays his salary—Dr. Salomón, Peruvian foreign secretary under the Leguía dictatorship—and exalts Coolidge's "gallantry" in condescending to visit the "natives of Cuba": "President Coolidge's voyage to Havana is the absolute negation of imperialism," says he, according to the Associated Press dispatch. "The U.S. government has not and never had any imperialist intentions, and now President Señor Coolidge is going to proclaim in the Sixth Pan-American Conference that he will never have any in the future. That is the best reply to the propaganda of vagabond elements against what they call a policy of aggression."

This juicy Associated Press cable immediately preceded the arrival of Sandino's shadow at the convivial banquet where Latin American submissiveness had an opportunity to outdo itself. Various foreign secretaries' ardent defense of the United States on that occasion was ample proof of troubled consciences and of the fact that Sandino was not fighting in vain. There was another load on the delegates' minds: until then only the United States, Honduras, and El Salvador of the twenty-one American republics had recognized the official government of Nicaragua. However, the vote of this trio had more weight than the recalcitrance of the seventeen others, and the Nicaraguan delegation was seated at the conference, which one way and another turned out to be less than a fraternity shindig of good Latin American alumni.

La Prensa of Buenos Aires published on March 9, 1928, some noteworthy cerebration by dictator Leguía which had been shared with the conference: "The invariable and unalterable policy of my government will always be favorable to the civilizing stance of the United States toward other American countries, whose liberty it defends and whose progress it protects without ulterior or selfish motives. I think that interventions represent no danger for [Latin] America, but rather a help to the weak nations that request it, in view of their internal conflicts."

Although the dictatorship delegations vied in intrepidly despicable defense of U.S. intervention, Sandino's shadow over the proceed-ings scored a resounding victory. As Bemis notes, it was the intervention theme that caused discord in the conference:

> The sharpest debates that had ever occurred in the history of Pan-American conferences took place in a special sub-committee to which this issue was referred. It resulted in a postponement of the issue: a resolution to refer the disputed projects and other subjects of codification to further meetings of the Commission of Jurists under the auspices of the Pan-American Union for study, the results to be considered at the next (Seventh) Pan-American Conference at Montevideo.[3]

Actually the balloon had gone up when Dr. Guerrero of El Salvador moved the following, among the dozen resolutions submitted on public international law and one on private international law: "No state has the right to intervene in the internal affairs of another." Mr Hughes parried the blow skillfully. "Intervention," he said, "where sovereignty is inoperative, is a principle of international law, and international law may not be modified by the resolutions of this conference. International law continues to be operative. The rights of nations remain in force, but nations have duties as well as rights." Just so. In other words the North American puritans meekly sacrifice themselves to care for the flock, gobbling any willful lamb that proved intractable to their protection.

The uproar caused in Latin America by this interventionist doctrine in the buff, threatening any country's sovereignty on the pretext of keeping order,[4] compelled the conference authorities to put the study of "Fundamentals of International Law and the States" on ice till the next meeting. When the Seventh Conference convened in Montevideo in 1933, Franklin D. Roosevelt was president of the United States; the august shadow of Sandino weighed as heavily as ever on the delegates there. The new president's professed sympathy for Sandino was well known, so that the solemn promise made by Secretary of State Cordell Hull drew little attention: "I can confidently state that, with our support of the general principle of nonintervention as it has been put forward, no government need fear any intervention by the United States under the Roosevelt Administration."

Dr. Guerrero's resolution had finally been accepted as part of the signed convention's Article 7, to this effect: "No state has the right to intervene in the internal or external affairs of another." While this certainly proscribed military intervention, nothing was said of other kinds, and the proscription was confined to "the Roosevelt Adminis-tration." In effect nonintervention proved no better than interven-tion, but it suited the turn of the screw in U.S. policy and soothed Latin American pride. However, it was something, and more than something in the light of things to come—for example, the miserable fakery of John Foster Dulles in overthrowing the "miracle" regime of America, the Arbenz government in Guatemala.

What is most certain is that the outcome of both conferences drew all Latin America's attention to the influence of Sandino's struggle in the Nicaraguan mountains. And the struggle did not weaken: on February 27, 1928, Sandino won a resounding victory at El Brama-dero. As he told it to Maraboto:

> By now graduate students of Yankee tactics, we emplaced our machine guns in strategic positions and sat down to wait. The whole brigade was on hand at the appropriate site. The moment came, our guns chattered till they seemed ready to melt with the heat, and the unhappy Yankees fell like grasshoppers. It was the greatest slaughter I ever saw. In desperation they fired wickedly like madmen. They climbed trees and fell from them perforated with bullets. They tried to attack the places our fire was coming from but couldn't make it. In full view of our men, they offered an admirable target. Their weapons—the ones that the bishop of Granada had blessed—were of no use to them. Our triumph was complete. Beneath the vast acreage of wind-dried sugarcane that was the battlefield lay hundreds of dead and wounded. We set fire to the dry cane at the four corners of the field. The vermin had to be cleaned out! The flames mounted fast, fanned by the wind. A smell of burning flesh filled the air. And in the chronicle of our struggles, this is known as the battle of Bramadero.[5]

The reference to the bishop of Granada, Monsignor Canuto Reyes y Valladares, was exact. In mid-February this servant of God blessed the arms of the U.S. battalion that was marching "to finish off the bandit Sandino"—which in no way deterred it from sacking a church on its way through Yalí and liberating a gold thurible. As for the firing of the surgarcane field, Maraboto explains that Sandino thought it useless cruelty to burn the wounded and ordered the fire put out so that they could be picked up, "because in spite of all, they are my brothers." And Sandino adds: "Before retiring from Bramadero we collected magnificent war booty, Lewis and Colt machine guns, automatic rifles, plenty of Thompson pistols, and cartridges in great profusion. I also picked up the gold thurible stolen from the Yalí church and gave it to some responsible Bramadero people to return where it belonged."

Bramadero was the most important battle fought in 1928. The many other encounters were in the nature of skirmishes, with losses on both sides of which the world knew little since the intermediary, Froylán Turcios, most direct recipient and broadcaster of Sandino's news, resigned from those duties. Maraboto suggests one possible reason for Turcios' defection: "His resignation had hardly been accepted by Sandino when Turcios sailed for France as his country's consul, and he is now in Paris. It is generally said that his appointment was the reward for quitting Sandino, an arrangement maneuvered by Yanqui imperialism through the Mejía Colindres regime in Honduras."

Turcios edited the well-known magazine *Ariel,* but his key importance for Sandino was his connection with people who sought to send arms and men to Las Segovias via Honduras, the only possible route. He was the recipient not only of news about Sandino's campaigns and of Sandino's messages to Latin American governments and peoples, but of messages that Europeans, North Americans, and Asians directed to the rebel chief. All messages, money, and arms passed through his hands and he was the channel by which volunteers made contact with the rebel cause. This made his defection a hard blow for Sandino, who commented: "As the struggle gets tougher, the North Americans scatter their dollars and build walls between us and the outside world to impose silence about us, so that since Turcios quit as our spokesman, little has been reported about events in Nicaragua. And that's how it's going to be till we win freedom or fall in battle."

Later, when Turcios tried to put on airs about his role in the patriots' struggle, Sandino would comment:

> I have read the interview given by señor Turcios, who seems anxious to hide his error; but I will publish the correspondence with him and oblige him to confess the truth. Far from señor Turcios having been our intellectual and ideological mentor, we in fact had to call his attention in a friendly way on July 10, 1928, to a running item he published in *Ariel,* putting himself in the most lamentable role of petty

chauvinist in the frontier dispute between Honduras and Guatemala. Admittedly Turcios immediately withdrew this unfortunate item.

The item in question was an announcement of the Cuyamel Fruit Company, the banana empire of Samuel Zemurray. At the time there was imminent danger of war between Honduras and Guatemala. Backed by Cuyamel, which wanted to exploit the territory in dispute, Honduras laid claim to the cultivated lands between Guatemala's Motagua River and the border, a sixty-four-mile stretch from the Caribbean for which the Guatemalan governments of Orellana and Chacón happened to have given a concession to the United Fruit Company.

While United Fruit, with interests in both countries, acted in a prudent and even conciliatory way, Cuyamel, confined to Honduras and in great need to expand, was blithely ready to start a war by whipping up Honduran nationalism.[6] The intervention of Roy David, U.S. ambassador to Costa Rica, prevented the cold war between the two countries—actually just a war between banana companies—from becoming hot. The low comedy of the situation was that Sam Zemurray, so jealous of Honduran sovereignty in its quarrel with Guatemala, had backed Nicaragua against Honduras when Honduras laid claim to the Mosquito Coast, which was being satisfactorily exploited by the Cuyamel subsidiary, Louisiana Nicaragua Lumber Company.[7]

There were certainly no clouds over Sandino's mind in the matter: he not only reproved Turcios for "putting himself in the role of parish patriot" but, looking further ahead, sent him a long note that caused a sensation throughout Central America. Still in Sandino's typical style, the document shows that marked progress in ideology which his circle of companions had recently observed. For its political value it deserves reproduction in full:

El Chipotón, 10 June 1928

To Froylán Turcios, Tegucigalpa

Esteemed maestro and friend:

I read with great surprise your editorial in the May 1 *Ariel* about the danger to Honduran territorial integrity involved in the frontier question with Guatemala. Your statements and the quote from the editorial in *El Cronista* of your city made my blood freeze for a moment. Then I realized that Yankee imperialist characters must be the ones poking up this fire in Central America.

Right now I feel more concerned about the serious problems among you people, leaders of our Central American Great Fatherland, than about the cause I'm defending with my few hundred Hotspurs, because I'm convinced that with our steadfast spirit and the terror we've managed to sow in the hearts of the pirates, our destination is obvious, while you people are surrounded by patricides who are always drawn by the smell of great causes to sow in them the seeds of treason.

Dear friend, in the name of Nicaragua, of Honduras, of Guatemala, and of God I implore you and all Central Americans of understanding and plain patriotism to try by all means possible to avoid heating up spirits and splitting our own ranks. You have an obligation to make the people of Central America understand that there should be no frontiers between us and that concern for the fate of each and every Latin American people is our common duty, since that fate is the same for all in light of the Yankee imperialists' policy of colonizing and absorbing us.

Geography has put the blond beast at one end of Latin America from which they watch all our political and economic movements with covetous eye: they know the volatility of our character, and manage to keep problems between one country and another simmering unresolved. For example the Guatemalan-Honduran and Honduran-Nicaraguan border problems; the canal problem between Nicaragua and Costa Rica; the Gulf of Fonseca problem between El Salvador, Honduras, and Nicaragua; the Tacna-Arica problem between Peru and Chile, and so on—a whole chain of important problems among us. The Yankees have studied us carefully and take advantage of our volatility and the state of our culture to keep us on the edge of danger as and when it suits them.

The Yankees are our peoples' worst enemies, and when they see our patriotic spirit urging us toward unification they give our intramural problems a vigorous stir to exacerbate hatreds among us, to keep us disunited and weak and hence easy to colonize.

We are well into the twentieth century, and the times have shown the whole world how the Yankees' slogans can be turned against them. When they speak of the Monroe Doctrine, they say, "America for Americans." Fine, well said. All of us born in America are Americans. But the imperialists have interpreted the Monroe Doctrine as "America for the Yankees." Well, to save their blond souls from continuing in error, I propose this reformulation: "The United States of North America for the Yankees. Latin America for the Indo-Latins."

Taking that as a slogan as should be done, the Yankees can only come to our America as guests, never as masters and senōres as they assume to do. I and my army would not be surprised to find ourselves in any Latin American country where the murderous invader plants his boots in the attitude of a conqueror.

Sandino was an Indo-Hispanic for whom Latin America had no frontiers. He ended with a "Fatherland and Freedom," sending Turcios "my heart, from which I speak to you in this letter."

In that year of 1928 Manuel María Girón Ruano, a Guatemalan general who had joined Sandino's army, repudiating that of his own country, was taken prisoner by the North Americans. They delivered him with fettered feet to the National Guard and he was summarily executed by order of Augusto Caldera. When Moncada's secretaries Cordero Reyes and Anastasio Somoza advised Guatemalan dictator Chacón of the execution, they did so in terms so insulting to Girón Ruano's memory that Sandino wrote:

> As for those waddling penguins Cordero Reyes and Somoza, a day will come when they can be brought on foot to Las Segovias to disinter General Girón Ruano's body with their hands and bear it on their shoulders to the port of Corinto, fulfilling our duty to repatriate the remains of this valiant *compañero* to rest in Guatemalan soil. And as for the chains in which he was buried, they would be just the thing to adorn the necks of certain people I know.

The enthusiasm for Sandino's battles and ideals that was aroused in Europe by such spokesmen as José Vasconcelos and Manuel Ugarte inspired, in July 1928, a letter that was a source of great pride for Sandino. It was from Henri Barbusse:

> General, I send you this greeting in personal homage and in that of the proletariat and revolutionary intellectuals of France and Europe, who have on many occasions authorized me to express on their behalf our admiration for the heroic figure of Sandino and his splendid troops.
>
> In you we salute a liberator, a magnificent soldier of a cause which, without regard to race and nationality, is the cause of the oppressed, of the exploited, of the peoples against the magnates. In you we salute the ardent youth of Latin America who are aroused to stand against the hangmen of the North, the beasts of Gold; we salute all the multitude of workers and Indians who throb impatiently to march against the imperialist and capitalist machinery imposed by foreign

hands, and to create in its place a radiant new world on the soil that is theirs.

At the vanguard of the struggle and of your challenged continent you, Sandino, general of free men, are performing a historic, indelible role, by your luminous example and splendid sacrifices. The hearts of all of us are with you.[8]

Spanish socialist Luis Araquistain said on a later occasion that one of the most treasured documents in his files was a letter dated July 31, 1928, in which Sandino wrote to him:

I have received your important work *La agonía antillana*, which you honored me by autographing in terms that fill me with legitimate gratification. The shining honesty and deep vision with which you present in this book the problems our brother Antillean republics face from Yankee imperialism, which only their national independence can resolve, move me to offer my warmest congratulations.

Although conditions in all the Antillean Republics are the subject of your study, based on personal observations, you deal with the dependent situation suffered by Central America and specifically Nicaragua, and this was to have been expected, given the identity of our problems in face of U.S. imperialist expansionism, which could not but be grasped by such a conscientious spirit as yours.

It is encouraging that the new generation in Spain should be writing such transcendent works, because it is a portent of reactionary Spain's entry into the new paths being taken by the social sciences. We in this continent who are concerned with higher human goals are not blind to the present struggle in Spain between past and future, between those in whom ancestral currents of domination run deep and those whose minds are free of prejudice.

We who seek the total revision of human values have fraternal embraces for all of you; and writing to you in Spain gives me the opportunity to say that if in the present historical moment our struggle is national and racial, it will become international as colonial and semicolonial peoples learn to unite with peoples of the imperialist metropolises.

Before the end of 1928 another letter went around the world: the one Sandino sent to Admiral Sellers, who for the first time condescended to stop calling Sandino a bandit and wrote:

Commander, U.S. Special Service Squadron
Flagship USS *Rochester*
Corinto, Nicaragua
30 November 1928

General Augusto C. Sandino, Las Segovias

Señor:

Although all previous efforts to get into communication with you, by peaceful means, have failed, I am again impelled to appeal to your patriotism to ascertain if it is not now possible to terminate the armed resistance to the forces under my command. In view of the situation, political and otherwise, now existing, there would seem to be ample proof that continued armed resistance serves no useful purpose and should you desire to consider a cessation of your activities or struggle with its attendant benefits, any communication you may care to send will be given attention and careful consideration.

D. F. Sellers
Rear Admiral, U.S. Navy
Commander, Special Service Squadron

Sandino replied:

Army Defending the National Sovereignty of Nicaragua
General Headquarters
El Chipote, Nicaragua
1 January 1929

Admiral D. F. Sellers, U.S. Fleet, Corinto

Señor:

Your communication from the above port to hand. The patriotism to which you appeal is what has kept me repelling force with force, since I totally reject any interference by the government of your country in the affairs of our nation and am demonstrating that the sovereignty of a people is not something to discuss but to defend with arms in hand. Unless this is recognized there will be no peace, and although you state in your communication that continued armed resistance serves no useful purpose, I formally declare to you that only continuation of this armed resistance will bring the benefits to which you allude, in precisely the same way that foreign interference in our affairs brings the loss of peace and provokes the people's anger.

Patria y Libertad,
Augusto C. Sandino

The method now being tried to bring Sandino to his knees was diplomacy. In view of this Sandino felt obligated to reply in the same language, and on January 5 he made public the conditions on which he would agree to a cease-fire, among them these imperatives: immediate and total withdrawal of its invading forces by the U.S. government, either by reason or by force; no inflated U.S. loan to be accepted; the Bryan-Chamorro Treaty and all its derivatives to be declared null and void; any interference by the U.S. in elections or any other area, to be vigorously rejected.

Sandino's "unreasonable" attitude decided the army of intervention to go the limit, and on January 15, 1929, this Associated Press cable appeared in New York's *La Prensa:*

> Reports received from advance detachments indicate that forty more soldiers under command of the rebel chief, General Sandino, died yesterday in attacks by U.S. forces in the Chipote sector. Attacks on the rebels will in future be conducted by airplanes instead of land forces, since the latter risk being killed in ambushes. The aerial attacks to date have been very effective, according to Colonel Louis Mason Gulick, commander of the occupation forces in Nicaragua, who said the rebels were scattering in terror of the effects of bomb explosions. The marines' objective is to cut off the rebel leader's retreat to prevent him escaping into the Caribbean down the Coco River. General Chamorro has offered Colonel Gulick the assistance of Conservative forces, stating that these would be more effective than the North Americans due to the rough terrain in Nueva Segovia.

This was the time for air power to concentrate on the liberating army's headquarters. El Chipote lies on not very high ground in the steepest mountain zone, a lone eminence protruding into a small wooded plain and flanked by two streams. On its slopes shelters had been dug which the air offensive succeeded in making useless, for this was the most blitzed target in the entire war. Day after day the squadrons dropped their deadly cargo against lively rifle and machine gun fire. Flying low to use machine guns as well as bombs, they exposed themselves sufficiently for the patriots to be able to bring down no less than seven, including one zapped with a Lewis gun by Sandino himself.

In such steep terrain the planes could only harass with their machine guns *sandinistas* who were caught on the plains, and who scattered to regroup in forested areas. At other times, when they were few in number, the *sandinistas* stood up motionless like statues or trees, hoping not to be spotted. When an airman crashed he tried to defend his life to the last moment, rejecting capture as infamous.

The invaders' normal air strength in Managua—thirty planes, extraordinary for the time—was finally increased to seventy. Their methods reduced all laws of war to a scrap of paper. Exasperated by this resistance that made them look ridiculous, they began executing every patriot who fell into their hands. Up to that time Sandino had preferred to set prisoners free, by way of constructive propaganda and to gain their goodwill. He decided to emulate the enemy when he saw how they treated not only his men but civilians: houses destroyed, earth scorched, in a tactic of indiscriminate extermination which only betrayed their impotence. The invaders bragged of giving their prisoners "the freedom they ask for" by shooting them; Sandino took to "losing" his "along the road." Thus the war became merciless on both sides. Like their human occupants, the entire Segovian heights, bristling like a Maginot Line, seemed to boil from their very entrails against the homicidal invader.

It had not always been thus: it was the invader who turned the mountain people into belligerents by treating them like rabid animals. Having no ideology of any kind, they had looked with meek curiosity upon these tall blond soldiers, who at first showed suspicious reserve but later were seized with destructive frenzy, seeing hostility in every hut and a guerrilla or spy in every inhabitant. As Belausteguigoitia writes: "Often they lined up their machine guns against houses they passed on the road, or against cattle they came upon here or there, with the idea of striking terror or desolation into rebel territory and making life impossible for the enemy."

So the time came when the whole people of the mountains were either fighting under Sandino or active in his round-the-clock spy network. Warlike passions were awakened, wrapped in hate and despair.

One day a U.S. aviator on routine reconnaissance came upon a man in a field in the attitude of cutting hay. The man looked like a *sandinista* soldier putting on a performance, and the aviator let loose with his machine gun. Sure enough, the man seized his rifle and started firing at the plane, jumping and running to avoid the bombs that the aviator was now dropping. One bomb blew away the man's arm and rifle; then the pilot saw him raise the arm stump and shake it at the plane in desperate fury. Then another bomb blew him to pieces. The airman who related the incident added that this man's gesture gave him the impression of an entire land protesting against armed occupation.

A correct impression, for Sandino's performance inspired the people's respect. News agencies reporting his "atrocities" didn't mention that, to preserve discipline and the honor of the cause, he applied to his army the same inexorability as to the invaders. Only liberal papers reported the shooting of Colonel Antonio Galeano, "a gallant soldier in battle," ordered by Sandino because Galeano "committed serious abuses, getting drunk and raping a young girl." Although in command of a troop and put in charge of a town, he was summarily executed. Sandino's comment: "We respect women and honestly acquired private property. The thieves and rapists are the Yankees."

Two generals, a sergeant, and a soldier were executed for serious abuses. General José Santos Sequiera's fate was amply publicized due to the fame he had earned inside and outside the country. Sandino thus explained it:

> One morning I arrived at a certain hut in a forest clearing which I used as a shelter. A whole night's work had completely exhausted me and I recall I was wearing a white riding habit. I had hardly entered the hut to rest when the North American airmen started one of their raids. Covered with a black cape, I hid in nearby thickets, and there I stayed dodging the bombs while my men machine-gunned the planes from further off. Then I saw quite close to me General Sequiera, who was my chief of staff at the time. He was aiming a pistol at me. I grabbed my revolver and ordered him to remove himself. I repeated the order and got it obeyed at gunpoint. Later Sequiera was convicted of treason, but although stripped of command he continued participating in operations. When he was surprised in another act of treason, he managed to escape toward the North American camp. He left our ranks as a deserter and some weeks later was captured and executed as an example to others.

In contrast, volumes could be filled with shameless and pitiless acts committed by the invaders and their National Constabulary auxiliaries. A pamphlet written by a school principal named Napoleón Parrales, *La barbarie yanqui y la vileza criolla* (Yankee Barbarism and Creole Vileness), seems to cry out to the heavens on behalf of the thousands of victims of the invaders' and their national collaborators' terror.

Assaults by drunken marines, assassinations for trivial reasons, rapes, the sadism with which *campesinos* were treated whether or not they were *sandinistas,* the complicated forms of death that were invented for prisoners to tickle the North American sense of humor, put in the shade the worst excesses by the resistance forces who, as defenders of their soil against a foreign power, had some justification. For neither in the heat of battle nor in rest periods nor around a conference table did Sandino ever fail to stress the legitimacy of his cause, resisting intervention as a simple Nicaraguan by every means in his power.

This report from Managua appeared in *El Gráfico* (New York), on March 1, 1929:

> In the place called La Pita in Jinotega, a group of U.S. marines entered the house of Cruz García, searched his furniture, and found some Springfield ammunition. This was enough for them to seize García, whom they found working, and beat him with their rifle butts until they drew blood. They took him to the house of Salvador Picado some 300 yards from García's place and shot him without further ado.
>
> The marines responsible are part of a detachment billeted in Poteca. Murders of this kind have occurred in settlements all over the mountains, in Jinotega and elsewhere, and this has helped to make Sandino's struggle all the more inflamed and drawn-out. The National Guard, under direction of the marines, also performs every sort of violence on the inhabitants of villages, settlements, and haciendas. According to statistics of U.S. troop activities in Nicaragua since General Sandino raised the banner of revolt, seventy villages and hamlets have been burned by the marines since May 31 of last year. The following places figure on the list: Quilalí, Jabalí, Plan Grande, Buena Vista, San Lucas, Ula, Esquinay, Susocován, Jumuyca, Santa Rita, Sábana Grande, Loma, Choto, San José, Santa Rosa, Manchones, San Jerónimo, Chipote, Remango, La Branca, La Virginia, La Conchita, El Barro, Santa Cruz, Pata Blanca, Palo Pristo, Ventillas, Murra, Los Limones, California,

Casas Viejas, Carrizal, El Pastoreo, Renacuajo, El Cacao, Santa María, La Paz, Pie de Cuesta, El Quebracho, and many others.

Such reports in the interventionist press as the following—an Associated Press cable datelined Tegucigalpa, April 8, 1929, published by the *New York Times*—suggest that the above account was not malicious: "U.S. planes from Managua which bombed suspicious rebel camps on the border also discharged bombs today over the city of Las Limas in Honduras; the city was almost completely destroyed."

Not to be outdone by their air force comrades, on June 5 drunken marines attacked the Managua cemetery and profaned the graves—an exploit which, condemned even by the official press, brought from President Moncada this excuse for his protectors: "I wish to say that Nicaraguans owe a great debt to the U.S. Marine Corps. . . . To err is human. Soldiers do this sort of thing all over the world, and we should say nothing about the affair of the cemetery."

Fatherland and Freedom

The bitter complaints which are heard in Latin
America against Wall Street are matched by the
constant, no-holds-barred attacks leveled by liberals in the United States and daily published by the
many radical newspapers in our country. Without
them these "trusts" would have already completely
swallowed all life in Latin America. But one should
not forget that these rights are purchased in the
countries to the South because there are people
there who will sell them. I remember that three
years ago I took a trip . . . giving lectures on inter-
American relations. . . . Well, on arriving in New
York I opened the *Herald Tribune* and found an
interview with the new Nicaraguan ambassador to
Washington. A year ago, this gentleman had been
thrown out of the presidency with the help of our
Marines. He called on liberal sectors in the United
States to help him obtain justice. He organized
meetings from one side of the country to the other
to send protests to Washington. But things were
worked out in Managua and the liberal *caudillo* who
had assured his U.S. counterparts that he only
wanted "justice" accepted the posting offered him
by his old enemy as ambassador to Washington.
And, can you imagine! He declares in this interview that the Yanqui marines were all very gentle-
manly and that they were only providing very useful services to Nicaragua and that to pull them out
of his country would be an act of discourtesy on the
part of the United States.

Samuel Guy Inman[1]

Much has been said about Sandino's "peculiar" religious ideas. We
know that when he was living in Tampico he fell in with Masons and
frequented theosophical and spiritualist groups. With a natural dis-

position toward mysticism and metaphysics despite the realism and enterprise he showed later in action, he was more influenced by intuition than by logic.

The Basque journalist Belausteguigoitia recalled Sandino saying to him: "Give me an *abrazo* instead of your hand. That's how we should greet each other. That way the fluids are transmitted much better." The *abrazo* was indeed the form of greeting between *sandinista* soldiers, except on duty when they bowed. They treated each other as "brothers."

Sandino always needed to pace up and down, and in San Rafael del Norte used for the purpose a dark room next to the guardhouse, protected by soldiers with submachine guns. The room had rifles stacked in one corner, a table and a few chairs, and a long bench on which members of his staff, or *campesinos* and workers seeking advice or help, would sit listening to him or attending his conferences with visitors. Nothing on the wall but a simple almanac and a photo of a landscape. His favorite seat was a rocker.

He had a soft voice with inflections that were more persuasive than commanding. His face was oval and bony, with a strong protruding jaw that accentuated the lines of his broad, firm, fine-lipped mouth, giving him an air of stubbornness and energy. His glance had that sad expression characteristic of Indians and mestizos whose small, black, incisive eyes carry long memories of slavery and pain. Sparse eyebrows, broad and somewhat protruding nose; small of stature like most Central Americans; dark complexion showing the preponderance of indigenous over European descent. Belausteguigoitia thus described him:

> His prematurely lined face reflected an expression so peculiarly his own, somewhere between profound reflection and intimate sadness. More than on the privation-worn soldiers who passed before him, his attention seemed to be fixed on something remote and invisible. There was about him none of the fierce air of a battle-hardened soldier with nerves on edge from war's dangers and inevitable cruelties. Rather was it the face of a man born to think and fantasize, a spiritual man cast by fate in the role of ringleader. . . . That indefinably profound look on that ascetic face, half saint, half thinker, revealed a man tormented in spirit but clear and precise in conviction. . . . The impression given by General Sandino, both in appearance and in talk, is

of great spiritual grandeur. Without doubt he is a devotee of yoga, a disciple of the Orient.

A characteristic habit was rubbing his hands with a handkerchief between them. He rarely gesticulated or changed his quiet tone of voice. He sent his soldiers on their way with a "May God guard you." When Belausteguigoitia lamented that his countrymen had sent no men or arms, Sandino said: "They've given us something more—the *waves* that come from moral support. That's worth more than if they'd sent a gunboat full of soldiers and ammunition."

Perhaps the best description is that of the Peruvian writer César Falcón who met Sandino in Mexico in 1930:

All eyes were turned on a spare and well-groomed man wearing a pistol and cartridge belt, certainly not the type one would nominate for a place on General Sandino's staff. One had to yield to the evidence: this big little man was General Sandino. But let him speak; he will talk about himself; there is no fear of losing his autobiography; his whole speech will be full of it. "I, *compañeros,*" are his first words. On this occasion he won't mention anything else.

But let's forget for the moment what he will be telling us and concentrate on his appearance, since no caricature is possible of this man who doesn't have a single characteristic feature. Short of stature (though we don't have to look at the floor to see him), spare without being thin, nervous, one would say he is all muscle. His face is desiccated, hard, bleached, like a rag that one has dried too long in the sun; we could say that all the outdoor weather to which the Yanqui planes exposed him have dehydrated his face. His eyes tell nothing; one might think they never saw anything. He doesn't know how to smile, though he often laughs; one might say that his laugh doesn't laugh: this is not tragic but certainly exasperating. Personally, Sandino isn't ugly nor unsympathetic; he is just insignificant, extraordinarily like everyone else.

Now we hear him speak and see him gesticulate. Still talking about himself. When he talks, his hands, his fatherland, and his heart don't get a moment's rest. He never says "Yanquis" or "Americans"; he says "the gringo," as Spaniards say "the Moor." "I'll never abandon my mountains as long as one gringo remains in Nicaragua, never abandon my fight while my people have no Law to respect. My cause is the cause of my people, the cause of America, the cause of all oppressed peoples." Although he doesn't know how to speak, he is expressive and fiery, saying all that he feels—sometimes what he doesn't feel (after all, as a good Latin American he's very Nicaraguan); he is a hundred percent the typical Creole, talkative, in general something of a braggart. I didn't ask him, but I'll swear he has one great weakness, the cockfights. Only with great effort can I remember just what he said, and I saw nothing in his face that revealed the formidable energy of this tireless fighter; all the weight of his fame has only driven his voice back into his throat; beyond that he's a simple, natural man, a true Creole. If his voice hadn't become so throaty, one would say there's nothing of the general about him.

Falcón's somewhat lethal irony does not make the portrait less faithful; indeed, it is enriched by his comments on Sandino's insistent cud-chewing of his own history, with which the reader is already familiar. Yet he only waxed expansive on the theme in connection with this struggle, remaining completely mum about his private life.

The quisling press also picked on Sandino's religious side to satirize. The churches, echoing such calumnies, fanned support of the intervention and condemnation of the resistance, with broadsides from every pulpit against the *sandinistas'* "bolshevism" and atheism. The legends woven about Sandino included clairvoyance in military situations. His predictions, logical as they were, awed his soldiers and helped surround him with an aura of mystery. General Carlos N. Quezada, who served under him, offered this example:

> I recall that when we were in La Culebra camp in the Chipotón area, word came from Las Carretas that a column of 250 Yanqui marines was advancing from Jícaro on Sandino's headquarters. With his usual serenity the general said, "I'm not worried about that column because it's a ruse to draw attention from other columns advancing from I don't yet know where." And as if by magic he distributed his forces on the Ventía heights commanding the river port of Wiwilí and at Santa Cruz, another Coco River port. Next day each of these detachments beat off a Yanqui column advancing through the mountains. At the same time the column from Jícaro about which we had had word pitched camp on the Santa Rosa heights, as General Sandino had predicted.

Is it any wonder that his men's simple minds transformed his intuition into clairvoyance? Or that their admiration for him should have imbued him with a sense of predestination about his mission?

Or that these feelings, mixed with hurried studies and a predisposition to mysticism, should have inclined him toward messianic fanaticism? In any case, it was thanks to that fanaticism that the resistance was able to continue unbroken. As he himself put it:

> Yes, every man fulfills a destiny; I am convinced that my soldiers and I are fulfilling the one that was assigned to us. That supreme will to set Nicaragua free has brought us together here. . . . In the beginning it was love. That love creates and evolves. But all is eternal. And for us life is not a passing moment but an eternity passing through the multiple facets of the transitory. . . . We are interpenetrated by the role assigned to us; in our army we are all brothers. . . .

And concerning his intuitions and premonitory dreams:

> At various times I have felt a sort of mental trepidation, palpitations, something strange within myself. Once I dreamed that enemy troops were approaching and that a certain Pompillo, who had been with me earlier, was with them. I immediately got up and gave the alarm, putting everyone at defense posts. Two hours later, still before dawn, the North Americans were beginning the attack. There is a part of our organism in which the organ of presentiment exists.
>
> . . . Talking often to the soldiers about justice and about our destiny, inculcating the idea that we're all brothers. It was above all when bodies weakened that I was able to raise spirits. Sometimes even the bravest languish. You have to know them, to choose them. And to chase away fear, making them see that death is a light pain, a transition. But those ideas are assimilated by interpenetration; and, yes, we are interpenetrated in our mission, so that my ideas and my voice can reach them more directly. The magnetism of a thought is transmitted. The waves flow out and are caught by those ready to receive them. In battle when nerves are tense a magnetic voice has enormous resonance. . . . Spirits are also in the battle, incarnate or nonincarnate. . . . Since its beginnings the earth is continuously evolving. But here in Central America, this is where I see a great transformation. . . . I see something I've never spoken about. . . . I don't think anything has been written about it. . . . In all of this Central America, beginning lower down, I see water penetrating from one ocean to the other. . . . I see Nicaragua covered with water. A tremendous depression coming from the Pacific. . . . Only the volcanoes remain above it. . . . It's as if one sea emptied into another.

To Belausteguigoitia, Sandino said:

I think faith is eternally childlike and creative. Childlike because it unites the real world with the world of marvels: it removes doubt, which is skepticism and old age, and returns us to the dream world of infancy when, as Wordsworth wrote, man retains the reflection of a nonmentality and an incarnation—as the theosophists say—that the years still haven't wiped from his mind. Creative because it makes man feel himself to be the miserable tenant of a life that will vanish like smoke, but the proprietor—the actor—of an eternal and ever-renewed drama.

These highly spiritualistic notions are in marked contrast to Sandino's other aspect, that of the fighter. Apart from his innate military sense which the invaders had reason to admire, he had rare powers of perception of both national and international social and political problems, powers that could have made him a good disciple of any tendency. This despite the ingenuousness to which his own public documents attest, ascribable as much to his generous heart and his spirit devoid of malice as to his deficient and belated political education.

But the essential point was clear as day to him, that no liberation struggle in Latin America could be undertaken without effective participation from all other victims of suppression, exploitation, and poverty. That ever since the colonial empire was surrendered by Spain, its Anglo-Saxon inheritors, through their economic imperialism, had become the basic obstacle to its development and to the progress of its culture and civilization. And that the cruelest expression of that imperialism negating our peoples' freedom came from the financial and economic powers of the United States.

It was in this conviction that Sandino addressed a long message to all the American governments which he assumed to be free of imperialist domination:

Señores Presidentes:

In view of the fact that your fifteen countries would be the most threatened if Nicaragua were permitted to become a colony of Uncle Samuel, I take the liberty of sending you this letter, inspired not by hypocritical diplomatic courtesies but by the unceremonious frankness of a soldier.

With such shame as they still possess the Yanquis seek to mask themselves behind an interoceanic canal project across Nicaragua, the result of which would be isolation of the Indo-Hispanic republics. Not in the habit of wasting opportunities, the Yanquis take advantage of the remoteness of our people to realize the dream they inculcate in their primary school children: that is, that when all Latin America shall have become an Anglo-Saxon colony, the blue of their flag will have but one star.

For fifteen months, to the chill indifference of Latin American governments, and left to its own resources, the Army Defending the National Sovereignty of Nicaragua has honorably and brilliantly confronted the terrible blond beasts and the terrible herd of Nicaraguan renegades who support the invader in his sinister designs.

During this time, *señores presidentes,* you have not acted in fulfillment of your duty. As representatives of free and sovereign peoples you have the obligation, either diplomatically or if necessary with the arms the people have confided to you, to protect against the numberless cold-blooded crimes committed in our unhappy Nicaragua in the name of the White House government, without any right and without any offense by our people except not wanting to kiss the whip that scourges them nor the Yanqui fist that strikes them.

Can it be that Latin American governments think the Yanquis will content themselves with the conquest of Nicaragua? Can it have been forgotten that out of twenty-one Latin American republics, six have already lost their sovereignty? Panama, Puerto Rico, Cuba, Haiti, Santo Domingo, and Nicaragua: those are the wretched six that have lost their independence and become colonies of Yanqui imperialism. Their governments do not defend their peoples' collective interests because they came to power not by popular will but by imperialist imposition; those who rise to the presidency backed by Wall Street magnates defend the interests of U.S. bankers. All that remains in those six unhappy republics is the memory of independence and the distant hope of regaining their freedom through the efforts of a handful of their sons, who fight on to rescue their fatherlands from the infamy in which the renegades have smothered them.

Yanqui colonization is advancing swiftly over our peoples without meeting any wall of bayonets, and thus the conquistador swallows with little difficulty each of our countries when its turn comes, since until now each has had to defend itself alone. If the governments of Latin America's leading nations had a Simón Bolívar, a Benito Juárez or a San Martín as president, our fate would be different, because they would know that once the blond pirates dominate Central America, Mexico, Colombia, Venezuela, etc., would be next.

What would become of Mexico if the Yanquis succeeded in their dastardly designs to colonize Central America? With all their virility the heroic Mexican people could do nothing, because Uncle Sam's monkey wrench would promptly tighten around their necks and the help they would hope to get from brother nations would be blocked by the Nicaragua canal and the Gulf of Fonseca naval base. They would have to fight the Yanqui imperium in isolation from the other Latin American nations and with their own resources, as is happening to us now.

The famous Carranza Doctrine proclaims that Mexico by its geographical position has to be—and in fact it is—the advance guard of Latinism in America. What, one must ask, is the present Mexican government's view of the present Yanqui policy in Central America? Can Latin American governments not have grasped that their prudent line in cases like Nicaragua's gives the Yanquis a big laugh? True, for the moment Brazil, Venezuela, and Peru have no intervention problem, as their representatives told the Havana Pan-American Conference in the debate on the right to intervene. But if those governments were more aware of their historic responsibility they would not wait for it to come to their own soil; they would go to the defense of a brother country that is fighting with courage and tenacity born of despair, against a criminal enemy who is 100 times bigger and armed with the most up-to-date weapons. Can governments which express themselves as Brazil's, Venezuela's, Peru's, and Cuba's have done, in such a tragic and critical hour, be sure of retaining tomorrow enough moral authority over these brother peoples? Will they deserve to be heard?

It is to the peoples of Hispanic America that I address myself now. When a government fails to reflect its people's aspirations, they who put it in power have the right to be represented by virile men with ideas of effective democracy, not by useless satraps whose lack of moral courage and patriotism puts a proud race to shame.

There are ninety millions of us Latin Americans. We should be thinking only about unification. We should understand that Yanqui imperialism is the cruelest enemy that threatens us—the only one that proposes by conquest to destroy our racial honor and our peoples' freedom.

Tyrants do not represent nations, and liberty is not won with flowers.

In order, then, to form a united front and halt the conqueror's advance into our fatherlands, we must start by deserving respect in our own house, and not permitting sanguinary despots like Juan Vicente Gómez and degenerates like Leguía, Machado, and others to hold us up to ridicule before the world as they did in the Havana pantomime.

We Latin Americans who retain some dignity must emulate Bolívar, Hidalgo, and San Martín, and the Mexican boys who on September 13, 1847, fell at Chapultepec, riddled with Yanqui bullets. They fell in defense of fatherland and race rather than bow submissively to a life of opprobrium and shame, the life to which Yanqui imperialism would condemn us all.

Patria y Libertad,
Augusto C. Sandino[2]

This limpidly quixotic document, indicting the Latin American officialdom to whom it is addressed, has no word of criticism for the peoples who were for the most part represented by volunteers in Sandino's army. Any friendly gesture in response would have kindled some hope, but the result was of course zero.

How long could this sort of struggle continue? With the withdrawal of foreign troops from Nicaragua as its sole aim, its possibilities were as remote as they were clear. The Latin American governments' unconcern made the struggle harder for Sandino, obliging him to curtail its objectives; but had he been able to broaden them, its repercussions and effectiveness—to judge by previous and subsequent experiences—might have been different.

Sandino needed to project the military struggle onto the political plane; to assure its survival by propounding an integral program of short- and medium-term social demands reaching beyond his own person or the possibility of military disaster. This in turn would have assumed the adoption of a combat plan anticipating a change of tactics by U.S. imperialism, which, as shrewdly analyzed by García Naranjo in the article I have cited in the notes to chapter 5, was about to substitute Mr. Morrow's suavities for planes dropping bombs. Many of Sandino's manifestos show he was not blind to this need, but turning to Latin American governments—in any tone of voice—was hopeless.

With his military potential declining, he faced a critical situation. Turcios' defection had cut all contact with the outside world, and the reactionary press made the most of it by announcing Sandino's death, which was calculated to disintegrate sympathetic movements in the Americas. This, together with Sandino's need to restore his broken health and his desire to appeal personally to friendly governments (above all Mexico), may have decided him to resign his command and leave Las Segovias. He may even have thought it possible that he could get into the United States to appeal directly to its people. His brother Sócrates was already there, addressing meetings in New York. In any case, with various versions in circulation as to what he had in mind,[3] on July 2, 1929, he arrived in Mexico.

But before leaving he had written directly to various presidents, in a further attempt to win Latin American governments' help or at least sympathy. To President Pío Romero Bosque of El Salvador he wrote on March 12:

El Chipotón, Nicaragua

My longing to free my country has impelled me to make representations to the four governments that remain in Central America, and I am addressing myself to the three others in the same way that I have the honor to do to yourself. Not being able to come personally, I do so symbolically. Enclosed you will find a leaf from the Segovian forests where Nicaragua's honor is at stake. The tree from which it comes is called *palanca,* lever. At this moment Nicaragua has a lever like that of Archimedes, and needs a fulcrum as he needed one. I ask you to consult with your people as to whether your country may be the fulcrum for which this section of the great fatherland is in search through myself. Archimedes could turn the world upside down. We, together, could stop being humiliated by the Yankee. If Nicaragua does not find in that brother people the fulcrum it needs, perhaps this note will take a place in their history. With my warmest wishes for the collective progress of Central America during your term of office.

Patria y Libertad,
A. C. Sandino

The most important letter was the one Sandino sent to Argentine President Hipólito Yrigoyen on March 20. Although neither Yrigoyen nor the foreign ministry paid it any attention, it became known when *La Nación* published it on April 5, with a preface noting that early in 1927 Sandino had already proposed mediation of the Nicaraguan conflict by the Argentine government. Leftist newspapers fiercely criticized the Alvear and the successor Yrigoyen governments for keeping the proposal secret, but failed even to get Sandino's letter acknowledged. The letter said:

On behalf of the Army Defending the National Sovereignty and of myself, I am privileged to advise you that our army will be honored to propose to the governments of Latin America and of the United States a conference between representatives of all America and myself representing the autonomist army, to be held in Buenos Aires. I am today addressing this proposal to the governments of Mexico, Guatemala, El Salvador, Honduras, Costa Rica, Panama, Colombia, Venezuela, Ecuador, Peru, Brazil, Bolivia, Paraguay, Uruguay, Chile, Cuba, the Dominican Republic, Puerto Rico, and the United States. Nicaragua will, as I have said, be represented by myself, and separately by representatives of what the governments of America recognize as the government of our republic, in the event that it accepts the invitation.

The object of this conference will be to set forth the original project of our army, which if put into effect will assure Indo-Hispanic sovereignty and independence and equitably based friendship between the America of our race and the United States. In presenting this project our army will speak for the right of the Indo-Hispanic peoples to express their opinion on the freedom and independence of the Latin American republics, which today suffer intervention from the United States, and for their natural God-given privileges that are the cause of our oppressor's pretensions.

The above project will also set forth the facts about the proposed construction of a Nicaraguan interocean canal. It is written in the destiny of our peoples that humble and outraged Nicaragua should be chosen to summon us all to unity with a fraternal *abrazo*. It is she who has been sacrificed, and she would gladly let herself be disemboweled if that would bring total freedom and independence to our Latin peoples of continental and Antillean America. The project rejects any sale of Nicaragua's rights over the canal that is proposed to open across her territory. The Nicaraguan canal should be opened because civilization demands it; but this cannot be decided by Nicaragua and the United States alone, for such an undertaking is of high importance for the inhabitants of our whole globe. To put it into effect, all of continental and Antillean America needs to be consulted, since the America of our race is making daily strides in industry and commerce. The right to an opinion as to the conditions in which the Nicaraguan canal shall be built cannot be denied to ninety million Latin Americans. Our Indo-Hispanic America has already been wronged once when she was not consulted about the Panama Canal; but we can still avoid another wrong with the Nicaraguan canal.

At the conference to which we invite all American governments, the question will be raised as to whether the Nicaraguan canal should be opened with exclusively North American capital. Should the conference concede this privilege to the United States, that country should in return sign a solemn pledge before the twenty-one Latin American governments' representatives that it will desist from all intervention in our republics and all interference in our internal affairs, and commit itself not to foment revolutions against the governments of Latin America, which have no desire to become footmen of the United States.

With such commitments we will avoid the contagion of servility in our governments and will emerge independent. If we permitted the United States to open our Nicaraguan canal without any commitment on their part to respect our peoples' sovereignty and independence, we would do a wrong even to the United States. With the Nicaraguan canal they would feel themselves stronger than God himself and would defy the whole world, which would bring destruction to the great nation of North America.

Señor Presidente: your government would do me honor by accepting our army's invitation to name your representatives to the conference we propose, and at the same time giving your esteemed approval to the conference being held in your capital city, cabling your decision to your representative in Honduras and through him to our army's special representative there. Should your government honor us by agreeing to attend such a conference and to extend to it the hospitality of your brother republic, we would ask you at the same time to receive a delegation from our army, to set a date for the governments of America and also your representative in Honduras to be notified of the conference, so that I may arrive in your capital on the date fixed by you.

On arrival in Tegucigalpa I will have the honor of placing myself under the Argentine flag and proceeding to the conference under its protection. As soon as our army's project has been presented, I will leave your brother republic accompanied only by my aides to return, should that still be necessary, to this same headquarters of struggle from which I now address you. I have the honor to subscribe myself your and the Argentine people's obedient servant.

Patria y Libertad,
Augusto C. Sandino[4]

Set to leave for Mexico on the invitation of its President Portes Gil, Sandino issued this final order to his subordinates:

El Chipotón, Las Segovias
1 July 1929
Generals Pedro Altamirano, Ismael Peralta, and Carlos Quezada

Esteemed *compañeros* and friends:

I have the honor to greet you and confirm my note of 20 May. I would also bring to your attention that as of this date generals Francisco Estrada, Pedro Antonio Irías, and José León Díaz are appointed to command our autonomist forces, as follows: commanding general, Estrada; second in command, General Irías; third in command, General Díaz. The above generals will explain to you the plan we are developing in line with our aspirations to see our country completely free. Their decisions will be observed as if they were taken by myself. The plan under development accords with everything we have achieved for the sovereignty of our nation, and you will understand that I cannot be explicit in writing, but generals Estrada and Díaz will explain all that has to be done.

Fraternally, *Patria y Libertad,*
A. C. Sandino

On the following day Sandino left for the border, arriving on July 4 in Honduras accompanied by Martí, captains Rubén Ardila Gómez, José de Reyes, and Gregorio Gilbert, and Lieutenant Tranquilino Jarquín. He passed through the Central American countries almost in secret: in the belief that he was fleeing and abandoning his cause, the governments gave him every transit facility. He stopped off in Tegucigalpa and sailed from the Honduran port of San Lorenzo for La Unión, El Salvador. A special train took him to La Garita whence he proceeded to El Congo, still in Salvadoran territory,[5] then by car into Guatemala and by train from Morán station to the Mexican frontier. Guatemalan police chief Herlindo Solórzano accompanied him in person through Guatemala to see he started no revolutions en route.

His stay in Mexico, which he had thought would be brief, lasted almost a year. Much of our information about it comes from Gustavo Alemán Bolaños, who carried on a lengthy correspondence with him. When he reached Vera Cruz his intention was to proceed to the capital, but he was forbidden to do so and "invited" to stay in Mérida, Yucatan. In a letter dated July 16 he expressed confidence that "our stay in this city won't be long," but by August 4 it looked longer:

The hope of securing in this republic what we need to continue our liberating war in Nicaragua is getting dim, but I'll try to raise money here in Mexico to secure it elsewhere. My being allowed into Mexico is due to a request from the president, Portes Gil, last January 6. This government has no commitment to help us, but coming here has been an opportunity to make progress in the undertakings I am after. Other versions circulated by the enemy are without foundation.

In pursuit of the said money I am very aware of the adage about not changing horses to put on a harness. Mindful of that, I won't make any political commitment and will conduct my search strictly on the basis of Latin American brotherhood or, if it suits any supporter better, of ensuring that the Nicaraguan canal project shall not be the Yankee pirates' property. But, I repeat, no changing of horses to put on a harness. . . . If this approach gets me nothing, I prefer to return to Las Segovias and continue defending our integrity with sombreros and spittle as weapons.

His letter to Alemán Bolaños on August 8 is more pessimistic:

I mentioned my early return to Las Segovias. But events are taking another turn, making me decide to stay in this republic long enough to resolve many matters connected with Nicaragua. . . . I had thought of returning to our camp this week, but as we haven't so far found even half a centavo divided in half, nor a pistol bullet for the cause of liberty in Nicaragua, I must wait a bit, if only for some replies that I consider hopeful for our cause. I do have one offer for purchase of weapons that would take us to victory. There may be a little demoralization in the forces I left organized in Las Segovias, but everything was carefully provided for.

On September 6, at his correspondent's suggestion, Sandino directed a manifesto to Nicaraguans:

In May 1927 Nicaragua's spurious sons Adolfo Díaz and José María Moncada [Chamorro had left the country] led the people into confusion by presuming to make them yield their dignity to the miserable Yankee invaders; but at that hour of collapse and confusion the Segovian column under my orders became the Army Defending the National Sovereignty, and it has forcibly beaten off the affront that the White House government sought to impose on the Nicaraguan people.

So long as Nicaragua has children who love her, Nicaragua will be free. And it has been loving children who in the whole people's behalf have transformed her from the nightmare she was for Latin American sister republics into the sister deserving all respect, through the fight to which that column committed itself on May 4, 1927.

Take heart, Nicaraguans! Liberation is at hand, but we will only be one in that hour if you emulate the army defending your sovereignty and join its ranks as soldiers ready for all, ready to kill or be killed. The hour approaches. The invader already thinks of packing up, convinced that our army is growing every day and that if at one time its ranks were only in Las Segovias, today they are in the cities of the interior. Each one of you, Nicaraguans, is a soldier in that army, because in each one, love of country is awakening in the form of dignity and energy for the redress of grievances.

Take heart, Nicaraguans! They, barbarians of the north, would bid you farewell leaving the imprint of their blows on your faces. Then so be it! Let the retributive action not be delayed, and let the account be squared blow for blow, eye for eye, so that the Yankees may learn the respect due to the freedom of peoples. There would be no forgiveness for you, Nicaraguans, if you turned the other cheek to the invader: your hands should fall like thunderbolts on the descendants of William Walker. Our autonomist army has amply shown what the force of right can do against the right of force.

Take heart, Nicaraguans! I will be with you in an hour that is approaching. The invader is already disheartened and feeling the weight of the people's anger. He is already packing his bags and withdrawing, striking blows as he goes. Happily you have given ample proof that you will not turn the other cheek. That is your duty.

The hour also approaches to square accounts with the creatures of the intervention—those who called for it and who have done their utmost to maintain it. It is for you, Nicaraguans, to take this task into your hands so that the army defending our sovereignty may meanwhile resume its activities. Do not waver. My temporary absence from Las Segovias means the absolute victory of freedom in Nicaragua. The day will dawn when you least expect it. Nicaragua will be free so long as she has children who love her.

But although his and his companions' expenses were covered by the Mexican government, Sandino was filled with uneasiness in a land that was not his, and chafed with impotence to help his compatriots in cities and towns who on their own account were organizing guerrilla movements or developing passive-resistance methods.[6] The slanders circulating in Mexico, portraying him as in cahoots with the enemy, made his golden prison the more odious. He mentioned this in his letter of September 8:

As for those who believe our flag of redemption has been lowered, I formed the opinion long ago that they are the eternal small-spirited pessimists of this world. The moans of "nothing can be done" are far from new to me and I never regarded them as anything but the voices of pusillanimity. These pessimists are always the ones who, when they see a task completed against all difficulties, clutch their brows trying to figure out what for them will always be unfigurable.

When some news agencies reported that Sandino had left Mérida surreptitiously, he wrote on September 9:

My departure, as reported by the press, is something I've never contemplated, nor have I resorted to anything in the nature of incognito. I'm always in the public view. As I told you, I will stay here for the time necessary, and I've taken all appropriate measures to prevent anything stopping me when the time comes. I'm only waiting for other *compañeros* [he had ordered generals Estrada, Irías, Díaz, Peralta, and Quezada to join him there along with colonels Reyes López, Dionisio Centeno, and Pedro Blandón and some captains]; you're aware of the reasons why they are to foregather here from Las Segovias—so that Colonel Martí, who has your address noted down, may leave.

It is my understanding that sincere leadership of our struggle (and I stress the word "sincere") will enable us to reorient the disoriented and those who are in error or confusion. And, as you say, it's of interest not to lose contact with small-minded patriots, and the manifesto I sent out will help in this.

In the same letter he made some political points:

I don't let myself be distracted by notions about presidential timber. In public and in private we handle even the smallest details of our orientation with common sense. . . . Neither extreme right nor extreme left, but united front, is our slogan. This being the case, it's not illogical that our struggle gets cooperation from all social classes without "ism" classifications.

This also makes it very logical that extreme left organizations support us, some of which could make some people think we preach a particular social doctrine. The principles we presented to the traitor Moncada, of which I sent you a copy, show that we have a program we believe appropriate for Nicaragua's social problems, and also for workers inept enough to be fooled by the careerists, to show them their position in the national struggle. Without such orientation toward their real problems, they will just be fodder for abject politicians.

With right practice in our actions, we'll always be able to distinguish patriotism from false patriotism.

Along with a copy of Emigdio Maraboto's pamphlet *Sandino ante el coloso,* Sandino sent these comments to Alemán Bolaños: "This pamphlet contains all the essentials of what we've done. It has two errors—that Sócrates Sandino and I are brothers of the same father and mother, and that the seller-out Díaz is Nicaraguan minister in Washington. On that first one, I'm my father's first son and my mother is Margarita Calderón; Sócrates' mother is Doña América de Sandino. On the second, you know as well as I do who represents the traitors in Washington—that idiot Sacasa." In fact, on February 1, Dr. Juan B. Sacasa had been reported in Guatemala's *La Prensa* as calling Moncada a "magnificent visionary," and on February 6 as having received his just reward: $6,000 "to prepare for his journey to Washington, as advance on $7,500 that is due to him." And it was this ambassadorship that inspired the complaint of liberal commentator Inman at the head of this chapter.

Martí fell sick in Mérida, depriving Sandino of his best spokesman to Central American nations. The young Colombian Ardila Gómez replaced him, but Martí's loss of health made Sandino as sad as a lost battle. He remained optimistic, however, and wrote on September 26:

Each day that God gives us, the chances for what we have undertaken get brighter, for important correspondence is raining on us from all directions. . . . The hermit's life that my enemies say I lead is something I might explain to you. My character is naturally retiring and I only talk a lot when someone touches me on that painful gland I have, my Latinamericanitis. It's true I don't go out much, but that's because I don't need to; I feel better staying in my observatory and I don't want them to think I go around drumming up popularity. . . .

And on October 8:

The arrival in Mérida yesterday of the White House's Lone Eagle, Lindbergh, seems an appropriate moment to publish in the local press my dedicatory remarks to you in giving you the typewriter that accompanied me in the first campaign.

You'll recall that when we captured that machine the Pan-American pantomime was on in Havana, and just before that was Lindbergh's so-called "goodwill tour." And a lovely coincidence: on the very day Lindbergh landed in Managua, the North American war planes were making desperate day and night flights bringing the pirate dead and wounded from Quilalí into Managua. The "goodwill ambassador" himself is witness to that since he, Lindbergh, helped lower those dead and wounded from the planes. For this reason we may be sure he left Nicaragua out in the account of his tour. Very good.

On October 19 he wrote to Alemán Bolaños correcting new rumors that were circulating about him, that he was "a prisoner." On the contrary, he said, he had "freedom of action in every sense" and "there'll be no difficulty about our leaving when the time comes."

General of Free Men

By cable from Managua, Nicaragua. February 11.
Several days ago I rode out of the camp of General
Augusto C. Sandino, the terrible "bandit" of Nicaragua who is holding the marines at bay. Not a
single hair of my blond, Anglo-Saxon head had
been injured. On the contrary, I had been shown
every possible kindness, I went, free to take any
route I might choose, with permission to relate to
anybody I encountered any and every thing I had
seen and heard. Perhaps my case is unique. I am the
first and only American since Sandino began fighting the marines who has been granted an official
interview, and I am the first bona fide correspondent of any nationality to talk to him face to face.

"Do you still think us bandits?" was his last query
as I bade him goodby.

"You are as much a bandit as Mr. Coolidge is a
bolshevik" was my reply.

"Tell your people," he returned, "there may be
bandits in Nicaragua, but they are not necessarily
Nicaraguans."

Carleton Beals[1]

What Sandino got in Mexico was not much. As he remarked on
September 9, 1929, there was no hostility toward him ("we didn't
expect it from the Mexicans who in any case cultivate frankness").
But his visit to the capital at the end of that year was little more
productive than his stay in Mérida.

When he decided to return to his country, just two submachine
guns—declared in the customs as "carpentry tools"—constituted his
whole arsenal obtained in Mexico. One G. Constantino González
had provided him with 1,000 Mexican pesos for his and his companions' travel expenses.

Failing in his attempt to unify all Latin American revolutionary movements, he had seen his best foreign allies drop out one by one: Turcios, Martí, the Peruvian Pavletich. He had missed meeting the Peruvian Haya de la Torre, who was expelled first by Chacón from Guatemala and then by the government of Panama; now he missed Alemán Bolaños in Guatemala.

Sandino entered Guatemala by train on May 1, 1930, under the name of Crescencio Rendón. He tried to find the Nicaraguan journalist who was so identified with his cause, but because of the haste and secrecy with which he had prepared for the journey he could not advise him of his arrival. Alemán Bolaños had gone to San Salvador, and Sandino had the brief pleasure of chatting with the journalist's wife and fondling his children.

At midday on the third he left by car for El Salvador and, passing through San Salvador on the fifth without stopping, took the Oriente train at Zacatecoluca to Honduras. Two days later he and his companions were back in Nicaragua.

Although no political changes were to be seen in his country, there was a visible transformation in the forces of the enemy: they no longer consisted mainly of U.S. marines, but of Nicaraguans under the invading army's instruction and command. The National Constabulary had become the National Guard. This turned into solid reality an apparently innocuous clause of the 1923 Peace and Friendship Treaty, endorsed and guaranteed by Washington, and brought into play a new psychological and a new military factor. The *sandinistas* now confronted their own brothers, and the National Guard troops, accustomed to the climate and terrain, used the same tactics as Sandino.

In their great self-esteem and contempt for their adversary, the North Americans had stood in the open to fight the guerrillas, bringing up rifles to cheeks as soon as the first shot rang out and thus forming perfect targets for Sandino's ambushed sharpshooters. The National Guard men, in contrast, immediately threw themselves on the ground. They advanced through the forest instead of along roads, avoided towns and villages, were always on the alert for espionage possibilities, and in general followed the methods that Sandino had developed.

Blood had been as copiously shed by the North Americans as by the *sandinistas,* in four years of war without quarter against an enemy who was as invisible as he was tenacious. In the United States there was a rising clamor of public protest and expostulation by the liberal press. Impatient voices rang out one after the other in the Senate. What better solution than to turn the war between invader and invaded into a civil war?

Five thousand men formed the first contingent to fight Sandino. Uniforms in the U.S. style; heavy armament, 400 machine guns; aviation totally in U.S. hands. This was the force to be sent against an army thus described by Belausteguigoitia:

> . . . Deprived, to an extent that defied belief, of the most primitive things it needed to function. Almost a third of the men marched barefoot; most days, not even one half-adequate meal; no one, from general to ranker, earning a centavo; yet with a spiritual power surpassing anything the Americas have known since the armies of independence, and perhaps surpassing them in ideological depth, for all the force's smallness and modesty.

To insure against "accidents" from the rear, the National Guard started with a ban on bearing arms: even the simplest penknives were forbidden. The consequence was an immediate rise in the urban delinquency index, since anyone obeying the order became a ready victim for delinquents.

At the same time the already exhausted treasury staggered under a 100,000-*córdoba* monthly budget for the National Guard, a load so far exceeding the country's potential that "unnecessary lines" of public expenditure had to be suppressed. What was most unnecessary? Education: why ask? So in 1931 and 1932 Nicaragua's schools and colleges were closed as a "war saving."

The so-called Military Academy "put out officers in six months." Added to the strange mix of Nicaraguan soldiers and officers and foreign generals and colonels was the National Guard's independent postal and telegraph system. The Guard was exempt from all responsibility to the national authorities, spent funds for which it did not have to account, and ran its own promotions and demotions. Thus the North Americans' one visible legacy to Nicaragua was implantation of the dominant military caste.

From then on the United States did not need to indulge in new military adventures. It only had to raise to the top tried-and-true military addicts of the U.S. way of life—preferably military attachés in Washington—to achieve the tranquility its self-sacrificing businessmen needed to carry on their deals without fear or risk.

This was the thought behind the nonintervention policy, later to be transmogrified into the "Good Neighbor policy," which evidently represented an important shift of the rudder in inter-American relations. Once again wisdom grew out of experience. The Big Stick policy was moribund, giving place to the smile and the pat on the back.

The first smile was the invaders' public promise in 1930 that, on the day after Moncada's successor (elected at U.S.-"supervised" polling stations) took office, not one foreign soldier or officer would remain in Nicaragua. Early in the previous year the United States' new president, Hoover, had prepared the ground with his famous "goodwill" junket on the cruiser *Utah*. There was less pleasure in his trip than so eminent a figure might have expected. In all the capitals he visited where dictatorships did not prevent it, there were public demonstrations repudiating imperialist policies. In Buenos Aires and Montevideo, Hoover was received with choruses of "Sandino! Sandino!"[2] This type of welcome must have been quite irritating, for he decided to throw the rest of his program overboard. But while word of these manifestations of popular sympathy reached Sandino, he could only wish bitterly that the solidarity might have taken more concrete form.

His failure to get arms in Mexico, the occasional hostility he felt in that foreign land, and the unconcern of Latin American governments had made his return to Nicaragua seem ever more urgent. Nineteen twenty-nine had been one of the saddest years in the history of Latin American liberties: a shameful year of government indifference and popular impotence; sad for the future, with another Republican president in the United States, signaling no end to the plunder and intervention policy, disguised though it was with meekness and repentance; bitter for Sandino, reduced to flickering hope of help that never came.

In June 1930, when he had not yet been back a month, he was again in the thick of battle with his soldiers. As ever, he is a good chronicler of his campaigns:

> In these plains and mountains our salvos of protest and alert against the brigand hordes have not ceased, and will not. Las Segovias has two imposing heights, El Saraguazca and El Yucapuca, which were our

centers of operation during the war against Chamorro and Díaz in 1927. In line with new plans, our army occupied El Saraguazca on June 18 with 400 men and ten machine guns, leaving in various places columns totaling over 600 men with sufficient weapons. On the morning of the nineteenth officers of the guard notified me of suspicious lights on the Chirinagua and Peña de la Cruz heights, moving toward the lower slopes of El Saraguazca as if trying to approach our advance detachments. I ordered the three mortar shots to be fired which were the general-alert signal. The battle began in the early hours of the nineteenth, in the direction of the San Marcos lowland. By noon the enemy was defeated on all flanks, the Yanqui who led the attackers being killed in the first assault. The enemy kept up almost constant fire till 6 P.M. when our exasperated men completely wiped him out.

A squadron of six planes that took part in the battle bombed and machine-gunned us furiously. But the counterattack was also furious and the enemy suffered many losses and desertions. On our side we mourned the death of Captain Encarnación Lumbi. The soldier Roque Matey of Talpaneca was wounded, and when the air bombardment seemed to have stopped at around 4 P.M., a bomb fell near me and a fragment caused a light wound in my left leg. I haven't given any importance to the wound and have continued directing matters connected with our army, since the wound doesn't even keep me from mounting my horse.

Latin America rejoiced over the new signs of life in Sandino and his return to combat. A price—in dollars—was again placed on his head. But he was still far from alone: distinguished Latin Americans like Vasconcelos, Ugarte, Haya de La Torre, Palacios, Mariátegui—even César Vallejo in Russia—were propagandists of his cause, and the multitudes throughout the continent still had confidence in its final victory.

Many newspapers and journals had by now become virtual *sandinista* house organs, and these fighting outposts were not confined to Latin America. In Washington itself, the Pan-American Anti-Imperialist League branch had organized demonstrations, one leading to disorders in which over 100 demonstrators were arrested. One of the signs they carried said: WALL STREET, NOT SANDINO, IS THE REAL BANDIT IN NICARAGUA. Another: WE DON'T APPEAL TO THE WHITE HOUSE BUT TO THE MASSES AGAINST THE WHITE HOUSE. Carlos Thomson wrote in *La Nueva Democracia*, New York:

> Sandino is in more than one sense the key man in the Nicaraguan situation. Whether Liberals or Conservatives come out on top, their

foreign policy will be rapprochement with the United States. In my opinion any government there, Liberal or Conservative, will try to go along with the White House. Of course there are people who sustain Sandino on the moral level, as he courageously sustains himself in Las Segovias. I believe that U.S. intervention has done something worse in Nicaragua than trample national sovereignty: it has corroded the Nicaraguans' moral fiber, broken their confidence in themselves, destroyed their capacity for self-government. Up to now I see no organized political group that can take leadership in Nicaragua's national affairs without first getting the United States' okay. And this, as I see, it is a wound to the Nicaraguan organism that will need many years to heal . . . and which will leave a scar on General Sandino and his Las Segovias army.

The *Daily Worker* had its say at some length, asking itself "Where is Sandino Heading?" and describing his worker and *campesino* army's "heroic resistance to the vandals" who were equipped with "planes, bombs, rifles, and cannon," and the "echo" of this throughout Latin America, whose "oppressed masses saw it as one effective means of defeating Yankee imperialism." In the United States, "revolutionary workers did not hesitate to acclaim the rebellion and give it their unconditional support." The paper saw Sandino as having been "forced by his army's international character to see the situation with some clarity."[3]

In Nicaragua it had been decided to hold elections on November 16, 1932. This set off another war, not between the invaders and Sandino but between Moncada, Liberal Party aspirant for a second term, and the top leadership of that party which repudiated him. Paralleling this was the struggle of both factions against the Conservatives, who naturally raised the electoral banner of our old friends Chamorro and Díaz.

The National Guard paid little mind to Moncada but by its very presence imposed the Washington electoral recipe of "supervision" by North Americans. This against the open opposition of Sandino, for whom such an election merely confirmed the subjection of national sovereignty to a foreign nation. Both Liberals and Conservatives were of course enemies of Sandino, or at least sought to demonstrate it with equal fervor to the interveners in hope of their support.[4] Moncada, in posssession of the presidency, tried to put a clause in the Constitution making his re-election possible and sent emissaries to Washington to sample the climate for this.

But since the State Department was now wearing a hands-off mask, it took this splendid opportunity to demonstrate as much officially, publicly repudiating any "unheard-of pretension." Moncada's fate was thereby sealed. Nevertheless, he played the faithful lackey to the end: when still more decorations were to be pinned on North Americans, he chose the government house for the ceremony in which such pearls as this fell from his lips: "Not being able to decorate the soldiers of the United States of America, I am especially privileged to decorate the *jefes,* the airmen, and the officers: in the one case for their leadership, in the other because in the very ether itself, fearless of storms and of the unknown, they self-sacrificingly perform their duty."

According to a United Press cable from Tegucigalpa on September 9, 1931, up to August 20 of that year the *sandinistas* had fought twenty-three battles, in one of which (at Wauspuck on the Coco River) they killed six marines and fifty-three National Guardsmen, and captured three airmen and 60,000 rounds of ammunition—a timely haul for the offensive Sandino was readying for November. Sandino's successes were also reported by the Associated Press a month earlier:

> WASHINGTON, D.C., AUGUST 12, 1931—Reports from Nicaragua sent to the Department of Marines in this capital by sergeants Gordon Heritage and Orville B. Simons state that their plane was riddled with bullets by the insurgents before crashing into a swamp in northeast Nicaragua, on July 22. Another U.S. marine aircraft accompanying them when the *sandinista* rebels opened fire got away with bullet-perforated wings. Heritage and Simons counted seventeen holes caused by bullets. Seeing that they could not gain altitude, they set fire to the plane and had to make their way through forty miles of scrub to reach Puerto Cabezas. The marines also abandoned the machine guns carried by their plane.

While in Mexico, Sandino had informed Alemán Bolaños of the whereabouts of his own and his army's records:

> Still without material support from any government or institution, I have made arrangements for the safety of our army's archives, which I consider a moral treasure of great historical value. I have deposited

them with a notary public in the Masonic lodge of Yucatán. As you know, another part of them is in the hands of Froylán Turcios, and my wife Blanca Aráuz de Sandino has another, the records of the Constitutionalist column I headed under Sacasa. The part deposited with the lodge is the most important. I would like to deposit with you the documents covering the period from then to my departure for our camp in Las Segovias, so that should I die tomorrow you may bear faithful witness to the integrity of our attitude.

Now, on July 16, 1931, he brought up the subject again to Alemán Bolaños after telling him that

the general condition of our army is far better than in previous periods, mainly because we have now awakened the conscience of our people, a welcome task which I imposed on myself. . . . Recently, working at night, we have made copies of important documents of our army which are now assembled in a file and could be published right away as a book or pamphlet. I've been ranging the outside world in my mind in search of the right person to entrust with publication of this work, and am happy to tell you that you are our army's choice. Accordingly, I'm sending you the file by express courier, carefully arranged, for publication with whatever commentary is appropriate. It's simply a matter of lighting the lamp of justice.

The documents never reached their destination. They were intercepted at the Honduran frontier town on Danlí, and these invaluable sources of light on the *sandinista* epic were lost.

At this point Sandino's battles were not all military: he was trying to convince his compatriots that abstention was the only revolutionary course open to them in the upcoming electoral farce. He issued this manifesto on July 28, 1931:

Everyone knows that our army is fighting against an army with the most modern equipment and all the material resources available to a government. Nevertheless, the rural areas of eight Nicaraguan departments are now under our control, and if we have not taken cities it is because this does not figure in our program, but we will assuredly do so when the time comes. Our tactic is to keep under vigilance the urban centers of departments where we are operating. The enemy is saying that food is running short in Las Segovias, but that is in the urban center where the mercenaries are holed up. In the countryside there is no hunger and our army has food enough and to spare.

Our expeditionary forces consist of eight columns, situated and commanded as follows: columns 2 and 6 under generals Carlos Salgado P. and Abraham Rivera, operating successfully on our Atlantic coast; column 1 under General Pedro Altamirano controls Chontales and Matagalpa departments; column 3 under General Pedro Antonio Irías controls Jinotega department; column 7 under General Ismael Peralta controls Estelí department; columns 4 and 8 under generals Juan Gregorio Colindres and Juan Pablo Umanzor control the zones of Somoto, Ocotal, Quilalí, and El Jícaro; column 5 under General José León Díaz controls León and Chinandega departments.

Our general headquarters is established in the center of the above departments. Our columns are mobilized with mathematical precision to the right and left of our headquarters.

Our army is the most disciplined, devoted, and disinterested in the entire world, because it is conscious of its lofty historical role. It is of no consequence that abject pens describe us as "bandits." Time and history will undertake to say whether the bandits are over there or in Nicaraguan Las Segovias, where human love and brotherhood prevail. Even when our army orders traitors to be shot, it does so from the highest love of liberty. Only those are shot who commit crimes against that liberty, trying to impose a slavery which we reject with sacred anger.

For the benefit of anyone wishing to see them, there are in our headquarters great quantities of documents, flags, and assorted objects formerly belonging to the army that seeks to exterminate us, all taken from the enemy in various battles. We too have suffered great losses, but we make no attempt to deceive the public as our opponents do, saying that our bullets only touch the brims of their hats.

The above information should suffice to keep the public on the alert and proof against the enemy's lies designed to confuse and befuddle. In fact July 24 marked the fourth anniversary of our army's first battle at El Ocotal against the army of the world's most grotesque imperialism. Yesterday as today, our enemy has impotently brandished all his weapons against us, including calumny, the most potent weapon of cowards.

I myself am in no way different from any rank-and-file soldier in the armies of the world. My voice is not arrogant, nor does my presence evoke terror as many might imagine. We have, however, fulfilling our duty as citizens, had the pleasure of seeing under our feet in humiliation a number of exalted chiefs and officers of the arrogant army of the United States, the would-be annihilator annihilated. We have shown, so far as was possible for us, that the force of right—wielded with force, yes—is greater than the right of brute force. My conscience is clear and I have the satisfaction of duty done. I sleep as contentedly as a happy child.

In another letter to Alemán Bolaños he wrote:

Moncada is surely the most dismal and dangerous of the men who are now astride of our people, with his fakery about public works, prosperity, and grandeur—as false as it is ridiculous. Even if it were all true, Moncada would only be giving out lollipops in hell from his presidential throne installed by the Yankees. The income from customs and other taxes loaded on the people goes to pay a National Guard in which bad Nicaraguans take orders from Yankee officers as numerous as they're inept. The railroads and highways that Moncada is giddily constructing are designed for ridiculous strategic purposes. Everything he does smells of sadness, disaster, and death. He, Díaz, and Chamorro form an accursed trinity of traitorous wretches. But it won't be long before our army sweeps them away with a broom of bayonets, along with their hangers-on.

What I'm going to say may not seem serious to you, but it is. Our army leads the world for readiness to sacrifice, for discipline and disregard for material wealth, because in full awareness of what it does it carries and maintains an ideal, both with respect to Nicaragua and to the brotherhood of man. There is no military pedantry to be found among us, nor dishonest ambition, and hence no traitors in the ranks of this emancipating army. I set this forth to you, good friend, because we know how servile pens seek to discredit us with the label of *bandoleros*. The real *bandoleros* are in the caverns of the White House in Washington from which the plunder and murder of our Spanish America are directed.

His language takes on tones of violent accusation in another manifesto:

Like a rabid but impotent beast, Herbert Clark Hoover, the Yankee president, hurls abuse at the head of the army that is liberating Nicaragua. He and Stimson are the modern assassins, as were Coolidge and Kellogg before them, the quartet whom the North American people have to thank for their country's fiasco, and who have earned the eternal curses of parents, sons, and brothers of the marines fallen on Segovian battlefields.

Coolidge's insolent swagger in 1927, in promising to disarm by force the army defending Nicaraguan honor, has cost the prestige of the United States of North America dearly. Now Herbert Clark Hoover, the president who won't survive after 1932 [a prophesy fulfilled—G.S.], has promised to capture Sandino and bring him to justice: an empty threat in light of the drubbing our army has just given the Yankees on the Atlantic coast, leaving Longtow littered with corpses [May 1931]. We have no guilt: we were simply defending ourselves.

And Nicaragua pays dearly for North American policy in our country. Since 1909 it has destroyed over 150,000 human lives of both sexes; it has plundered more than two-thirds of Nicaragua's capital, and it was ready to colonize all Central America when a frightful crisis took it by surprise and paralyzed it. What is the word for men who have done and threatened these things to us?

But looking more closely at the unhappy Hoover regime, it had to dig out an office boy from the Bowery to become secretary of state, and, for lack of a man, it has sent to Nicaragua as minister an old wreck by the name of Matthew Hanna, whose wife—a German as it happens—now runs the Yankee legation in Managua. But the government of the pirates will soon be changed and all these characters will be shot out like rockets.

The reference to Mr. Hanna is more significant than this document makes it seem. The activities of his wife, much younger than he, were the talk of the town in Managua. Addicted to balls and to young National Guard officers, she had chosen one as her favorite partner—Anastasio Somoza, whom Sandino had earlier dubbed "the penguin."[5] She proclaimed herself the "de facto ambassadress" of the United States, and later history would show how her protégé—shoved upstairs by adultery, treason, assassination, and terror—sustained himself through more than twenty years as dictator of Nicaragua.

In Sandino's conversation and proclamations, references to Indo-America became more and more frequent. A communiqué of October 20, 1931, said:

As we have said, we have no government, neither Indo-Hispanic nor any other. Nicaragua is directly and solely represented by our army. For this reason, our expeditionary columns have been ordered to collect from nationals and foreigners what is needed for their maintenance. On many occasions our columns on arrival in some hacienda or estate in national territory have taken merchandise and provisions that are found there, and there have even been cases where our brother soldiers took shoes and clothing from their owners, because our soldier brothers have greater need of them and it is unjust that men who are bringing liberty to Nicaragua should go in rags. This has caused many scoundrels to call us *bandoleros;* but history will do us justice, not overlooking the fact that the capitalists from whom we take are primarily and directly responsible for what has happened in Nicaragua, because they brought the Yankee mercenaries into our national territory.

He replied similarly to criticism of his intentions in proposing the conference of governments. Nor did he neglect the politics of war, as this recommendation to "Pedrón" Altamirano indicates:

Avoid setting fires at all costs; there is no need to create ruins. Good enough if the lads take along screwdrivers to detach doors and windows and burn them along with belongings that need to be destroyed, as a punishment and to disseminate fear. This is a very practical and effective procedure which you should inculcate in your lieutenants. Burned houses constitute an accusation; houses without doors provoke smiles and the punishment remains visible.

Nineteen thirty-two began for Sandino with more of the same battles. His army remained vigilant and resolute; the interventionists maintained their efforts to put an end to resistance; and the territory not controlled by Sandino was deep in preparations for the election which would this time be "supervised" by Admiral Woodward. Sandino issued this manifesto about the election:

To our Nicaraguan compatriots:

The gringos will not cease in their efforts to humiliate our country up to the day they leave. The Conservative Díaz-Chamorro ticket is their handiwork: the Yankees want a new term for the *yanquistas,* but for the eventuality that Liberal *yanquistas* might suit them better, they ordered Moncada to put up Sacasa as candidate and pretended to accept Espinosa's protestations of *yanquismo.* The are anxious to avoid unruly demonstrations when they leave, and whoever wins will strive to prevent any. Should there be trouble they expect either Díaz or Sacasa, as the case may be, to implore them to land and occupy the country again, but this they don't want to do because the Army Defending the National Sovereignty of Nicaragua continues to make Yankee power look foolish.

Compatriots: proceed with dignity and remember that you have been victims both of the Yankees and of these politicians. Anyone following these individuals to polling stations sentineled by Yankees will only pay lamentable homage to foreign bayonets, by giving them the final touch of shine, to the shame of Nicaragua. To expect national dignity from Chamorro and Díaz, or from Espinosa and Sacasa, is foolishness of the worst kind, especially when the Army Defending the National Sovereignty of Nicaragua is approaching in triumph.

Tell the intrusive admiral who is herding you like cattle: Out! Do your duty. Do not obey a single order of the marines in this electoral farce. No one has to go to the polls and there is no law to make you. Show yourselves to be worthy of freedom. Let not Liberal Party members believe that a Conservative victory will last a day longer than the time necessary for the people, together with the Army Defending the National Sovereignty of Nicaragua, to liquidate it. Let not Conservatives fear a victory for the ticket headed by Sacasa, for the punitive hand of that army is within striking distance and he will never remain president beyond January.

This is the true situation, compatriots, and you have been shown the road to follow.

But for Liberal or Conservative Nicaraguans who had collaborated with the invaders, the elections were not the only worry. The marines were departing with the problem of Sandino's army still unsolved. U.S. officers still ran the National Guard, and even so it was suffering defeat after defeat; but without them, how were the guerrillas to be dealt with? To calm these fears a certain Captain Trumble, head of the Military Academy, publicly announced that within weeks of the symbolic deoccupation, "some twenty or twenty-five" marine officers would return "as employees of this government to act as technicians and instructors of the National Guard, whose continued functioning in Nicaragua is of great concern to the representatives of the Washington government."

By way of filling the cup of gall to the brim, in October 1932 Moncada named as Nicaragua's envoy extraordinary and minister plenipotentiary to European governments one Irving Lindbergh, a North American who had been acting as collector of customs in Nicaragua on Washington's behalf.

Following an announcement in the Managua daily *La Nación* that surplus U.S. materials would be auctioned off, *El Comercio* published a statement by a Lieutenant Lincert, secretary to General Berkeley, to the effect that the marines were "offering to sell certain belongings and the houses we built in the Campo de Marte, in the belief that we were going to be left there for life." Built at a cost of some $4,000 each, including light and water installations, the houses were being offered to the Nicaraguan government for $200 apiece.

On October 14, thanks to Sandino's efforts, the Nicaraguan Workers Party (PTN) called an electoral general strike. On the same day this cable concerning the marines' departure was published:

> It is known that Rear Admiral Woodward will leave Nicaragua early in December, that is, as soon as he has said his last word on the new president of the Republic. He will make his report to President Hoover on 20–25 December. Payment to Rear Admiral Woodward of 25,000 *córdobas* due ot the electoral mission will round out the total of $150,000, in liquidation of what he has already received on account, deducting among other sums the value of the automobile purchased on credit by the government, amounting to $3,000, and the installation of electricity in the rear admiral's house, amounting to $300.[6]

Sacasa's nephew, Debayle, Nicaraguan chargé d'affaires in Washington, said there on October 17 that Nicaragua owed its "present financial and political stability" to the U.S. intervention and asked in a radio talk that the "supervision" be continued after the elections. Meanwhile another nephew—this time of Pedro Joaquín Chamorro who signed the famous treaty with Bryan—declared in Managua's *La Prensa* his faith in the "frank and sincere policy" of the United States and his assurance that "the Conservative Party accepts the intervention without doubts or suspicions of any kind." Which did not prevent him from commenting in the same newspaper on November 7, when the electoral victory had gone to Sacasa:

> We have been defeated by our flag, the pro-North American flag. To the Nicaraguan people's honor, we must say that they turned their backs on Conservativism, because they saw it as shielded behind pro-North Americanism and feared that our victory would bring back this evil which is tending to disappear forever from Nicaragua. We have felt for some time that the Nicaraguan people are not only disillusioned by pro-North Americanism but have decisively made up their minds to get rid of this factor of our public life as far as that is possible. Many politicians have perceived this but not all have wanted to accept it. Despite the fact that the Nicaraguan people's feeling are

beyond a doubt, we have stuck to this flag, thinking and expecting that beneath its shade everything would come our way. But the Nicaraguan people have justly punished us, teaching us at the same time a lesson we can never forget.

This was a time of many comings and goings of U.S. diplomats to and from Nicaragua. Mr. Julius Lay, minister to El Salvador, visited his colleague Hanna. In Tegucigalpa on his way back, *El Cronista* quoted him as saying: "Sandino is still being a nuisance despite the U.S. Marines' and the National Guard's desperate efforts to overcome him; but the marines, tired of fighting in vain for so long, will be leaving shortly."

On October 4, when rumors were circulating about Mr. Hanna's departure for Washington, the disastrous Emiliano Chamorro visited the legation and spent more than an hour with the minister. Rumors built up, some to the effect that Hanna was leaving because of "matters connected with the elections," others that it was "for fear of the *sandinistas* breaking into this city."

With a voting list of 150,000, the elections won by Sacasa brought 98,550 to the polls: a third of the voters followed Sandino's advice to abstain. Sandino's response was to designate General Juan Gregorio Colindres as provisional president of the Republic of Nicaragua in the "Liberated Area of Las Segovias." To lend this a legal touch, *sandinista* columns made forays into urban centers beyond the Segovian departments, where they appropriated judicial and municipal seals, sacked local authorities and put in new ones, and generally made themselves a threat to the capital. Columns under General Umanzor took San Francisco del Carnicero on the Lake Managua shores in October, causing panic in the capital only three hours' march away and giving rise to reports of Hanna's departure. Umanzor withdrew after abducting official seals to validate *sandinista* administrative and judicial measures. Equipped with them, Sandino solicited recognition of his government from the various American countries.

The request addressed to the foreign minister of El Salvador said in part:

It is equally notorious that the recent presidential elections in Nicaragua, controlled by North American power, were carried out by official agents of the U.S. government, which nullifies them in the consensus of nations. Consequently, the Provisional Government of Nicaragua in Las Segovias requests: first, nonrecognition of the government to be installed in Nicaragua as a result of these elections; second, express recognition of this free government of Nicaragua in the region covering the departments of Nueva Segovia, Estelí, Jinotega, Matagalpa, and part of the departments of León, Chinandega, and Chontales (more than half of the Republic). All this as an act of racial and national solidarity for the present and for the immediate future.

Naturally no American government paid attention to this request. On the basis of a banquet for the presidential candidates given before the elections by Rear Admiral Woodward, Sandino voiced a suspicion that there was a secret agreement between the invading troops and whoever would win for the marines' prompt return in case of need. As if to confirm this, the new National Guard commander Anastasio Somoza—another nephew of Dr. Sacasa—threw a banquet for the North American brass and his uncle, at which he toasted the happiness of Nicaragua "and the good relations that happily exist between Nicaraguan patriots and the high command that founded the Guard and that will possibly continue collaborating with it." Other toasts offered were General Matthews' for Dr. Sacasa and Dr. Sacasa's for Mr. Stimson.

The best comment on the election came from León University students in a November 15 declaration to President-elect Sacasa, saying in part:

General Augusto C. Sandino in the mountains is the decency, the honor, and the dignity of our nation. He does not pursue wealth and privileges, nor aspire to public offices, nor seek sinecures in his struggle. General Sandino is not a *bandolero*. We say so and most of the Nicaraguan people, who still retain their traditional bearing as free men, say so. Sandino's road is the road of victory or death. In any case, it is the road of glory. Will you, Dr. Sacasa, allow the only man who kept our country's flag pure and clean to continue being calumniated? He preferred to maintain our Constitution out under the sky in the forest while Sacasa's soldiers sold themselves to the will of the Yanqui for ten pesos per man.

11
The Yanquis Went Home!

Those whose puny souls
Had no room for the grandeur of our mountains,
Oh, motherland! They sold you without ever owning
Anything but their miserable hearts.

How could their merchant sleep not be troubled
By your tropical sun's divine splendor?
How could the opal blue of your lakes
Not put an end to their fantasies?

Sandino has saved you. He took your dishonor
Upon his bleeding titan's shoulders
As your redeemer, and called out to history.

And the nations saw Nicaragua
Pay her account, the price of her sale,
With her blood and with her glory!

Anonymous

The end was near. The marines' voluntary departure only seemed to make sense on the basis that some other ploy was being cooked up to end Sandino's resistance. But the objective fact that they were going confronted a leader who had made their presence the heart of his whole campaign. Having always insisted that his struggle had no ideological, political, or social motivations, only patriotic ones, it was logical to assume that with the U.S. withdrawal peace would come to Nicaragua.

Nineteen thirty-two had not differed from other years in the extent of military actions. The campaign summaries described almost daily encounters between *sandinista* and U.S.-National Guard troops. For example, in April:

> On the fourth, ex-National Guardsmen who had fought with the enemy in Quizalaya on the Atlantic coast rose against the Yankee filibusters who commanded them; a force under gringo Lieutenant

Charles Lebowasky was sent against them and wounded the renegade sublieutenant Carlos Rayo. As a result of this mutiny our army inherited twenty-one Springfield and Lewis rifles, some bombthrowers, twenty-one hand grenades, a Thompson machine gun with 1,600 rounds, and 5,000 Lewis rounds. These were handed over by exguardmen Sebastián Jiménez, Felipe Briceño Jr., Francisco López, and Aurelio Flores, who are now in our ranks. The arms were received by generals Estrada and Morales and Colonel Sócrates Sandino.

On the eleventh three artillerymen of the same enemy unit, Antonio García, Balbino Hoys, and Antonio Cornejo, passed over to our army with their weapons–one Bronis and two Thompson machine guns, hand bombs, and Springfield rifle ammunition. This was received by General Colindres.

On the fifteenth Captain Heriberto Reyes engaged in a bloody three-hour combat at San Lucas in Ocotal jurisdiction, in which thirty traitorous dogs and one of the pirates commanding them perished. On our side, we mourn the death of brothers Alberto Cruz Rodríguez and Fausto E. García.

On the twenty-first our forces under General Morales attacked the new enemy detachment stationed in Quizalaya; this time the enemy was stronger but we nevertheless routed them after an hour and three-quarters of fierce battle. We mourn the death in this engagement of three brothers, Sergeant Major Francisco Montenegro, Captain Celedonio Gutiérrez, and Lieutenant Marcelino Rugama, and of the young León University student Octavo Oviedo, son of a magistrate of that name. Generals Morales and Estrada continued their advance into the interior of the Atlantic region. We also have reserve forces on that coast. Wounded in the above-mentioned engagement were lieutenants Rafael César Zamora, Orlando Baldizón, and Santos Godoy, and the engineer Larios M.

On the same date at Santa Barbara, Jinotega jurisdiction, Colonel Juan Altamirano defeated the enemy who left on the battlefield five traitorous dogs and one Yankee pirate. Later that day Altamirano's forces attacked another column at Chaguitillo, where the enemy was completely routed and we obtained 3,000 Springfield rounds and two .45 pistols. We had no casualties and the enemy succeeded in removing his dead and wounded.

Also on the twenty-first forces under the command of generals Carlos Salgado and Juan G. Colindres and Captain Reyes engaged the enemy at La Puerta, Ocotal jurisdiction. After resisting for three-quarters of an hour, the enemy was defeated and left on the battlefield two dead Yankees and twelve traitorous dogs. We obtained a Bronis machine gun and five Springfield rifles, all with ample ammunition, and had no casualties. At 4 P.M. that day our units under the same command had another encounter with enemy reinforcements at Los Leones which lasted till nightfall. Five traitorous dogs and three Yankee officers were found on the battlefield and we obtained twelve Springfields, three .45 pistols and bombthrowers with six grenades, and many important documents for Nicaraguan history which we have sent to our friend Alemán Bolaños. On our side we mourn the death of brothers Pío Melgar and Estanislao Maradiaga; Manuel Valladares was wounded.

On the twenty-third at Los Bellorín General Sandino and Captain Heriberto Reyes had another encounter with the enemy, who left seven dead on the field.

The battles fought in April in the interior of Nicaragua by General Umanzor, colonels Tomás Blandón, Perfecto Chavarría, and Ruperto Hernández Robledo, General José León Díaz, and others have already been reported by the enemy, admitting their defeats.

In May the liberating forces reported:

On the first General Salgado had another bloody encounter in Ciudad Antigua. On our side, brother Federico Tercero of San Marcos de Colón, Honduras, was killed. On the same day General Colindres attacked the enemy at Los Bellorín. The battle lasted three hours and the enemy left on the field thirty-six dead and a package containing fourteen woolen blankets, three capes, two uniforms, a pair of shoes, and a tent. On our side we mourn the death of brother Juan Pablo Bellorín, owner of the property where the battle took place.

I take this opportunity to inform our compatriots abroad that our army, today as yesterday, is convinced that Nicaragua will only be freed by bullets and at the price of our own blood. That we will prevent any foreign-supervised electoral farce that may be attempted in Nicaragua, and will under no circumstances recognize anyone elected in that manner, however it may be camouflaged, even if I am implored to do so on bended knee.

Nicaraguans interested in their country's liberation are well received by our army, but without party banners and accepting the discipline we have established. Our attention has been drawn to the proposals of Moncada whereby the sadly famous Bryan Treaty and the treaty establishing the National Guard would be included in the

Constitution. The last Nicaraguan may fall, the country be reduced to ashes, but those treaties will never be legal.

These operations were recorded for July:

Outstanding battles during the month were as follows. Our Atlantic Division forces under generals Francisco Estrada and Simón González attacked and took the U.S.-owned Vaccaro banana plantation in Puerto Cabezas. The enemy encamped there received immediate reinforcements but our lads drove them off, taking trains and motorcars and ammunition, rifles and machine guns. They set fire to the buildings and next day an air squadron bombed our column, but one plane was brought down. In a bloody ensuing battle lasting almost till nightfall, the enemy suffered losses estimated at over 100 men.

We were informed that twenty Yankee amphibians landed off Puerto Cabezas to pick up U.S. families resident there. We see this as a prudent proceeding, since the fate awaiting the North Americans there is dark.

On the fourteenth our forces under Colonel Ruperto Hernández Robledo and Sergeant Major Francisco García had a bloody encounter with the enemy at Los Achiotes, Jinotega department, in which three traitor-dog lieutenants and nine Yankee pirates lost their lives. Arms and ammunition were obtained.

At La Rocía, León department, on the sixteenth our forces under Colonel Zacarías Padilla had another bloody encounter and took much armament and provisions.

Generals Estrada and González of the Atlantic Division have just informed us that strong U.S. forces have crossed into Nicaragua from the Honduran Mosquito Coast. How the Honduran government, which calls itself strictly autonomist, permitted this, we are at a loss to know. The report adds that these troops have headquarters in a banana plantation belonging to the Yankee concern United Fruit, in the Honduran port of Trujillo.

This item, from Managua's *El Comercio,* rounds off Sandino's military year:

Lieutenant Lee, a U.S. officer known as "the tiger of Las Segovias," has arrived in Managua aboard a U.S. Marines plane flying from Jinotega. . . . We visited him in the hospital. His head and right arm were covered with bandages from serious wounds received in the battle on the Peña Blanca road. "The National Guard patrol of forty men was commanded by Captain Puyed," he told us, "with myself as second in command. We were caught in an ambush which the *sandinistas* had strategically prepared, moments after the expedition crossed the Pijuguay River."

Already in March of that year efforts had begun to iron out the differences between Sandino and Nicaraguans who, directly interventionist or not, wanted the struggle to end. As happens in all of Latin America, the national bourgeoisie allied with imperialism needed a climate of order for the tranquil development of their business—a constitutionally based peace that Sandino's resistance made unstable. And although the old politicos would never forgive Sandino for setting himself up as a symbol of national conscience—a conscience that accused them of duties undone, of treasons committed, and of a patrimony surrendered—they sought to approach him for an orgy of forgiveness, after which all would be friends and good business would be resumed.

And so was formed the committee of notables that came to be known as the Patriotic Group: such men as Juan Francisco Gutiérrez, Rosendo Argüello, Salvador Buitrago Díaz, and Octavio Pasos Montiel, joined later by Pedro Joaquín Chamorro (no less), Ramón Solórzano, Pablo Hurtado, and Federico J. Lacayo. With Sofonías Salvatierra as their chief soloist, this choir assembled to move for total amnesty, under a plan whereby presidential candidates should pledge themselves to respect the losing party in the November elections.

Superfluous to add that Sacasa and Chamorro accepted the plan, solemnly signed the pledge and, to make it even stronger, resolved to sign agreements assuring coexistence of the government parties. But when they made this intention known, Moncada, who still ruled, was less than happy. He repudiated the plan in this third-person manifesto:

> Not solely because of *sandinista* declarations which are deemed subversive has the president reluctantly ordered the imprisonment of certain persons, but because ever since the results of the elections for the Supreme Authority were known, certain publications have sought to compromise the country in its relations with the United States of America with which Nicaragua maintains the most sincere friendship. Having accepted its supervision in good faith, and knowing that the marines are withdrawing from Nicaragua, the frankest cordiality should exist between both sides.
>
> It is evident that outbreaks of *sandinismo* have been occurring in the

interior for some time. And although one cannot prejudge the attitude of President-elect Sacasa with respect to this transcendental matter after January 1, it is known that the present government neither can nor should tolerate *sandinista* or communist writings, nor meetings, nor subscriptions, aimed at negotiating with the author of the ruin of Las Segovias and, in part, of the country.

Within a few days and with the president-elect's permission, if he so desires it, those enamored of the unhealthy ideas preached by *sandinismo* will be able to negotiate with it. Meanwhile the government has the duty of being consistent with and loyal to the government of the United States and its own convictions.

This ponderous document plainly declared those who would negotiate with Sandino to be enemies of the United States, and informed the invaders that the new president was one of them. It was the last shot fired by Moncada against his one-time subordinate Sandino, and an attempt to wing Sacasa with the same bullet.

On November 23, 1932, with the authorization of the president-elect, his brother Federico (father of Somoza's wife), and Julián Irías, Sofonías Salvatierra fixed the first rung in the ladder that would lead to the hero's assassination. He addressed this letter to Sandino:

> . . . In pursuit of this lofty and firm goal, we are promoting a movement of reciprocal understanding by the parties which has resulted in various agreements toward coexistence of said parties in the functions of state: representation of minorities, constitutional reform, pacification. All of which tends in an open manner toward effective resumption of the full exercise of sovereignty. With feet planted on this road of goodwill, the Liberal and Conservative directorates have agreed to send a joint commission to confer with General Sandino, as proposed by the Group. This commission of the parties has already been appointed, and the Group, for its part, independently of the parties, has named a representative to go wherever you are, and it is to me that this representation has been confided.
>
> The chief purpose of this letter is to learn whether you are disposed to confer with the party commissioners and with the representative of the Group, in terms respectful of yourself and on an eminently patriotic basis, and to learn where such peace talks may be held.
>
> I hasten to assure you that prior to writing this I talked with the heads of the Liberal Party, and that I am also in discussion with prominent Conservatives interested in the matter. By way of assurance

that all this patriotic negotiation is leading toward our definitive independence, I will tell you that when I asked the Liberal leaders *if the parties are acting freely in negotiating peace with Sandino,* they immediately replied: *with absolute freedom.* [Emphasis here and below in original.] Thus if we take into account the total withdrawal of the Yanquis next January, the Liberal leaders' reply, and their manifestly genuine wish to reach an understanding with you, plus the Conservative press's flat declarations *against intervention,* everything indicates a plain reaction in the different sectors of party politics against the old interventionist policies, and that Nicaragua is standing erect for the free motherland. Everything indicates that the blue and white flag that you have raised so high will from now on be rooted in every Nicaraguan's heart; that the hand now extended to you by the parties and independent citizens, in token of glorious peace for the free motherland, shows how all sectors of our nation are making a reassessment now that our soil is being rid of intervention, and are turning toward you with the open arms of a brother.

Let me take this opportunity to tell you about the family. All those in Niquihomo are well. Don Gregorio has some heart trouble but enjoys good health due to looking after himself well. Josefita Rivas was here in Managua a few days ago and told us that her lot are in good shape. Tell Sócrates that Ameriquita is getting gray-haired thinking about you all. They'll all be happy when they read this letter and know I've written you.

I'm addressing this to Esteban Albir of El Ocotal to send on to you either by Alfonso Irías or José Idiáquez or Ramón Raudales. I and other friends await your reply at the earliest possible moment, trusting that when you let me know the place and date of the conference you'll indicate how I get there with due facilities and reciprocal security taken care of. With respectful greetings to doña Blanca, an *abrazo* to Sócrates, and to you the sincere and unchanging affection of your kinsman and friend,

Sofonías Salvatierra

While Sandino's reply was awaited, Sacasa assumed the presidency on January 1, 1933. The U.S. troops had begun leaving Nicaragua in December 1932. But before half of January was out the National Guard had been caught making its first subversive move. Sacasa, in token of his confidence in Salvatierra and the importance of the negotiations undertaken, had named him secretary of agriculture.

Sandino received the letter in the second half of December and dispatched his reply on the twenty-fourth. Confident of the benevolent climate that the letter seemed to indicate, Sandino sent his pregnant wife to San Rafael del Norte to have her child there. Captain Policarpo Gutiérrez, who commanded the Guard at San Rafael, had her arrested, but not before she had wired to Sacasa, who ordered that she be freed and given guarantees. Gutiérrez ignored the order. "I am not concerned with the president's orders," he replied; "he gives them in Managua, the Guard gives them here."[1] The apparent comedy was all too serious. As events would soon show, the National Guard under the command of the pet of the U.S. minister and his wife was the real ruler of Nicaragua.

Unaware of this, Sandino replied to Salvatierra:

> I take this happy opportunity to send you and the Patriotic Group of whom you speak our highest congratulations on your labors for restoration of our national independence, the one and only cause for which the army I am honored to command fights and will fight.
>
> We see no obstacles to acceptance of the joint commission of persons concerned with pacification of Nicaragua, so long as they bring the official delegation of the government that wishes to legalize its rule of the Republic. Any kind of commission not vested with official powers is unacceptable to us. Dr. Sacasa should seize the opportunity that is offered him to reach an understanding with our army, in order not to continue, as he otherwise will, a puppet for the amusement of children. We are entitled to speak with authority about Dr. Sacasa, since he abandoned us in the worst moments of our nation's history. As a person, the said doctor merits our esteem, but it is our duty to remind him of his past as a public man.
>
> On the basis of a possible patriotic understanding, we have named señores don Salvador Calderón Ramírez, Dr. Escolástico Lara, Dr. Pedro José Zepeda, and General Horacio Portocarrero as our delegates. Today we send them a patriotic call to serve, and ask you to receive them. I also ask you to write to them personally whatever you deem appropriate. Meanwhile I submit to you that if Dr. Sacasa decides to treat this matter officially, our delegates' expenses during the discussions should be charged to the national treasury, since neither I nor they have the necessary resources.
>
> We are sincerely grateful for your news from Niquihomo. My wife,

Sócrates, and I send our fraternal *abrazo* to your distinguished family and yourself.

Patria y Libertad,
Augusto César Sandino

In authorizing peace talks with representatives, Sandino expressly laid down that the talks should take place "if the government of Sacasa is free and has no public or private commitments to the United States of North America." He demonstrated his severe concept of sovereignty by expressing frank reservations about Sacasa as a "puppet," and even accusing him of desertion of duty when the country most needed him to fulfill it. And Sacasa, knowing that behind the insolence Sandino spoke the truth, took no offense. He replied denying any public or secret agreements with the United States and insisting that as of that day, January 8, not one soldier of the intervention remained in Nicaragua, "not even guarding the legation."

On the tenth Salvatierra obtained from the illustrious Juan F. Gutiérrez, Buitrago Díaz, Rosendo Argüello, Alberto Reyes, and Federico Lacayo a declaration to round out his own message to Sandino. One noteworthy statement in this was that "with regard to the economic-financial question, that is banks, railroads, and customs collection, we think they imply no obstacle to peace, since under the shelter of peace and of the new spirit that has now entered the Republic's soul, obstacles will be easily removed and the fullest success assured."

Salvatierra left for San Rafael del Norte on the twelfth, accompanied by Sandino's father don Gregorio, Gregorio's wife doña América, and General Alberto Reyes. They arrived next day and found Sandino's wife already at liberty. From San Rafael they sent a request for an appointment, which Sandino granted in this note on January 17:

> This will serve as your pass for the benefit of our scouts and expeditionary columns that you may meet on the way. You will make the journey with the Castelblanco brothers, with whom Blanquita will put you in touch. As there will no doubt be a number of persons in your group, you might be stopped by some of our units in the area who don't know of your presence, having been out of touch with us. It

would therefore be advisable for you to carry a white flag, which would immediately identify you for those of our forces who have instructions to respect it. The Castelblanco brothers will bring you to the place where I am, which is about a day's journey.

I consider it every good Nicaraguan's highest duty to bring peace to Nicaragua, but peace that brings dignity and not slavery. . . .

> *Patria y Libertad,*
> Augusto César Sandino

The peace envoys left on the nineteenth for Sandino's camp and arrived after thirteen hours' march. Don Sofonías thus described his first impressions:

Sandino's first words indicated that I must proceed with the caution that a difficult and unexplored subject calls for. Accustomed to absolute and uncontradicted command in seven years of war, and perhaps also because of his dominating nature, he was in no mood for objections and rectifications. Nevertheless an idealistic light shone through the bluntness and military roughness of his temperament. I got the point that the way to an understanding with him was to avoid direct argument, rather to follow along with his reasoning. The very idealism with which he tinged his words gave me the opportunity to formulate my arguments and ideas about unity. Thus I avoided any collision, always dangerous with Sandino. The wisdom of this course became clear as Sandino in short order began showing his disposition to unbend when treated with kindness and consideration. . . .

From dawn on, Sandino's men kept up chants of "Long live General Sandino! Long live the Army Defending the National Sovereignty! Death to the traitor dogs! Down with the Yanquis!" This entire ritual, over and over again, on the smallest provocation, without omitting a word and always with the same intonation. I could see the situation this army was in. No clothes, almost naked, no blankets against the humid chill of the Nicaraguan north, no medicines—and with rain never letting up. How did they survive, how could they endure it? Yet they had been that way for years, visibly resolved to stick it out.

Salvatierra returned to San Rafael on January 23 with a proposal known as the Peace Protocol:

The undersigned, general and supreme head of the Army Defending the National Sovereignty of Nicaragua, submits the following

Peace Protocol to be confirmed by our delegates on signing the definitive peace:

1. The political program to be pursued by Dr. Sacasa in his four-year administration must be known in detail. We must be assured of absolutely no foreign intrusion into the finances of Nicaragua, and what will be done about the National Guard; also whether Dr. Sacasa has signed agreements of any kind with the U.S. interveners.

2. That on the initiative of the Executive, the Nicaraguan National Congress will decree a new department comprising vacant national lands between the Chipote zone and the Atlantic coast, with the name of Luz y Verdad and with the following boundaries. . . . It is to be understood that creation of this new department in no way implies sinecures for our army, still less for the undersigned, and that the aim in view is general aggrandizement of the Fatherland.

3. That on the initiative of the Executive, the National Congress will decree integral maintenance within the Luz y Verdad department of materials of war that the Army Defending the National Sovereignty of Nicaragua has used during the war dignifying our national honor; and that all civil and military authorities of said department will be appointed from among members of our army. We desire the war materials that we have assembled with the blood of patriots to remain at the disposition of the Luz y Verdad departmental government as the best guarantee of order in our Republic, and because the undersigned will remain in that region where we will be ready to repel any aggression by anyone against the constituted government of Nicaragua.

4. That on the initiative of the Executive, the National Congress will decree the removal from national archives and the burning of all documents in which our army's patriotic attitude is described as banditry, and will legalize the attitude assumed by the undersigned and his army on May 4, 1927, when the U.S. government arrogantly threatened to disarm Nicaraguan armies by force if they did not submit to its despotic caprice. These points—removing and burning documents that calumniate us, and congressional legalization of the undersigned's attitude—are matters of national dignity, which once attended to will permit Nicaragua to stand up as a free, sovereign, and independent Republic.

5. It should be stated in the definitive peace agreement that the Army Defending the National Sovereignty of Nicaragua requests revision of the Bryan-Chamorro treaties, since they were notoriously entered into by a Nicaraguan government imposed by U.S. intervention. Furthermore the Army Defending the National Sovereignty of

Nicaragua demands that the projects for a trans-Nicaragua canal and for a naval base in the Gulf of Fonseca be declared of Indo-Hispanic nationality. To that effect, a Congress should be summoned with representatives of the twenty-one republics of our race's America and of the United States, in the capital city of the Argentine Republic, which will decree nonintervention in the internal affairs of any Indo-Hispanic republic, respect for their sovereignty and independence, and promotion of a more fraternal rapprochement which will bring us together in the common freedom of the peoples of this continent.

A two-week truce was agreed, commencing January 23, during which talks for a final armistice would be begun between the government's and Sandino's representatives.

The National Guard, true to its line of not showing the president too much respect, proceeded to violate the truce. Nor was it alone in continuing to prefer war. In various ways efforts to abort peace were made by a part of the Congress, most of the cabinet, most of the press, the dominant classes of Jinotega and Matagalpa ("two cities," commented Salvatierra, "whose wealthy inhabitants so craved war that they descended to mortal hatred of myself because I wanted peace without bloodshed"). But above all by the Guard, mental and physical inheritor of the hatred of Sandino so studiously imbued by the invaders.

On the pretext of repairing telegraph lines, Guard units marched from Jinotega to attack General Adán Gómez, who controlled the Zaraguasca heights some two miles from the nearest telegraphic line. The ensuing battle cost casualties on both sides and had the virtue of showing up once more who really held the reins in Nicaragua. At the same time it was reported that *sandinistas* were being shot on the pretext that they were bandits. One such victim in Jinotega, and five in Yalí, showed how fast the Guard was assuming the role of the courts, even supposing that the victims really were bandits.

The extent of the Guard's obedience to Sacasa in carrying out the truce was shown in this telegram:

> To Colonel J. Rigoberto Reyes, Chief of Central Area, Jinotega: General Sandino through his wife doña Blanca has accepted the armistice from 12 noon on the 23rd inst. and we have also accepted it. However, in view of the advance made by his troops, General Sandino has been advised that his forces must not intercept communications

between cities, nor cut telegraph lines, and that he should withdraw them from places where there is danger of clashes, such as Zaraguasca. If he doesn't, let me know. A Somoza, Director in Chief.

This was leading nowhere and clashes continued to be reported. In the face of that situation, Salvatierra met with Sacasa again and asked for a plain statement of his peaceful intentions. Sacasa repeated them and the agriculture secretary decided on another trip to Las Segovias. He took a plane piloted by Julio Zincer, an admirer of Sandino, landed on the twenty-ninth at Jinotega, and again rode to Sandino's headquarters on horseback. They talked on the thirty-first, leaving the discussion inconclusive overnight. On February 1, with no previous sign of such an intention, Sandino told Salvatierra and his comrades-in-arms that he was willing to go to Managua for a personal meeting with Sacasa.[2]

The government envoy was enthusiastic about the idea and sent dispatches ahead to give the news. This telegram went to President Sacasa:

General Sandino has definitely decided that before entering upon specific talks, he will come with us to Managua to talk directly with you. He wants the talk to be brief and the peace of Nicaragua to be settled in these first five days of February, without further delay. The plane will arrive tomorrow, the second, in the morning. Please give ironclad orders to the National Guard not to be present on the landing field and to take a position of full guarantees, for we are all guaranteeing the life of General Sandino and his return to this camp. Essential to keep this in strict confidence and that a car come unostentatiously to take us directly from the landing field to the presidential palace. Respectfully, Sofonías Salvatierra.

Together with his brothers Federico and Crisanto the president replied pledging security and guarantees that the liberator's person would be respected. Before leaving, Sandino paraded his troops and said to them:

Brothers: we have fought for our country to be free of foreign intruders. The Yankee has gone but he is crafty: he thinks he'll be returning soon, hoping we'll continue the fight. He is wrong. I believe peace has to be made in these five days, and to make it I have thought it best to go and reach a direct understanding with Dr. Sacasa. In my place, for the days when I'll be gone, I leave General Lara, a man of León like Dr. Sacasa. If instead of listening to us, Dr. Sacasa should be disposed to imprison me, I will kill myself, and if I don't, each of you is authorized to spit in my face as a traitor.[3]

The plane set down in Managua on February 2. The news spread throughout the capital; government house was filled with citizens as eager to meet Sandino as to see how his mission would turn out. When the hero was alone with the president, they agreed on the general structure of peace. That same night at 11:15 the following agreement was signed:

> Salvador Calderón Ramírez, Pedro José Zepeda, Horacio Portocarrero, and Escolástico Lara, representing General Augusto César Sandino, and David Stadhagen and Crisanto Sacasa, respectively representing the Conservative and Liberal Nationalist parties, fully convinced of the supreme necessity of peace for the Republic, have agreed on the following harmonious accord based on the sincere love that Nicaragua's future inspires in them and the high sentiments of honor to which the signers pay homage.
>
> 1. The representatives of General Augusto César Sandino declare, first and foremost, that the crusade undertaken by him and his army has assisted the liberty of the Fatherland; consequently they desire at this moment to affirm, on behalf of their principal, his total personal disinterest and his irrevocable resolve not to demand or accept anything that could belittle the motives of his public conduct. He wishes to establish as an unshakable principle that he aspires to no financial or material gain.
>
> In view of these manifestations of high disinterest, the representatives of the Conservative and Liberal Nationalist parties pay homage to the noble and patriotic attitude of said General Sandino.
>
> 2. General Augusto César Sandino through his delegates, and the representatives of both parties, declare: that by virtue of the departure of foreign forces from national territory, an era of basic renovation in our public life is opened; that this is of transcendent importance for our national destiny; and that, disciplined by a painful experience, they deem it imperative to fortify the collective sentiment of autonomy which moves Nicaraguans with unanimous enthusiasm. In order to deepen this most noble tendency, the undersigned agree to make respect for the Republic's Constitution and basic laws the foundation stone of their respective political programs, and to maintain by all rational, adequate, and juridical means the full resplendency of Nicaragua's political and economic sovereignty.

3. The delegates of General Sandino and of the parties recognize the need to cement in practice the peace of the territory of the Republic, through fruitful dedication to work by the men under General Augusto César Sandino's command, and through gradual laying down of their arms. To the end of assuring normalization of these men's lives in constructive activities under protection of the laws and the constituted authorities, the following measures will be taken:

(a) The Executive will place before the National Congress the initiative of full amnesty for political and related common crimes committed during the period from 4 May 1927 to the present day, this to include all individuals of General Sandino's army who will lay down their arms within two weeks of promulgation of such decree, and equally all those who with General Sandino's authorization shall promise to lay down their arms within three months, and also 100 persons of said army who may temporarily retain their arms to protect the idle-land zone where all who have belonged to said army will have the right to settle and work.

(b) To represent the administrative and military authority of the Government of the Republic in the Northern departments, especially the zone where individuals of General Sandino's army are to settle and work, and also to receive gradually the arms of these men, the Executive will appoint as his delegate don Sofonías Salvatierra, to whom General Sandino will deliver within twenty days of this date no less than 25 percent of the arms of any description in possession of his army.

(c) The idle-land zone referred to in (a) above will be sufficiently extensive and located either in the Coco or Segovia river basin or in a region satisfactory to the Government and to General Sandino, in any case not more than ten leagues distant from towns in which there is now a municipal administration.

(d) The commanders of the safeguarding force of 100 armed men, which will be authorized to continue in existence, shall be appointed by the Government as emergency auxiliaries, and be chosen by agreement with General Sandino from among competent members of his army; but if after one year from promulgation of the amnesty decree the Government should deem it advisable to maintain said force of 100 men or less, appointment of the command shall be the authority of the President of the Republic.

(e) The Government shall maintain throughout the Republic, and especially in the Northern departments, for a minimum of one year, public works in which there will be job preference for individuals of

General Sandino's army who request it and who submit to the normal established regimen of such works.

4. Signing of this agreement implies cessation of all forms of hostilities between forces of the two sides, that is, of the Constitutional Government of which Dr. Juan B. Sacasa is president and of General Augusto César Sandino, for the more immediate guarantee of Nicaraguans' lives and property; and once this agreement is definitively signed and sealed, with the approbation of General Sandino and acceptance of the President of the Republic, all of General Sandino's men shall be under the protection of the constituted authorities and hence obligated to cooperate in the conservation of public order.

5. To facilitate the disarming of part of General Sandino's forces and provide them with provisional protection, the town of San Rafael de Norte is designated for this and General Sandino undertakes to maintain order for such time as the Government deems convenient.

In certification of this agreement, two copies are being signed in the city of Managua, on the second day of February, nineteen hundred and thirty-three.

Amid the delirious enthusiasm of all present, who distributed embraces and cheers to representatives of the two sides according to preference, national and foreign correspondents photographed the historic act of reconciliation. Sandino received an embrace not only from Sacasa but from National Guard chief Anastasio Somoza, before the camera which would preserve for posterity the kiss of Judas.

12
"A Free Country or Death!"

The figure of Sandino belongs among the greatest in the pantheon of our race. The greater his figure, the greater it is comprehended in these wretched times. And it is no transport of lyricism that makes me thus appraise him, but the memory of an elegant cinema hall in one of our America's plush cities. On the screen airplanes supposedly of the North American army were machine-gunning a party of natives in the tropical jungles—*sandinistas,* though the titles did not make this plain; and the entire hall, filled with elegant folk, madly applauded the dapper airmen who purported to be North American officers subduing the degenerate horde of patriots.

José Vasconcelos[1]

The first demonstration of governmental goodwill was made by the Congress, which voted an extraordinary credit of 120,000 *córdobas* for costs of pacification and public works. But there were no dividends due to the aggressive hostility of the National Guard in San Rafael, who took advantage of the disarming of their old enemies to harass and mistreat them.

On the very day of his arrival in San Rafael, Salvatierra learned of the Guard's preparations to entrench at Yucapuca, a height by the road that Pedro Altamirano's men would be taking to San Rafael. Thanks to Salvatierra's prompt intervention that particular clash was avoided, but not the wounds and bruises the Guard inflicted on *sandinistas* returning home with safe-conducts and no arms. On February 15 in Pueblo Nuevo, discharged *sandinistas* were killed by Somoza's troops. The next day Salvatierra wired to Sacasa:

> I have the honor to transmit to you the following message which I am sending to the director in chief of the National Guard and to Major Baca in Ocotal: "Deeply deplore clash Guard with discharged *sandinistas* in Pueblo Nuevo. All this is incomprehensible. It has been endlessly repeated that these are not so-called *bandoleros* but people

disarmed of weapons which will pass into the government's hands; stated and restated that they should not be treated in warlike fashion. These people were disarmed when come upon. It is necessary to help Dr. Sacasa, president of the Republic, with patriotism and goodwill to end this critical situation. I already reported that the first discharged men had no safe-conduct and that Doroteo Hernández is one of these. Consider, General Somoza, the difficulties of all kinds confronted by this delegation, not to make them worse. Truly yours, Salvatierra.". . .

I appreciate, señor President, the complaints that the director in chief sends me, but would also appreciate his informing me of the orders he issues. As you see, the situation is serious because one of the greatest fears of Sandino and his people is that once disarmed they will be killed. The reports he makes to me always contain tranquilizing explanations, but when a Pueblo Nuevo incident occurs I don't know how to explain it. I have the greatest possible goodwill to serve the Republic and your government in this supreme task, but I begin to wonder if I am not an obstacle to a policy I don't understand, an obstacle I am ready to remove with all honor. . . .

At Sacasa's prompting, Somoza finally decided to recommend observance of the armistice to his subordinates, "reserving repressive measures solely for cases where they are inevitable and well justified."

On February 22 Sandino proceeded to deliver the stipulated arms in the presence of the Guard's Colonel Reyes and of Salvatierra. The weapons were 14 Springfields, 55 Concónes, 199 Krags, 23 Winchesters, 8 Mausers, 28 Infume and 8 Remington rifles, 6 shotguns, one .22 Remington rifle, 2 Mausers without butts, 2 Krags without butts, 1 buttless Springfield, 10 Thompsons, 9 Brownings, and two Lewis machine-guns with 3,129 rounds of ammunition. He said he had an unspecified number of rifles in the mountains, but what he was delivering was the major part of the weaponry and he pledged to deliver the rest within the next two months.

Sandino's politically unforgivable good faith or ingenuousness put him at his enemies mercy. He surrendered himself stripped of defense in the belief that his own honesty was shared by all, that his sincere desire for peace was understood, respected, and returned. But he not only surrendered his own life but the lives of those who had accompanied him through his years of hazardous and continuous struggle. Back in their homes or on the road there they were beaten, hunted, jailed, tortured, and finally killed, in a sadistic orgy of the kind unhappily filling the history of Central American peoples.

When Sandino went the second time to Managua at the end of May, to insist with Sacasa that the agreement and guarantees for his disarmed men be observed, it was spitefully rumored that he came for money. The error into which he had fallen, in failing to stipulate in the peace pact the conditions set forth in the initial protocol, made him appear to renounce his aspirations for a Nicaragua free of the Bryan-Chamorro pact and of the crippling economic agreements. As always he put his trust in "honor," still innocent of the fact that that is a bad word in politics. And because Sacasa had made verbal promises, Sandino acclaimed an agreement which in fact only signed his death warrant.[2]

On a visit to Sacasa on February 6, Vicente Sáenz had put forward the possibility of denouncing the Infamous (Bryan-Chamorro) Treaty and the General Treaty of Submission (Peace and Friendship, 1923) in conjunction with El Salvador and Costa Rica and with the backing of Sandino's troops. "The entire people would back you, doctor," he said, "in the event that the traitors tried to make something of it." His plea had left Sacasa irresolute and weak. "Here," he said, "things are very different, my friend. I don't dare. I incline toward the procedures I've always followed, which can be summed up in the word prudence." Prudence did not save him from being overthrown, after Sandino was put out of the way.

Sandino, returning from the second Managua journey, received the hard blow of his wife's death after she had given birth to a daughter on June 2. More blows followed on the political front and from the Guard's increasingly unbridled actions. In Las Segovias the "fugitive from justice law" continued to be applied with *sandinistas;* women were raped, as in Apalí; prominent officials were scorned, and the president's orders publicly ignored. On February 6 even Chamorro's daily had been stirred to editorialize: "In these hours Sandino is ceasing to be a military problem for the country" while "the National Guard is becoming day by day the real problem of national peace."

Sacasa went about his business with no suspicion of the coup that was being prepared. He was playing bullfight simultaneously against Sandino and Somoza, in the belief that maintaining their presumed rivalry was his best guarantee of stability.[3] The no less ingenuous Salvatierra thought that if the quarrel between Sandino and Somoza were resolved, the danger of clashes would vanish. To this end he arranged interviews, "cordial interchanges," in which "reciprocal declarations would be exchanged and photographers would be present, all with the knowledge and approval of the president." Such an interview took place on the occasion of Sandino's third journey to Managua at the end of November and beginning of December 1933. On December 9 Sandino returned to Wiwilí. The next journey would be his last.

Early in February 1934, when Somoza celebrated his birthday, he was feted for a whole week, named "Somoza Week" in his honor. Details of the festivities filled the pages of Managua newspapers, perhaps crowding out news of the Guard's advance toward the Wiwilí camp where most of Sandino's discharged men were concentrated. The danger in which they stood caused Sandino to write to Sacasa. An exchange of letters resulted in another trip by Sandino to Managua.

The trimotor plane which brought Salvatierra to Las Segovias to pick up Sandino landed at Jinotega. From there Salvatierra wired Federico Sacasa to expect him with Sandino the following day: "General Somoza is here with me," he added, "sends his regards, and says if there is strong feeling for it in Jinotega he will with pleasure accompany General Sandino tomorrow."

Sandino felt uneasy. That sixth sense he sometimes talked about warned him of danger. When he met Salvatierra on the night of February 15, he said:

> "I'm being surrounded. For about a month now the Guard has been taking up positions around Wiwilí. What's this all about? The president is deceiving me."
>
> "No," [said Salvatierra] "the president is loyal."
>
> "Well, his subordinates are doing whatever they like. The Guards say they're going to destroy me. Destroy . . . destroy . . . as if we didn't know what we have to do! Destroy men who are working and teaching the country how it should work, those fellows who are a charge on the public treasury, those improvised petty officials who do nothing but eat and drink! General Somoza plans to destroy me. And what good is General Somoza? Good for the job he has, after that nobody sees him

again. Well, yes, I'm a leader—disarmed perhaps, but with one word from me the people will rise up, because they believe in me. I don't want war, but how is it possible that these people won't be allowed to live in peace on their own soil? The Guard is killing them, killing them every day. The proof that I want peace is that I'm going at Dr. Sacasa's call."

Despite his forebodings he boarded the plane for Managua, accompanied by Salvatierra, generals Francisco Estrada and Juan Pablo Umanzor, Sócrates Sandino, and some sympathizers. He had an interview that same evening with Sacasa and Sacasa's brothers Crisanto and Federico, in which the guarantees he would be given against the Guard's aggressiveness were spelled out.

As there were still unsurrendered weapons in Las Segovias, Sandino recommended to his men that they defend themselves as best they could, and said that if his presence was the cause of all the tensions, he was ready to leave the country. "It isn't my business," he told Sacasa, "whether there's a Guard or not, nor who should command it. I myself as a citizen have to pay taxes to maintain the army or the Guard or whatever it's called. All I want is that we should be given constitutional guarantees and that the Guard be constitutionalized."

Sandino's statements, all of a legalistic and conciliatory character, were published, although one paper twisted them so maliciously that it had him saying that only three powers existed in Nicaragua, the government, the Guard, and himself. Obviously such a notion could not be pleasing to Somoza. Yet Somoza had no qualms about embracing Sandino on Sunday the eighteenth in the presidential palace. On the nineteenth Sandino sent Sacasa this memo on the talks that had transpired between them:

Señor President, Your Excellency:
    As you know, in the peace accords signed on February 2 by you and myself as supreme chief of the Army Defending the National Sovereignty of Nicaragua, in the presence of Conservative and Liberal party delegations and of four delegates who signed, it was stipulated in Article 2 that the Liberal and Conservative parties would give preeminence in their respective political programs to respect for our Constitution and the Republic's basic laws, and to maintaining by all rational and juridical means the full resplendency of sovereignty and political and economic independence for Nicaragua.

It is my understanding, señor President, that the Liberal Party came to power when the country's political and economic independence was very constricted, and that it is for this very reason of nonindependence that a nonpolitical military institution exists in Nicaragua with regulations alien to our Fundamental Charter.

I realize your fervent desires to reorient the country within new laws; but there is the problem of the existence of the National Guard with its unconstitutional structure and procedures, and at the same time of the emergency guard you have in Río Coco under command of generals Francisco Estrada and Juan Santos Morales. This latter force is constitutional from the moment when you authorized it as president of the Republic and commander in chief, and it is by your authority that it will or will not continue.

However, señor President, since under the same accords you are under obligation to give effective guarantees of the lives and interests of the men who fought under my command in the recent campaign against the U.S. interventionist forces in Nicaragua, and since those indispensable guarantees cannot be effective without correcting the National Guard's illegal structure and procedures, I wish to reiterate to you the proofs of my frank and loyal cooperation, in the event that I can contribute in any way to the maintenance of peace.

So that the development of your governmental program may face no difficulties from the men who fought with me, and that I may facilitate your regulation of the National Guard's structure and procedures in accordance with the Constitution of the Republic, I will influence the men of my army to the end of our giving you a unanimous vote of confidence, to strengthen your authority in making more effective the guarantees to which the February 2, 1933, accords entitle us, and in effecting regulation of the National Guard within a determined time.

The essential object of this letter is to learn how you propose to guarantee us: not only constitutionalization of the Guard, but other ways of guaranteeing the lives and interests of all the men under my orders in our recent campaign against interventionist forces. Always your faithful servant in the future,

A. C. Sandino

Sacasa's reply was dated February 20:

Señor General Augusto C. Sandino
Esteemed general:
    Regardful of the thoughts in your kind letter of yesterday, I am

pleased to assure you that I of course concur with you in the highly patriotic objective of the Peace Agreement we signed on February 2, 1933, with the direct intervention of the Conservative and Liberal Nationalist parties of the Republic.

Although your personal appreciation differs substantially from mine on the various points covered in your letter, I do not consider it pertinent to enter into specific details since I have abundant goodwill to satisfy your wishes fully and reasonably in whatever tends to improve the functioning of the National Guard, created to sustain the Republic's institutions; and to give effective guarantees to every Nicaraguan, without distinction of any kind, under protection of the Constitution and laws.

To be precise, a regime of justice on the part of authority, and an ordered life of peace and work for the inhabitants, are indispensable for the conservation and full resplendency of our national autonomy.

For this reason I have always been disposed or, better said, determined, to throw my weight in the direction of early correction of the National Guard's organic law and regulations, and this will be effected within the first half of this year, to adjust them to the Constitution and to the administrative system legally established in the country.

It is my pleasure to inform you that while those necessary reforms are being made, and in order to inspire greater confidence in you, I will send to the Northern departments a delegate of the Executive and of the General Command, under whose direct orders the public forces of that region will be placed, and to whom I will assign the special task of collecting all arms now outside of the Government's control, and also of solicitously attending to the protection of the men who fought under your command.

I send you this letter with the greatest regard to satisfy the wishes you have expressed, in consideration of the patriotic attitude that has been unshakably demonstrated since we signed the Peace Agreement, and also of your spontaneous manifestations with respect to the strengthening of my authority, for which I sincerely thank you.

> Yours faithfully,
> Juan B. Sacasa

On February 21 this supposed arrangement was brought to public attention. It was in fact only a repetition of vague statements by the government, which Sandino was in no condition to elucidate through the fog of promises and fancy words with which they were adorned.

The newspapers published both letters and the fact that Sandino would return next day to his native village, Niquihomo.

At 5 P.M. on the twenty-first Sandino and his father went to the presidential palace accompanied by generals Estrada and Umanzor. Invited by the president to dine, they remained until 10 P.M., in the company of General Portocarrena, the probable government emissary to the Northern departments, and of the president's brothers. The tragedy occurred as they left.

As usual the newspapers gave very few details of it. The central figure was a declared enemy of the United States, and it is logical to suppose that the news agencies' interest was not to broadcast to the world the new crime committed against Nicaragua, in the person of its noblest and most selfless son. To do so would inevitably throw suspicion on the enemies whom he had just defeated.

However, two believable versions exist, provided by men who participated—one passively, one actively—in the events. The first was Salvatierra, an unwitting instrument of Somoza's machinations.[4] The second was Abelardo Cuadra, one of the soldiers who committed the crime.[5] The versions do not differ significantly in their details or in their conclusions.

These two testify that on the evening of February 21 the National Guard held a council of war in the residence of its chief, Somoza. The invitations noted that a "very important matter" was to be discussed. Sixteen persons participated, including General Gustavo Abaunza, National Guard second in command; Colonel Samuel Santos; majors Alfonso González, Diego López Roig, Lisandro Delgadillo, Policarpo Gutiérrez; Captain Francisco Mendieta; lieutenants Federico Davidson Blanco, Antonio López Barrera, Ernesto Díaz; Sublieutenant César Sánchez; General Camilo González; and Lieutenant Abelardo Cuadra himself.

Somoza turned up at the meeting at dusk. "I come," he said, "from the American Embassy, where I have been conferring with Ambassador Arthur Bliss Lane. He has assured me that the Washington government supports and recommends the elimination of Augusto César Sandino, considering him as it does a disturber of the country's peace."[6] A document was then drawn up, committing all present as perpetrators of the murder in case any of them might turn betrayer.

Sandino stayed in Managua at Salvatierra's home and had to pass near the airfield to get there. The plot was for thirty picked men from companies 15 and 17 of the Guard, under the command of majors Delgadillo and Gutiérrez and lieutenants López Barrera and Federico Davidson Blanco, to proceed in truck "GN No. 1" to the airfield and await Sandino there. All went according to plan, with one variant: the squad was informed that Sandino was at the presidential palace with generals Estrada, Portocarrero and Umanzor, Santos López, Gregorio Sandino, and Federico and Crisanto Sacasa, chatting with the president and Salvatierra.

Sandino had in fact, after dinner, been engaged in discussing the exploitation of gold deposits in the Coco River area: registration of a public company was outlined, to be authorized by Dr. Alejo Icaza Icaza as soon as Sandino would return again from Niquihomo. All the guests left the palace at 10 P.M. President Sacasa gave Sandino a farewell embrace, and Sandino invited General Portocarrero and Calderón Ramírez to keep him company in the car that would take him home. They excused themselves on the ground that they must wait with Sacasa for General Somoza, with whom they had to arrange details of the delegation shortly to go to Las Segovias.

Federico Sacasa accompanied the guests to the door. Sandino, his father, and Salvatierra took the back seat and generals Estrada and Umanzor sat in front with the driver. The presidential palace stood atop Tiscapa Hill, at whose feet was the National Guard's Campo de Marte. As the car approached the sentry post known as El Hormiguero, it was blocked by an apparently stalled vehicle which a group of soldiers seemed to be fixing. Sergeant J. Emilio Canales, who was in charge of the group and carried a Thompson machine gun, ordered the car to halt and the driver applied his brakes. Estrada and Umanzor, scenting an ambush, took out their arms. Sandino dissuaded them from firing, since neither his father nor Salvatierra was a "fighting man" able to use a weapon.

Major Delgadillo, disguised as a Guard corporal, then came up, told them they were under arrest and demanded their revolvers. They were led on foot to the Hormiguero guardpost and detained in its patio under the muzzles of submachine guns.

It so happened that President Sacasa's daughter Maruca was behind them in another car and witnessed Sandino's arrest. She protested, saying that Sandino had just been her father's dinner guest, but seeing it was useless she returned to the palace and told Sacasa what had happened. Sacasa immediately phoned to the Campo de Marte but by Somoza's orders his calls went unanswered.

Through all this Somoza was comfortably ensconced within the Campo de Marte, listening to a recital by the Chilean poet Zoila Rosa Cárdenas. It was the first such performance ever in the Campo de Marte. The plan as it had developed was to attack Salvatierra's house where Sandino's brother Sócrates then was, and simultaneously kill Sandino. The signal for the attack was to be shots fired from a place known as the Campo de Larreynaga.

Sandino tried to avoid his fate, which he foresaw, and convinced Major Delgadillo to send in a message to Somoza. According to Salvatierra, Sandino said:

"Why do this, if we're all brothers? We've made peace and are regenerating Nicaragua through work. All I've done is fight for Nicaragua's liberty. Three nights ago Somoza embraced me in token of harmony, and before then I visited him in his home and Somoza visited me. He gave me a signed portrait and I've done the same to him. Call General Somoza, let him come and tell me what he wants, let him talk to me. . . ."

Delgadillo returned from inside the Campo de Marte to tell Sandino he had not been able to get the message through to Somoza. Sandino had been jumpy up to then, in contrast to Estrada's serenity and the immobility of Umanzor, a descendant of Indians and Africans. But when he understood that his death had been decided, he regained his habitual calm.

Sandino's father and Salvatierra were told to remain there, while Estrada, Umanzor, and Sandino had to climb into the "GN No. 1" truck. Salvatierra interceded, asking the commander if he was obeying orders of the president of the Republic. Before the man could answer, Sandino said: "No, it's a military order and that is obeyed immediately." Suiting action to word, he climbed first into the truck. There were no farewells.

The truck with the three generals squatting in it headed for a place called La Calavera (The Skull) in the Campo de Larreynaga. Salvatierra remarked later: "I didn't believe they would kill Sandino. I thought they would put him out of the country . . . make him withdraw his letter to the president and commit himself to immediate surrender of the arms. . . ."

But Sandino was assassinated. When the three condemned men got off the truck, Sandino asked for a glass of water and that he be allowed to urinate. Both requests were denied, and Estrada remarked: "Don't ask these fellows for anything, general, let them kill us." Sandino refused to let his pockets be searched; Umanzor stepped forward to give the contents of his to the nearby sergeant.

Standing with hands in pockets, Sandino said: "My political leaders have played jokes with me." Then death came. The three martyrs— Sandino to the right, Umanzor in the middle, and Estrada to the left—sat on a rock to await the hail of bullets. Major Delgadillo was supposed to give the order, but since he was a brother Mason of Sandino's he shrank from being present at the massacre and, retiring to a prudent distance, put Sublieutentant Carlos E. Monterrey in command of the squad. He contented himself with a shot in the air as signal to open fire.

A bullet penetrated Sandino's head through the brain, another his left breast. Estrada was finished off with two in the chest, Umanzor with five in the head. The bullets came from machine guns. Hearing the shots back in El Hormiguero, Gregorio Sandino said: "Now they're killing them. It always happens: try to be a redeemer, and you get crucified." According to Salvatierra it was about 11 P.M. At 1 A.M. on the twenty-second, "the U.S. minister Arthur Bliss Lane arrived at the jail and invited us to come with him in his car to the legation, whose hospitality he offered us. I got the president on the phone and told him I'd rather go to the presidential palace. Dr. Sacasa approved, and the foreign diplomat had the amiability to accompany us. When I reached the palace I heard the whole story."[7]

In fact Salvatierra learned more, that there had been a second death squad at the airfield near his house. When the shots that dispatched Sandino and his comrades were heard, Salvatierra's house—from which his wife and daughter were miraculously absent— had been attacked with machine guns. Those there at the time were Salvatierra's son-in-law Rolando Murillo, Sócrates Sandino, and General Santos López. López defended himself with a submachine gun and was the only one to escape, though wounded. The other two, and a ten-year-old who was crossing the street at the time, were riddled with bullets. These Somoza forces were commanded by Major Policarpo Gutiérrez and Lieutenant Federico Davidson Blanco. The bodies were taken to the Larreynaga camp, where they were stripped of all objects of value. Apart from his suit, Sandino's body yielded the Guard a watch with gold chain and a diamond ring. Only in death had they been able to lay a hand on him. The remains were then thrown into a ditch abutting the lake, "almost in front of the first building overlooking the lake . . . in that part of the Zacarías hospice that faces eastward," where "there are two blocks of huts used at that time as soldiers' dormitories."

They were not the only ones massacred. Somoza had woven his plot in three parts. That same night, at about the same time, the National Guard completed the encirclement of Wiwilí and proceeded to slaughter Sandino's disarmed men who lived there with their families. Krehm gives the figure of 300 men, women, and children dead.[8] Vicente Sáenz says the figure was "several times higher," counting in the massacre at Jinotega where the troops did not even bother to bury the victims: ". . . for twenty-four hours the crows, dogs, and swine of the neighborhood treated themselves to a prolonged feast of human flesh."

José N. Castro adds this to the story of Sandino's murder: "Some days later, at a banquet in the U.S. embassy, drunk as Nero, Somoza publicly declared he had felt obliged to kill Sandino to preserve the peace of Nicaragua."[9] This seems by no means fanciful. Salvatierra in his invaluable book notes that when Sacasa faced Somoza with the deed, Somoza replied that "the crime had been committed by a few Guards out of hatred for Sandino." When the president demanded that the assassins be named and punished, the State Department's cynical servant replied: "I can't do it, because I would lose authority over them." His ludicrous explanations—such as "I can't change the orders of my subordinate" cited by Krehm—would seem to have been dreamed up by a lunatic for the exclusive benefit of imbeciles, were they not backed by a cynicism that negates any possibility of rational or ethical comprehension.

Four days later, on February 25, Somoza called together his general staff and officers, who chorused their oath of loyalty to President Sacasa. To get from Sandino's assassin a commitment of loyalty in the diplomatic corps' presence, Sacasa decreed himself to be the commander in chief of the National Guard and then publicly turned over the office to Somoza, availing himself of the occasion to reprove the Guard in moving tones for its behavior on the night of the twenty-first. To show how deeply this touched him, the Guard's general staff chief Abaunza commented loudly to another officer: "Okay, these bastards are satisfied, let's drink to that."[10]

One further example of Somoza's macabre humor comes from Salvatierra, who notes that "shortly after Sandino and the others were killed, Somoza went to inspect the victims' destroyed and profaned bodies." Ex-President Moncada, for his part, was reported in Managua to have toasted the massacre on the night it occurred, saying that "only by killing Sandino could we have security." A perfect match for his statement to *La Noticia* on March 11 that the accord between Sacasa and the Guard was the best means to avoid civil war.

On February 24, with the proper solemnity of a National Guard chief, Somoza ordered a tribunal to investigate "the deplorable events on the night of the twenty-first." The ensuing fiestas and tributes to Sandino's assassin—precisely for having assassinated him—challenged in brilliance and duration the celebrations on the occasion of "Somoza Week," instituted to commemorate his birth. The cream of Granada and León society vied in honoring him and showering him with gifts, thus celebrating the disappearance of the one man who had imperiled their interests and privileges, indissolubly linked with imperialist extortion.

And while the assassin rejoiced and took pride in his feat, tasting in advance the power that would fall ripe into his hands with small delay, there came from Washington the voice of President Roosevelt, erecting with a phrase the greatest monument Sandino could have wished:

"If I had been a Latin American, I too would have taken up arms against the intervention."

13
The Assassin at His Banquet

Anastasio Somoza, the genial dictator who now
curbs the liberty of the people for his own good,
revels in the friendship of Washington. The doctrine of the Good Neighbor has enjoyed no more
pleasant vindication than was afforded by the spontaneous ovation offered Somoza when he visited
Washington in 1939. He was met at Union Station
by President Roosevelt and members of the Cabinet, the proper guns were fired, the military bands
played glad music, and the streets along the line of
march were lined by tens of thousands of government employees granted three hours of liberty to
express their unstudied welcome. Mr. Somoza's
happiness was complete when the Export-Import
Bank pressed 2½ millions upon him.

Hubert Herring[1]

Who was Somoza? How did he manage to climb the ladder to the top
rung and put all his virtual competitors in his pocket: the career
military men; the lawyers for import and export concerns, everlast-
ing candidates for Central American presidencies; the embassy crowd
in Washington, always favored by official power; above all Díaz and
Chamorro, never the men to yield up a sinecure without a struggle?

We have already mentioned one of the probable explanations: his
influence with Ambassador Hanna through Mrs. Hanna, which got
him the top job in the National Guard. No less important was his
having been private secretary to ex-President Moncada. For before
Mr. Hanna arrived in the country, Somoza had already won some
spurs by his identification with the father of the Tipitapa betrayal,
which may also explain the personal hatred he aroused in Sandino, as
shown in the events culminating in the treacherous massacre. Another point is his marriage to President Sacasa's niece, which of
course did not deter him from throwing Sacasa out the window when
opportunity arose.

Somoza's grandfather Bernabé was a folkloric figure in Nicaragua. His nickname, "Seven Handkerchiefs," referring to what he needed to wipe the blood off his hands, spoke of a less than artistocratic past which had its epilogue on a gallows in the city of Rivas. But his father had nothing of the bandit. He was the owner of a modest coffee plantation which brought in enough to provide suitable education for his sons. Anastasio, born in 1895, had flunked in primary school and was sent to the United States to study business. He was in the Pierce Commercial College of Philadelphia, where his studies were likewise uncompleted but he could at least acquire some picturesque English—"fantastically incorrect and fluent," according to William Krehm who interviewed him. Employed as an auto salesman, he seasoned the job with an enthusiasm for cards and carousals. He married Salvadora Debayle, enabling him to add to his surname that of one of the country's traditional families—a family constituting, along with the Sacasas and Sevillas, the clan with the keys to the country in its pocket.

His dad endowed him with a small grocery business in his native town of San Marcos, which his passion for cards brought to bankruptcy. He then got a job as inspector for the Rockefeller Foundation;[2] then as an installer of electric wiring in León; then as an electric meter inspector. In 1921, with his old friend Camilo González—later chief of his personal guard—he was caught counterfeiting gold coins. Thanks to the Debayle family's intercession, he wriggled out of a trial that would have had unforeseeable consequences for his future.

At the time of the *chamorrista* revolution in 1926, Somoza tried to get into the act by taking over his town, San Marcos. In the scuffle he got a memorable beating, providing him with a promotion to a military rank which would start him up the ladder from sharpshooter to general, by one of those meteoric ascents that are customary in Our America.

The next step was acting as interpreter in the conference that led to the Tipitapa Peace. Thus the casual and apparently unproductive stay in the United States began to pay dividends: like Adolfo Díaz, his elementary English opened the door to State Department personages—in this case Colonel Stimson—and to the under-the-blackthorn peacemaker who knew no language but his own. Thanks to this, Somoza got wise from the first moment to the treason hatched by Sacasa's war secretary with an eye on the big prize, the presidency of the Republic.

When that prize in fact landed in Moncada's lap, he treated Somoza in turn to the foreign undersecretary job. It was in this role that he advised the Guatemalan chancellery of the death of General Girón Ruano, who had abandoned a military career in his country to join up with Sandino, and who was shot by the National Guard with his feet and hands chained in the presence of United States troops.

From there Somoza's "military career" took him to the top of the National Guard, the outfit replacing the "Constabulary" of Yankee origin and recalling the Indian military organization under British command—known as sepoys, from the Persian *cipalu,* and with the same mission of safeguarding the invaders' interests against their own brothers—but with North American flavoring. We have traced his activity at the head of the sepoy army culminating in the murder of Sandino and his people.

This gave him a pretext to add yet another feather to his already much-plumed hat: that of writer. In this area he attributed to himself the paternity of the book *El verdadero Sandino,* whose language and style betray the pen of his general staff chief and former counterfeiting comrade, Camilo González. The book purports to reveal unknown aspects of Sandino's personality, and to explain and justify the need to commit crimes against him. Undoubtedly—since he mentions the book—it was the source of information of the tourist John Gunther when he wrote that Sandino "plundered much of the country and eluded capture for years."[3]

The last step remained to be climbed: the presidency. With so irresolute an incumbent as his uncle-in-law, it would cost Somoza little to forget the two oaths of fealty sworn before Sacasa and before the diplomatic corps. With a weaker memory than the main protagonist, the diplomatic corps lent itself contentedly to intervening when "Tacho" led the National Guard in rebellion in Managua and León in May 1936 and had Carlos Brenes Jarquín named provisional President. Brenes Jarquín cozily prepared the electoral apparatus that would put Somoza on the throne from January 1, 1937.[4] One opponent suspected aloud that Sacasa had lent himself to the maneuver to show his impotence vis-à-vis his nephew, and that he had been equally impotent when the events of February 1, 1933 occured. What is certain is that there was no resistance to the rebellion and clearly there had been none to Somoza's presidential ambitions. The opposition expatriated itself at the kind invitation of the Guard, and to the U.S. ambassador's astonishment "Tacho"—"amazed by such a conclusive demonstration of democratic popularity"— garnered 117,000 votes to 1,096 for Leonardo Argüello.

Time's well-informed correspondent Krehm relates that when he was in Managua in 1944 and decided to check for himself the truth of the denunciations of Somoza's jobbery, he had no need to resort to opposition politicos: he only had to interview businessmen "in the strict sense of the word" to prove that the president owned most of the main businesses in Nicaragua. Bypassing the tragicomic details provided in Krehm's book and in Germán Arciniegas' *Entre la libertad y el miedo,* these were some of the "democratic occupations" of don "Tacho": private sale of cattle to Panama; clandestine sale of cattle to Costa Rica; monopoly of tallow distribution; the La Salud pasteurization plant in Managua; ownership of the San Albino gold mine; an extra whack of $175,000 a year from the 2.25 percent "additional contribution" by U.S. mining companies; ownership of fifty-one cattle ranches, forty-six coffee plantations, and the big Montelimar hacienda; 50 percent of the shares in the Nicaragua cement factory, 41 percent of the shares in the Salvadorean magnate Gadal María's cotton factory, 50 percent of the shares in the Momotombo National Factory producing matches, whose sale was assured by barring lighters; proprietorship of the daily *Novedades,* of most of the country's sawmills, of the buildings housing the legations in Mexico and Costa Rica, of various Miami apartment houses, of the Chinandega, Tipitapa, Jinotega, Estelí, and La Libertad electrical plants, of the Las Mercedes tract beside Managua airport, etc., etc.

This is clearly a pallid reflection of Somoza's multitudinous interests, above all abroad, where he stashed various millions of dollars for a rainy day. Nicaraguans have done a tally of them from A to Z, the X representing the unknown quanity of businesses running under the names of his numerous and well-heeled relatives.

The illegal traffic in cattle to Costa Rica was carried on under the blind eye of the National Guard, with the commercial transactions in the charge of Victor Wolf, a friend of Costa Rican ex-President

Calderón Guardia.[5] The sale of 5,000 head of cattle to Panama in 1943 brought Somoza—not Nicaragua—a net profit of $20 a head, and there were similar profits from Peru. The National Guard itself celebrated its chief's sagacity in doggerel:

> Whatever has horns in Nicaragua,
> Has four feet, and says "moo"
> Belongs to Chief Tacho Somoza
> And nuts to you.

The reader will ask how it was possible, at the United States' backdoor, during the presidency of the great democrat Roosevelt, for such political adventurers to flourish—not in Nicaragua alone, to Our America's disgrace. And how could the people that produced a Sandino submit docilely to the yoke of a petty tyrant, whose sole talent was obsequious servility linked to infinite unscrupulousness?

The Good Neighbor policy became a trap for the unwary. It was enough for any aspirant to power to chant hallelujahs to Democracy, and in its name overthrow a government that was legally constituted (but with a tendency to free itself economically from the yoke of U.S. investors), or show preference for British, German, or Japanese investors: the White House would back his coup d'état, he would immediately be recognized in the name of the nonintervention principle—the same that determined the death of Spain in the thirties—and the new tyrant would be cordially and officially invited to Washington.

In Somoza's case U.S. intervention had served to lift him to the throne. Nonintervention, curiously, would serve to keep him there. We have mentioned the Pan-American Conference in Montevideo in 1933, attended by Roosevelt and by Cordell Hull who proscribed intervention by any nation—American or not—in any American country's affairs. Subsequent events showed that doctrine to be the safeguard of another sort of intervention, differing very little from the military kind.

Somoza was not the first, nor was he an exception. Received with all honors by Roosevelt, he won the U.S. president's complaisance by promising to respect the people's democratic will—and, logically, the U.S. investments and positions in his country. Sandino's assassin basked in the favor of the president who had justified the heroic action of Sandino. Not to be outdone, Somoza made this public statement qualifying him for a gold medal in apple polishing: "I think of remaining in the presidency not less than forty years. But if the United States were to give me the least hint about leaving, I would clear out at once, asking only complete guarantees for myself."[6]

No wonder Gunther describes him as "the cleverest politician between the Rio Grande and the Panama Canal." At the time of the U.S. elections in 1940, Gunther relates, Roosevelt's new triumph made Somoza so happy that he decreed a two-day national holiday. Clearly so democratic a President, who liked to call the U.S. minister "Boy," could do no less than defend his popularity from the ebullience of the people: thus, as Gunther tells it, "Somoza has machine guns mounted outside his palace, and travels in a bullet-proof car preceded by a station wagon jammed with armed guards." The jocular details which Gunther (and even less intelligent people than he) celebrate as "local color" would be most entertaining, did they not at the same time show the tragic face behind all this exploited picturesqueness. When Arciniegas stresses such description, with occasional accompanying "sociological" comments for the use of U.S. academic cretins, he does no more than show the influence of those more interested in anecdote than in history, in farce than in drama—in what the eye can see through boudoir keyholes than in the vision of a man of letters who commits his opinion and ideas in defense of a cause.

With all of his fancy for platitudes and superficial analysis of peoples' problems, Gunther cannot dodge the evidence of the facts when, following his eulogies of "democrat" Somoza, he notes that "a peon is lucky if he gets 15 cents per day" and that "a policeman gets about $3.00 a month, and a good cook about $4.00. Somoza's salary is gargantuan by those standards. It is in the neighborhood of $100,000 per year."[7]

The police repression ranked with that of the great masters. From the time when he killed Sandino, Somoza had to face growing opposition by the Nicaraguan Workers Party (PTN), by the students, and by Conservative and Liberals disgusted by his egotism. His adoption of the methods that gave fame to the jails of Hitler, Mussolini, and Franco—his good friends despite his chumminess with Roosevelt—earned him another garland to add to his collection: a reputation for the most perfect police force in Central America. (Guatemala's dictator Ubico insisted Somoza was bragging; *his* was the best.) The era of limitless and pitiless persecution began in 1937 when a portrait of Somoza in silk, a special gift from Hirohito on the fourth anniversary of Sandino's death, was burned in the hall of Léon University. Octavio A. Caldera and various students and workers were arrested and savagely tortured; their bones turned up in Corn Island, the place to which workers and *campesinos* opposing the regime were thenceforth relegated.

After the visit to Roosevelt, the visible result of which was the Eximbank loan and a new agreement for a project replacing the Nicaraguan canal (known as the Rama Highway[8]), Somoza felt comfortable and secure. He boasted that his pilgrimage had put those of all other Central American presidents in the shade. On the basis of the new agreement he proceeded to acquire lands all along the probable route. But the Nicaraguan currency, the *córdoba,* was so weak that its devaluation could not be delayed. This also provided Somoza with something to get his teeth into. The immediate consequences were growth of the already efficient black market and further pauperization of the people, whose opposition grew in proportion.[9]

The "democratic" elections of 1936 assured power for Somoza until 1941. But World War II created politico-social problems which had to be faced from a different angle. Nicaragua was emerging from the depression, and the high market prices of gold and coffee were a favorable sign. But both were monopolized, gold by U.S. companies under the Fletcher family's control, coffee by consortia mostly under direct control of the tyrant. Popular resentment had an opportunity to show itself when the Corn Island deportees returned: in the Pacific coast area labor union groups of some signficance began to form, and united in the Managua Workers' Confederation (CTM), which was not under the official thumb. In 1940 the CTM had eight affiliated unions representing some 3,000 members, among them the League of Campesinos, the Bluefields Woodworkers' Union, and the Managua Workers' Federation.

When this movement began to look like an electoral threat, Somoza summoned a constituent assembly of his adherents which suppressed municipal elections, changed the Constitution to extend the presidential term of office from four to six years, and authorized the dictator to remain in office till 1947. Opposition leaders were again jailed or deported, under the benevolent "good neighbor" gaze of Ambassador James Bolton Stewart (whom "Tacho" liked to call "my steward").

In 1940 a workers' confederation manifesto commemorating the sixth anniversary of Sandino's death prompted new repression by the National Guard, who arrested and jailed the chief labor leaders for seven months; the roundup was completed at the May Day celebration, from which fifty-five more leaders were hauled to prison. This caused union and political activities to go underground. They emerged in 1943 when Enrique Espinosa Sotomayor inspired the creation of the Independent Labor Party with socialist tendencies.

Most illustrative of Sandino's importance are the events subsequent to his death; or more concretely, subsequent to the fate that befell his country Nicaragua, ruled since then—save for brief intervals—by Sandino's self-declared assassin. Between 1913 and 1929 U.S. investments in Nicaragua grew from $3 million to $24 million; in the same period, trade with the United States grew four times. This economic dependency had its political sequel: up to 1945, Nicaragua had ratified twenty-six of the forty-two Pan-American conventions while the United States had ratified twenty-seven.

President Sacasa told Vicente Sáenz in February 1933 that his country's debt amounted to $3 million. Yet Mr. Cumberland, the expert sent by the State Department (and known in Haiti as an agent of the Bank of Boston), had reckoned four years previously that Nicaragua needed $12 million, half of which would go for liquidating existing debts,[10] and in the intervening years that debt had expanded due to occupation costs and the loan required for military activities. Taking these facts into account, we would not be off the mark in calling the presidential calculation erroneous or false.

The U.S. financial catastrophe and depression of 1933 shook the feeble foundation of Latin American countries—among them Nicaragua—which could not overcome their colonial monoproductive condition. Their agricultural structure militated against the flowering of infant industry at the backdoor of more important centers. Yet as a result of World War II, what industry there was gave birth to a labor movement which followed our countries' tradition of dividing into antagonistic groups. Of the new groups the most important were of the communist tendency, whose leading figure in Central America was Agustín Farabundo Martí, and the moderate trade union–cooperativist group called Organized Workers of Nicaragua (OON).

Salvatierra, then the agriculture minister, was responsible for the latter's creation in 1924. He brought together some 1,200 workers— a respectable number under Nicaraguan conditions—divided into fifteen sections and oriented by an official organ, *La Evolución Obrera*. In 1931 Salvatierra managed to put through a labor code of modest pretensions, which became effective when he went into exile in Seville after his friend Sandino's death. After February 1934 the organization fell into Somoza's hands; Somoza turned it into a puppet opposition to the PTN, to which his opponents belonged and whose history contained periods of complete or partial clandestinity.

The census on May 23 of that year showed a population of 1.3 million, of whom 257,878 over the age of ten worked in agriculture and cattle raising—208,040 as wage earners and the rest as owners or renters. The total of arable land—crossed by two lakes, over 30 lagoons, 94 rivers, 78 major tributaries, and over 600 ravine streams flowing in winter—was 3.35 million *manzanas*,[11] of which only 678,606 were cultivated while 165,000 were used for cattle grazing.

The simplest analysis of Nicaragua's economic situation shows that (1) as a monoculture nation it had been reduced to dependency on the United States, which was reflected in its political situation; (2) the important exports, gold and silver, were monopolized by U.S. concerns; (3) the same was true of coffee, cacao, and forest products; (4) its dependency did not permit it to diversify crops to free itself from imports—i.e., corn and wheat, whose production thirty years earlier had satisfied internal needs; (5) it was therefore obliged to contract periodic loans, since its trade balance was always unfavorable; (6) all this constituted a system of vassalage vis-à-vis its powerful "good neighbor."

On December 31, 1940, according to the U.S. secretary of commerce, direct U.S. investments amounted to $8.858 million, of which 28 percent was in mining and in mining profits without capital investment.

To produce gold equivalent in value to $7 million or $8 million a year, 6,796 Nicaraguan employees received average wages of five *córdobas* (US $0.65) for an eight-hour day under wretched conditions. The government took 3.5 percent of the profits, to which was added the 2.25 percent "additional contribution" pocketed by Somoza. The chief "civilizing" and "progressive" U.S. mining concerns were seven in number:

1. Siuna, in the Zelaya department, the richest mine exploited by La Luz Mines Ltd., property of the Fletcher consortium, under laws of Ontario Province, Canada.

2. Compañía Minera el Jabalí in Santo Domingo de Chontales, 125 kilometers from Managua, with (like the above) its own hydroelectric plant and private airport.

3. Bonanza, exploited by the Neptune Gold Mining Company under the laws of the State of Delaware, United States. Also with its own hydroelectric plant and airport.

4. Centro Minero San Ramón, exploited by the Neptune subsidiary Compañía de Minas de Matagalpa.

5. India Mines Ltd., exploiting the mining centers of the same name in Santa Rosa, León department, under U.S. laws.

6. El Limón, in León department, property of the same firm exploiting the India Mines.

7. Centro Minero San Gregorio, not far from Santo Domingo de Chontales. The firm exploiting it got the concession of an immense agricultural area, depriving Nicaraguans of its use.

The low taxes paid by these firms, quite unrelated to their fabulous profits from cheap labor, were among the explanations of the regime's budget deficits. Somoza learned much from his protectors, especially how to appropriate others' land legally. After 1936, using "persuasive" or pseudolegal methods, he annexed for himself large areas belonging to minor or major *latifundistas*;[12] 40 percent of small landowners became farm laborers, and areas where some 200 families lived were transformed into private estates for the dictator and his favorites.

He also turned to his own profit four continuous drought years, running small owners into debt by denying credit from government agencies. The debtors had to resort to usurers or banks controlled by Somoza's straw men, who proceeded to take over the lands through the courts.

In 1946, 749 proprietors owned 879 coffee plantations containing Nicaragua's 33,121,500 coffee trees. At harvest time, 20,000 persons worked in them under subhuman conditions, despite the rising coffee price—6 centavos gold in 1940, 14 in 1945, and 26 in 1946.

As for sugar mills, there were twenty-two in the country employing some 10,000 workers at harvest time. Although production was sufficient to cover internal needs, statistics showed a permanent lack of local consumption due to the product being exported refined to the U.S. or neighboring Central American countries. Production was 274,500 tons in 1943, bringing the export monopoly a profit of $208,650; in 1944, $407,729.

Nicaragua's timber wealth was in the hands of two U.S. concerns, Long Leaf Pines Company and Cukra Development Company. They did not publish their balance sheets but separately declared annual profits of $1.2 million, of which 4.5 percent ended in the government's coffers and 2.5 percent in the president's. There are thirty-five varieties of exportable timber, from pine to cedar and mahogony; a parallel branch of exploitation embracing agricultural products for food and industry reported no smaller profits. Such products include cinnamon, achote, agave, garlic, sesame, cotton, bamboo, cacao, peanuts, sisal and hemp, sugarcane, white cane, castilla cane, fistula cane, onions, vegetable wax, coconuts, coyol, espabel, figs, rubber, gourds, mangrove and pine trees, quinine,[13] medlars, roots, tobacco, cassava, etc., as well as thirty-six varieties of fruits, twenty-five of vegetables and greens, and sixteen of forage products.

The United States imports from Nicaragua gold, silver, mineral soils, coffee, rubber,[14] timber, sesame seed, ipecac, bananas, corn, medlar gum, balsam, coconuts, hides and leather products, and cheese. These imports of course vary with the United States' fluctuating needs, leading to a permanent budget instability by no means exclusive to Nicaragua. The Rio Economic Conference in 1954 showed that the U.S. political economy punishes most countries of Our America with its imperialistic orthodoxy. They are powerless to shake off the hangman's rope that holds them in servitude and backwardness.

It was to demonstrate some of this that Carlos Dávila wrote his *Nosotros, los de las Américas*. Dávila, who replaced Alberto Lleras Camargo as president of the Organization of American States, can hardly be called a communist. But all his conclusions confirm that the United States methodically relegates our countries to colonial dependency, for exclusively imperialistic reasons.[15] Its price-fixing policy was put to the test during the last war. Strategic considerations and the closed Eastern production market determined the State Department to promote rubber cultivation in Nicaragua, and in 1944 the value of its production, $1,078,096, was the highest in the Americas. But with the war's end in 1945, interest declined and production sank to $846,836—at prices fixed by the State Department. The Allies' victory reopened the traditional U.S. source of rubber, and the State Department agreed with Nicaragua that exploitation of its rubber trees should stop. So at the end of 1945 and in 1946 rubber trees were cut down in such a way as deliberately to prevent large-scale production.

At the same time the war greatly inflated the prices of basic necessities in Nicaragua, as in all of our countries. In nine years from 1937 wheat flour rose 400 percent, corn 700 percent, rice 600 percent, beans 1,000 percent, potatoes 300 percent, meat 600 percent, milk 800 percent, eggs 800 percent. Meanwhile 1940–1948 statistics showed clothing up 145.55 percent, housing 132.82 percent, fuel and light 184.67 percent, and wages and salaries remaining stationary through the same period.

These were the wages: carpenters, masons, and fitters 48 *córdobas*,[16] peons or helpers 21, for a 48-hour week; in the textile industry, weavers (average for men and women) 5 *córdobas* for an 8-hour day, spinners 9, peons or helpers 4; shoe workers, per month, 39 in first category, 36 in second; liquor industry, average per week, 40 *córdobas*. In breweries, skilled workers 36 *córdobas* weekly, electricians and mechanics 48, machine room foremen 87, peons, draymen, and helpers 32 maximum. Mines, average 6 *córdobas* per day, 4 for helpers, 22 for contract workers, 14 for foremen and highly skilled. Sugar mill harvest workers 8 *córdobas* daily, cane cutters 3–4. The top daily wage for farm laborers and cattlemen never exceeded 3 *córdobas*.

Despite the moderate inflation beginning in 1947, wages and salaries remained fixed. When the workers refused to work, invoking Article 77 of Somoza's own Labor Code which established the minimum wage, he forcibly repressed the mine unions' protests. Simple comparison of wages and living costs shows the justice of the

Nicaraguan people's protest against a situation from which only Somoza, his relatives and friends profited.[17]

At the same time, bank deposits and fund disposals confirmed the bullish trend of the 1941–1945 period. Nicaragua's colonial situation was like a thermometer of the effect of the war on the U.S. economy. Disposable bank funds amounted to $14.6 million in 1944 and by the end of the war's last year, 1945, had dropped by $4 million. Budget surpluses in that year enabled the debt to Britain, estimated at $2 million in 1940, to be reduced to £387,840, which the U.S. customs inspectors were pressing Nicaragua to repay. Income from the Pacific Railroad brought the state $5.5 million in 1945 as against $800,000 in 1935, due to the rise in freight and passenger traffic, which in normal times gave jobs to 2,980 workers.

According to the Pan-American Union's Economic Research Department, between 1928 and 1944 Nicaragua's total income rose from $25 million to $61.375 million, or by 145 percent. The United States in the Roosevelt period did not reduce Somoza's economic support conditioned on the current rules of the game.

Thus it was no surprise when the friend of Hitler, Hirohito, Franco, and Mussolini again altered the Constitution to include the Atlantic Charter; still less so that, making the most of the change, he tried to include a clause whereby the constitutional "no re-election" principle would be suspended in case of war. But for him the Atlantic Charter was a two-edged sword, as it was for El Salvador's Hernández Martínez and Guatemala's Ubico. The U.S. propaganda broadside against the Axis bore an "admission free" sign and was recommended for diffusion throughout Latin America. Indirectly it was a slap in the face for the principle on which the dictators rested their power. Yet they could not apply the brake without exposing themselves or running the danger of being considered enemies of the Allies.

Nicaragua, then, presented the bizarre image of a bloody dictatorship filling its mouth with ultralibertarian slogans; so that its own preachments started revolutionary fires, which were quickly suffocated. When Somoza's old friend and later opponent Carlos Pasos was preparing a speech for the Liberal convention in León, where he was to make public the complete list of the president's businesses, Somoza warned him through a friend: "I know he has a speech prepared for the convention. If he insists on making it, he had better not forget to go armed. I'm not the type to be overthrown with speeches."

To make sure, he arrested Pasos. Then came word of successful revolutionary movements in El Salvador and Guatemala, which sparked students to seize the university, and the good ladies of the capital, who had never before uttered a rebellious peep, to parade their distaste for the dictator through the streets. Somoza responded by jailing the students and marshalling the whores of Nicaragua for a counterparade. After this the Atlantic Charter was carefully filed away and the National Guard could resume its loyalty to its traditions.[18]

Fear of suffering the fate of his neighbor dictators induced Somoza to veto the clause which would ensure his re-election, and to offer his opponents all kinds of guarantees and sinecures. When they turned down his offers, he put out feelers to the most revolutionary citizens, who were chagrined to see types like Emiliano Chamorro and Carlos Pasos capitalizing on the resistance to the dictatorship. But the Left wouldn't play either: it replied with the famous street actions of June and July 1944, which failed to unseat Somoza but at least elicited from him a public statement that he wouldn't try for re-election. Worker, *campesino,* and artisan organizations took advantage of the commotion to rebuild their decimated cadres and launch them into the social struggle. This bore fruit in the January 12, 1945, Labor Code under Decree 336,[19] which in fact regulated technical aspects of labor in relation to wages. Nicaragua had already ratified in 1934 the 1928 convention on methods of fixing minimum wages, which fell into disuse in 1938 when the president decided membership in the International Labor Organization was a big headache.[20]

The idyll lasted till May 1945 when Somoza's secretary, unveiling a lifesized statue of his chief, proclaimed that he had not been "elected" in 1939, only "designated" by the Constitutional Assembly for another term. Somoza promised to step down whenever the Caribbean highway was completed. Two thousand workers promptly offered their services gratis to complete it in a hurry, and opposition demonstrations intensified, now backed by U.S. ambassador Fletcher Warren; so Somoza named as candidate the longstanding aspirant,

Leonardo Argüello, and in fact installed him in regulated elections. He even had the audacity to resign command of the National Guard.

But Argüello, although lacking political savvy, had a good enough memory to suspect his patron's intentions and tried to rob him of his ascendancy over the Guard by reshaping its officer corps. When Somoza objected, Argüello gave him twenty-four hours to leave the country. The Nicaraguan Socialist Party, Independent Liberal Party, Labor Confederation, and *sandinista* student groups tried to persuade the president of the need to proceed warily against Somoza, but traditional groups pushed him provocatively into quick action lacking any assurance of success.

The maneuver seemed to have the backing of Mr. Warren, representative of the "democrat" Spruille Braden, who some days earlier had offered Argüello an 8 million *córdoba* loan to liquidate the deficit of the Somoza administration, in exchange for the usual "investment guarantees." Argüello had turned it down, and announced his intention to free himself from the economic yoke in a speech before Left parties on May Day. This gauntlet to Somoza was enough to seal his fate without further ado. Sandino's assassin asked three days' grace in obeying the order to remove himself. Before the time was up, on May 26, after twenty-six days of Argüello's presidency, the candidate for exile ordered the Guard into action and personally informed Argüello, drowsing in his bed, that he was no longer president.

Urgently convoked at 3 A.M., the Chamber declared Argüello "mentally incompetent" and gave him time to take refuge in the Mexican Embassy. One of "Tacho's" uncles, Benjamín Lacayo Sacasa, was named to succeed him. Carlos Pasos and Emiliano Chamorro, Somoza's opponents till that moment, came to his assistance in the coup d'état. The success of the provocation was complete: popular reaction was stifled by the National Guard and the Steel Helmet brigades, and the provisional president called constituent elections for August 1947. When the constituents foregathered, the Constitution was again changed without opposition, the Labor Code abolished, and octogenarian Victor Román y Reyes—who of course was another uncle of Somoza's—named as president.

The explanation of all the hurry lay in the imminence of the Ninth Pan-American Conference, and in the nonrecognition by American governments which, however, extended recognition after the farce—

with the sole and honorable exception of Guatemala. From then on, the tally of violent deaths of opposition leaders kept growing. Luis Horacio Scott, Julio Aguilar Martínez, Rito Jiménez Prado, Octavio Escobar, and Luis Felipe Gabuardi Lacayo are some of the hundreds of martyrs of liberty in Nicaragua who fell at the same National Guard hands that slew Sandino. Another, who fell in August 1947 along with some companions, was Sandino's friend, the glory-covered General Juan Gregorio Colindres. History does not list the hundreds of Nicaraguans jailed and the thousands exiled—some 30,000 to Costa Rica alone.

The ending of the war brought insecurity and pauperization to Nicaragua's workers and *campesinos*. It closed down many lucrative businesses, artificially created with no real roots in the characteristics of a country whose monoculture made its economy fragile—reduced by the demands of U.S. imperialism to a source of raw materials. The crisis that hit the United States in 1947 had its repercussions in Nicaragua from April of that year, when urban construction in Pacific cities was paralyzed by lack of materials and cash to cover wages, which dropped by 39 percent.

We have mentioned what happened with rubber. This was followed in May by reduction of work hours from eight to six in textiles, cement, shoes, furniture, and clothing. Wholesale and retail establishments laid off 45 percent of their employees, whose unemployment favored the competition for low wages, with an immediate effect on the tobacco, liquor, brewing, match, and sugar industries. In July, between two and three thousand men and women employees of the highway and other administrative departments were fired. There was a 50 percent drop in commercial activity. The closing of some mines "for lack of equipment and impossibility of obtaining it" was a new source of unemployment, aggravated by the dire situation of *campesinos* deprived of their means of sustenance by Somoza's and his clique's monopolization of lands.[21]

The reduction of U.S. purchases operated on the Nicaraguan economy with the force of capitalist logic, and although the price of coffee—35.5 percent of all Nicaraguan exports in 1948—remained the same or showed a tendency to rise, this alone could not remedy the situation. If capitalism's cyclical declines always hit colonial and dependent countries harder, the damage was the greater when a rapacious administration had concentrated transformation and light industries in a few hands and reduced their incentive to grow. A few people reaped the benefits and the vast majority received minimal and unstable incomes, limiting their buying capacity, discouraging production, and braking development of the incipient local bourgeoisie.

Finally, the vicious functioning of the Mortgage Bank—created basically to extend farm credits and stimulate production by the *campesinos*—served only to expand the government's interests to a point where in 1947, after four drought years, the bank could grant no more credit. The Credit and Mortgage Section of the National Bank had a similarly nepotistic policy, offering its reserves to the maximum to the regime's pets. For its part, the Anglo-American Bank, in the five years ending 1947, registered the concentration of capital in the following hands:

1. General Anastasio Somoza, secretary of war, navy, and air and chief of the National Guard.

2. Dr. Victor Román y Reyes, president of Nicaragua.

3. General Francisco Gaitán, chief of the National Guard general staff.

4. Rafael Huezo, manager of the National Bank of Nicaragua.

5. Dr. Luis Manuel Debayle, brother-in-law of Somoza, ex-foreign secretary, and ex-secretary of health and public assistance.

6. José Beneti Ramírez, ex-secretary of the treasury and public credit, president of the National Insurance Company, and ex-private secretary of the President of the Republic.

7. Colonel Julio Somoza García, brother of Somoza, secretary general of the National Guard general staff and military commander of the Carazo area.

8. Dr. Jesús Sánchez R., lawyer of the National Bank, ex-treasury secretary, partner of Somoza in the cement plant, and lawyer for all his commercial and industrial enterprises.

All this without considering the continuous flight of capital through dollar deposits and investments outside the country, above all in the United States—a drain that explains the mysterious decline of the *córdoba*, and a flight of capital continuing in the period of Román y Reyes' presidency.

And after the uncle, who? Once again the nephew, "democratically" elected (how could it be otherwise?) in 1950 to become lord and master not only of Nicaragua but also of the destinies of Central American neighbors, in his capacity as Cerberus for the Department of State.

His army's modern weapons, his aerodrome and bases always ready and equipped for any emergency, his lack of scruple, his unconditional submission to the United States, made him—along with Trujillo—the hangman of all liberation movements undertaken by Central American peoples: undertaken not only in their longing for independence from the politico-economic claws of imperialism, but in their most modest attempts to improve their wretched living standards and conditions of existence.

14
Sandino's Glory and Renown

How fiercely the people tear at the bit!
One day they lit their captive match, angrily prayed
And in the full roundness of their sovereignty
Reclaimed their birthright with spontaneous hands.
The despots' trump card—a padlock
With their dead bacteria inside it.
Battles? No, passions! And passions preceded
By agonies of people yearning to be men!
Death and passion of peace, the people!
Death and passion of war among the olive trees,
understand?

César Vallejo

When the day had come, it was the time not to die.

The sun rose like a beating drum, and the prostrate man listened to the voice, which was his own secret voice but he didn't know it then.

When the day had come, the prostrate man stood up (small as he was, giants envied his stature), shook his clothing, and marched smiling (with the face of a happy child) toward destiny.

When the particular day for rebellion had come and Job himself stopped cursing his birth cry, the prostrate man, transformed into a hero, discoverd that his voice, which he thought was a hermit's, was the magnified echo of clear and far-off voices that intoned the same credo.

Not then the clamorous voices of a brotherhood on a mountain peak. Ancestral feats have ever blended into a harmony with future dreams. Yes, and even with dreams undreamt, for what we yearn for is already half of what has yet to come. Those dreams have always striven not to crush the heart's present happiness.

When the day had come, all that is wise and just in a death was committed to the fists of the man no longer prostrate: his submission to life could be redeemed by a pure gesture in death's face.

The hero knew that the day had well and truly come, that the prophecy was true, that his mission was a great river on which generations of fire would overturn violence and scorn. The hero stopped despairing, and like an old father-god, leaned head on breast and rejoiced for mankind.

It happened in Latin America. As if to say, it happened in the world. True, it had happened often there as elsewhere; so that everything seemed a repetition, though all was re-created: the signs, the years, the balance, and certainly the battle.

Thus it was easy to be confused and hesitant and, in signaling the symbols and the footprints, to say for example "I am sure of Harmodius and Aristogeiton, of their names and swords,"[1] not suspecting how gravely one could be wrong. Or to think of Numancia[2] and despair of raising up a single name that would embody the fruitful agony of the fever for freedom.

So although it happened in Latin America, it belonged to the history of the world and its people: it was the same battle, old as the tree, always renewed and always the same in its Gracchi, its Spartaci, its Viriatos[3] and its Communards, its Babeufs, and its Servetuses,[4] its John Browns, its Tupacamarus and Pumacahuas,[5] its Saccos and Vanzettis.

When the desolate hero sought the hand that would enrich his cause, all Latin America poured forth its sons rank by rank: sea, earth, and air were astonished by this exodus that violated the norms of tourism and troubled the souls of scribes and priests.

Volunteers of Latin America, said those who took pride in them. Volunteers for death, said the pessimists. Volunteers for liberty, they themselves proclaimed. Was it not admirable that such a brotherhood should make itself a torrent and demolish walls?

And to make all complete, the poet across the seas—the one who said, "Each man is too much to be alone"—placed on the hero's head the matchless and eternal title: "General of Free Men."

Then what had been a cry became a symbol and what had been a passion, a banner; what had been agony became history. And when the day had passed and winds had carried away the cries and sighs and roars, the hero, close now to the profound death which he had regained, knew that so long as there was anyone to recall and love his memory, the footprint of his battle would not be lost.

I come to speak through your dead mouth.
Give me silence, water, hope,
Give me struggle, iron, volcanoes,
Let me cleave to the bodies as magnets.
Come into my veins and my mouth.
Speak with my words and my blood.

Pablo Neruda

Sandino was not only personal, desperate, and romantic rebellion by one man. Sandino is within each *campesino* who thinks with fury, as he wipes off his sweat, about the land that isn't his; within each mulatto who suffers and resents racial contempt; within each black who knows that it is the skin, not the heart, that hangs in the balance. Sandino is within every worker who, in a union or in the dungeon where the hangman immures them, toils at the task of justice. Within each student who writes or distributes the leaflet—always the same student, the same leaflet, from one age to the next.

Sandino lives among those who fought in Venezuela to put an end to the heirs of "bison" Gómez; among the miners who, in Cochabamba and La Paz, without tactics or strategy defeated the tactics and strategy of the Bolivian army, carrying on the torch of their brothers massacred at Catavi; among the peoples of the Guyanas who no doubt have their own redeeming Sandino. So many Sandinos, too, are those anonymous Guatemalan heroes who in 1944 put an end to the clown who believed himself Napoleon; who installed Latin America's miracle regime and sustained it till they could do so no more and were betrayed, sold out, and crushed in June 1954.

What if he had defects? They don't bother us. He made mistakes? What else is new? As if his formidable effort by its mere intention (and he didn't stop at intentions, as our northern friends well know) were not worth all the faults to be found in him by those who see history through a keyhole. As if his courage were not sufficient response to the clumsy subversion that Wall Street's adorers impute to him.

The passing years are the best judge. They slowly but remorselessly bury the memory of those who, by the injury they did to Sandino, did it to Latin America. And by contast, Sandino's epic of yesterday is today a legend and will tomorrow be a myth. All through Our America, signs of the immortality of his message shine out. As long as it exists, Our America will be no easy prisoner of the pirates and the merchants.

Our peoples saw rising from total anonymity a man who had been a *campesino,* a blue- and white-collar worker and a miner, whose one aspiration was to continue in any of these tasks once the goal that made his name famous was reached. They felt that dark dream of freedom to be theirs. They felt involved in the quixotic adventure against an enemy who, superior in numbers and arms, was shamefully whipped by a handful of daredevils. A handful meeting machine guns with sardine-can grenades, airplanes with antique rifles from the Cuban war, omnipotent force with guerrilla tactics, and the invader's mercenary spirit (his soldiers fought for pay) with the inflexibility of unpaid men who came from the ends of the earth to swell the general's free ranks.

In Sandino, the peoples of Our America saw old debts being collected from the original conquistadors and from the modern ones. They felt that their language, their race, and their unjust fate were taking revenge on those who had enslaved them on their own earth. They saw the road reopening which, once followed to the end, would vindicate, ennoble, and liberate them. Our America had faith in Sandino. It knew that his was not the gesture of a belated romantic but the call of all its peoples to rebel in common battle.

For that reason Sandino triumphed. Not only because the invaders ended by having to retire, but because he showed that our peoples possess within themselves what it takes for liberation, and showed himself as an example of that possibility. With the fixation of expelling the invaders from his country, he directed everything to this single end, unsuspecting that they had subtler means than armed brutality. That, in the last analysis, was but the circumstantial expression of a policy that had won its basic objective before his rebellion exploded: bases in the Gulf of Fonseca, the concession for a canal, and above all, the means to dominate the nation's economic life and make it a dependent colony of their vast economic empire.

Sandino neither would nor could see beyond his immediate objective, to stop the intervention. That once achieved, he thought, Nicaraguans—and by extension Latin Americans—would solve their problems, the parties would be honest, the military less ambitious, the businessmen more honorable, and the workers and *campesinos* less despoiled. His political ingenuousness made him commit gross errors, one of which cost his life.

Yet history offers few examples of such material disinterest linked with guerrilla genius; of such modesty that when he spoke of his country's destiny he sinned with pride; of a political naiveté that did not blind him to the identity of his people's executioners; of timidity that did not stand in the way of his courage; of human, fraternal feeling that did not silence a gun; of a haughtiness that took pride in possession of a manual job rather than in personal splendors. Men like Sandino reconcile slaves with hope and the oppressed with destiny. Such men recognize defeats, turn the fiercest battles in their own favor, physically fortify the weakest. Such a man endows the word "hero" with its highest significance.

With his death, his personal battle became all America's patrimony. You will not find him in the official books which raise the withered patrioteer's flag to hide the sinister reality of betrayal, sellout, and submission. Nor in the cult of spreading names through the continent's streets, plazas, and cities, careful not to reveal the unpublished pages of its hallowed men of straw; and likewise omitting the jails, tortures, firing squads, loans, concessions, military interventions, scramble for markets, and imperialist division of territories, and the criminal disunity of our peoples' discussions, a disunity fomented and maintained to keep us in weakness and inertia.

Which is the Latin American history of infamy.

The infamous American history whose chief figures in order of appearance—Spain, Britain, the United States—turned our lands into dependent colonies, our governments into operetta puppets, our people into asocial beings, our culture and civilization into a strange goulash without guide or cohesion, our future into a terrifying question mark.

The American history of infamy.

Sandino rose against it with nothing but his fists and his fury at feeling himself a slave. He triumphed, yes, in the limited plan he set himself, but he did not end the slavery of his compatriots. At the most, the enslavers changed tactics, and secular oppression continued, constant, shameful, insulting. And Sandino paid for his rebellion with his life. His magnificent life that filled with glory seven years of the history of a scorned continent—a continent that did not reject him, recognizing in him the beloved son who justified it and pointed toward a future free from oppression and bitterness.

No effort is lost, no gesture is sterile; behind every affirmation is the will to resist; in every rebellion is the instinct of justice; in times of oppression the ability to rebel is the one freedom that is not lost. Hence Sandino did not pass in vain through his Nicaragua, nor die uselessly for his Latin America.

Afterword

After forty-three years of opprobrium and infamy, at the price of thousands of lives, *los muchachos* have won the day in Nicaragua.[1] All the Somozas have fled and the *sandinista* National Liberation Front has taken over a devastated land: a land made much poorer by Anastasio II, last of his bloody line, who thus fulfilled his ghastly prophecy of a year earlier, "If I have to go, I'll go over a mountain of corpses."

When this book first appeared, in September 1955, I saw it as reflecting no more than my modest determination to denounce. I wrote it in the heat of moral and political indignation at the overthrow of Jacobo Arbenz Guzmán, constitutional president of Guatemala, in June 1954. My study of the woeful Guatemalan events meant exploring the overall problems of Central America and the relations of its five countries with the nation whose aggressions covered a century of history since "filibuster" William Walker. It was in the course of that exploration that I came upon the figure of Augusto Calderón Sandino, who moved, captured, and held me.

Preparing the second edition, corrected and amplified more than twice, I found myself with spoken and written materials that called for a second book, *El pequeño ejército loco*—The Mad Little Army— documenting the role of Frank B. Kellogg's and Calvin Coolidge's oil policy in the State Department–White House intrigue of December 1926. Since it was at Mexico that Kellogg and Coolidge pointed their guns, Mexico became unforeseeably involved in the Nicaraguan tragedy. And another unforeseen phenomenon in the history of those days was this man Sandino. Not a wholly new one, however, for he had been preceded a decade earlier by the noble lawyer-general Benjamín F. Zeledón. Zeledón died in action on the day— October 4, 1912—when U.S. army and marine forces, commanded by Colonel Joseph Pendleton and Major Smedley Butler, stormed El Coyotepe and then took the town of Masaya, where Zeledón attempted a symbolic stand against what immediately followed: foreign occupation of Nicaragua.

Sandino saw himself as Zeledón's successor. "The Bryan-Chamorro Treaty," he said, "produced the revolution of 1912 which culminated in the killing of that undefeated and glorious general, Benjamín Zeledón. At that time I was a kid of seventeen and I witnessed the crushing of Nicaraguans in Masaya and other parts of the Republic by North American filibusters. I saw Zeledón's body buried in Catarina, a town near my own. His death gave me the key to our country's plight in face of North American piracy; so we see our war as a continuation of his."[2]

After Sandino's premeditated and treacherous death, his murderer prepared to take power; took it in January 1937; and directly or through straw men held it for himself and his heirs—Luis Anastasio and Anastasio Jr.—until July 18, 1979. So that the term "dynasty" is no more exaggerated than in the case of Haiti's Duvaliers. The murder of Sandino, with the complicity or silence of the United States which picked Somoza to head the National Guard, was the first step toward making Nicaragua a family fiefdom and an economic, political, and military appendage of Washington.

Many years had to pass before the people, enslaved by external and internal "gringos," would find the tools to heave this spurious mixed vassalage off their backs. And among the tools they found useful, it seems, were my two books. As a journalist committed to Our America's cause, I am grateful for having lived to see Sandino's triumph through his children and grandchildren—the people—who took up on a mass scale the torch held almost alone by Zeledón and his disciple. Their fatherland's honor and dignity have again been redeemed.

It is also exhilarating for me that twenty-five years after the appearance of this first youthful work, a publisher of such prestige as Monthly Review Press finds it worth translating and publishing. I ask indulgence for the small vanity of a political militant, and for the professional kind of vanity, as the one responsible for unearthing from an obscure letter by Henri Barbusse the most beautiful of all possible military ranks conferrable upon Sandino: "General of Free Men." The inspiration for my book on "The Mad Little Army" came from another letter I unearthed, by the Chilean poet Gabriela Mistral.

What I tried to re-create, as a simple chronicler of the Sandino epic, has become his people's inheritance. In them Sandino rides again, shaking off the dust of calculated oblivion with which yesterday's and today's invaders covered him. On horse or mule or foot, he has returned to dwell in his fatherland forever. He does not belong to us, nor only to the Nicaraguans, but to all of Our America for which he fought, suffered and died. But all his is the honor and glory of a resurrected Nicaragua, restored to life by its illustrious patriots' virtue and valor. A Nicaragua where today he is justified and gratefully loved by the *muchachos,* who are his *muchachos.*

No better note on which to conclude these reflections than José Martí's lines written nearly a century ago:

"When there are many men lacking decency, there are always others who have in themselves the decency of many. They are the ones who rebel with terrible force against the robbers of their peoples' freedom—hence robbers of their decency. Such men are the embodiment of thousands, of a whole people, of human dignity. Such men are sacred."

How much decency is embodied in a Zeledón, a Sandino, a Rigoberto López Pérez, a Carlos Fonseca Amador; in a handful of men and women, known or unknown, who rebel against the thieves with the dignity and honor of their country! Sacred are their names, and with them goes the hope of Nicaragua, of our new America!

Gregorio Selser
Mexico, September 1979

Notes

Chapter 1: The Eagle Over His Quarry

1. Nicholas J. Spykman, *America's Strategy in World Politics* (New York: Harcourt, Brace, 1942), pp. 63–64.
2. This right was canceled in 1937 under an agreement between Presidents Franklin D. Roosevelt and Lázaro Cárdenas.
3. Edward C. Kirkland, *A History of American Economic Life*, 4th ed. (New York: Irvington, 1969).
4. John T. Flynn, *Men of Wealth* (New York: Arno, 1971).
5. Stewart H. Holbrook, *The Age of the Moguls* (New York: Doubleday, 1953).
6. Lorenzo Montúfar, *Reseña histórica de Centro-América,* vol. 7 (Guatemala: La Unión, 1887), document 1, pp. 519–20.
7. Vicente Sáenz, "Pasado, presente y porvenir de Centroamérica (II)," *Cuadernos Americanos* (Mexico), no. 6 (November-December 1944), pp. 40–41.
8. Germán Arciniegas, *Entre la libertad y el miedo* (Mexico: Ediciones Cuadernos Americanos, 1952), p. 232.

Chapter 2: Filibusters in White Gloves

1. Samuel Flagg Bemis, *The Latin American Policy of the United States* (New York: Harcourt, Brace, 1943), p. 114.
2. Under this treaty, Britain with its large territorial claims in Central America (Belize/British Honduras, Mosquito Coast, Bay Islands) and the United States with none (but about to make treaties with Nicaragua and Honduras) agreed not to "obtain or maintain any exclusive control of the proposed" Nicaragua canal and to "extend their protection to any other practicable communications . . . across the isthmus. . . ." Nor would either "occupy, or fortify, or colonize, or assume or exercise any dominion over Nicaragua, Costa Rica, the Mosquito Coast or any part of Central America." Notes the *Encyclopaedia Britannica* (11th ed., vol. 6, p. 475): "The phraseology reflects the effort made by the United States to render impossible a physical control of the canal by Great Britain through the territory held by her at its mouth. . . ."
3. A *Gaceta Oficial de Honduras* article on May 30, 1857, indicates that the Hondurans also perceived this: "When one considers the ideas expressed by our colleagues *El Heraldo* of New York and the *Unión* of Washington, one can see that we have not advanced a step toward tranquility and individual and territorial security. According to the *Unión,* the present U.S. administration proposes to exclude all intervention by Britain in Central American affairs and ignore the existing treaties between both governments, arrogating to itself the exclusive right to run our business without intervention from any other country on earth.

Who has given the United States such rights over us? Does a nation, or do individuals, perchance have more right to butt into a neighbor's affairs than a more distant friend has? . . . If the United States wants an honest intervention in Central American affairs, such as is required by friendly relations between two countries, by justice and equity and common decency, why this egotistical jealousy toward an intervention from another quarter? If the North Americans have honest intentions, what is it to them that another nation also mixes in our affairs, when we have the same friendly relations with both and participation in our well-being is equally open to all? The only logical conclusion is that their insidious policy conceals a direct interest of little advantage to us, that all their ideas conceal a fact of grave importance, as their editors put it. And what is that fact of grave importance? The absorption of Hispanic America. For that is what was agreed at the Ostend Conference; that is what suits their aggrandizement and interests; that coincides with the desires shown by their people; that is the meaning of the designation for the new cabinet of men whose views are well-known throughout the world; that is what both the Northern and Southern U.S. press is saying; and we have proof of it in the protection given till now to the filibusters by that same government. . . ."

4. Isidro Fabela, *Los Estados Unidos contra la libertad* (Barcelona: Talleres Gráficos Lux, [circa 1920]), p. 165.
5. Harry Elmer Barnes, preface to C. D. Kepner Jr. and J. H. Soothill, *Banana Empire: A Case Study of Economic Imperialism* (New York: Russell, 1967 [1935]).
6. Scott Nearing and Joseph Freeman, *Dollar Diplomacy* (New York: Monthly Review Press, 1966 [1926]). (Translator's note.)
7. David R. Moore, *A History of Latin America* (New York: Prentice-Hall, 1938).
8. Vicente Sáenz, *Rompiendo cadenas,* 2nd ed. (Mexico: Unión Democrática Centroamericana, 1951), p. 187.
9. Vicente Sáenz, *Norteamericanización de Centro América* (San José de Costa Rica: Talleres de la Opinión, 1925), p. 51.
10. Quoted in Nearing and Freeman, *Dollar Diplomacy,* p. 152.
11. "I visited the Secretary of State with the express purpose of stating my government's position in the matter of the difficulties with . . . Nicaragua, and so informed him. In a previous talk with him I had brought to his attention the effort of my government to maintain neutrality and its intention to observe the Washington Treaty and Conventions. And as I confirmed this I could not but observe that what I said in no way pleased him. . . . Worried about the way he took it, I went to Undersecretary Wilson. . . . Looking further into the State Department's strange reaction to our attitude, I regretfully deduced . . . that by violating our territory . . . Zelaya was considered to have won a triumph . . . at irreparable cost for the revolutionaries. . . . They believe here that the Costa Rican government is quite indifferent to the violation of its territory. A candid move would be well received and would save us from embarrassing situations. We are in danger of losing sympathy."

Chapter 3: The United States Invents Quisling

1. Letter of January 7, 1915, cited in U.S., Congress, Senate, *Congressional Record,* 69th Cong., 2nd sess., 1927, 63, pt. 2: 1557.

2. U.S. Department of State, *Papers Relating to the Foreign Relations of the United States,* 1909, p. 452.

3. Ibid., pp. 455–57.

4. José Santos Zelaya, *La revolución de Nicaragua y los Estados Unidos* (Madrid: B. Rodríguez, 1910), p. 139.

5. Zelaya commented in his book: "Those men could not be treated like prisoners of war taken from the enemy in an international conflict; they were filibusters at the service of an internal revolution, paid to create havoc and death; foreign mercenaries who came to augment our misfortunes not for love of a country that was not theirs, but to get money from rebels and traitors who were staining the national soil with blood."

6. Scott Nearing and Joseph Freeman, *Dollar Diplomacy* (New York: Monthly Review Press, 1966 [1926]), pp. 154–55: "When Brown Brothers and Company learned of these plans they offered to the State Department to float the Nicaraguan loan. These bankers had entered into an agreement with the George D. Emery Company to collect their claim from Nicaragua, which had been settled for $600,000 in September, 1909, just before Zelaya fell. On February 2, 1911, Brown Brothers and Company wrote to Secretary of State Knox: 'We understand that the Government of Nicaragua is considering the advisability of obtaining a new loan for the purpose of refunding her present indebtedness and of providing for other governmental needs. We also understand that, in order to secure such loan upon advantageous terms, the Government of Nicaragua is desirous of enlisting the good offices of our own Government and of entering into engagements with it which shall furnish a satisfactory basis for such security as may be required. Should this information be substantially correct, we beg to say that, as bankers, we shall be glad to have the opportunity of negotiating for such a loan. Apart from our general interest in a matter of this kind, we beg to add that we are interested in the George D. Emery Co.'s claim against Nicaragua, under the protocol of September 18, 1909 and that we have, therefore, a peculiar interest in the readjustment of that country's finances.'"

7. The Secretary said that "the officers and men participated in the bombardment of Managua, a night ambuscade in Masaya, the surrender of General Mena and his rebel army at Granada, the surrender of the rebel gunboats *Victoria* and *Noventa y Tres,* the assault and capture of Coyotepe, the defense of Paso Caballos bridge, including garrison and other duty at Corinto, Chinandega and elsewhere" (U.S. Naval Department, *Annual Report,* 1912–1913, p. 38). Nearing and Freeman, *Dollar Diplomacy,* p. 164, note that on September 4, 1912, "the State Department notified the U.S. ambassador in Managua that 'the American bankers who have made investments in relation to railroads and steamships in Nicaragua, in connection with a plan for the relief of the financial distress of that country, have applied for protection.'"

As for Major Smedley Butler of the U.S. Marines, his statement as a general testifying before the Congress in 1935 would become famous: "I spent 33 years and 4 months in active service as a member of our country's most agile military force—the Marine Corps. I served in all commissioned ranks from a second lieutenant to Major-General. And during that period I spent most of my time being a high-class muscle man for Big Business, for Wall Street and for the bankers. In short, I was a racketeer for capitalism.

"I suspected I was just part of a racket at the time. Now I am sure of it. Like all members of the military profession I never had an original thought until I left the service. My mental faculties remained in suspended animation while I obeyed the orders of the higher-ups. This is typical of everyone in the military service.

"I helped make Mexico and especially Tampico safe for American oil interests in 1914. I helped make Haiti and Cuba a decent place for the National City Bank boys to collect revenues in. I helped in the raping of half a dozen Central American republics for the benefit of Wall Street. The record of racketeering is long. I helped purify Nicaragua for the international banking house of Brown Brothers in 1909–12. I brought light to the Dominican Republic for American sugar interests in 1916. I helped get Honduras 'right' for American fruit companies in 1903. In China in 1927 I helped see to it that Standard Oil went its way unmolested.

"During those years, I had, as the boys in the back room always say, a swell racket. I was rewarded with honors, medals, promotions. Looking back on it, I feel I might have given Al Capone a few hints. The best *he* could do was to operate his racket in three city districts. We Marines operated on three *continents*."
(Reproduced in *Common Sense* [New York] 4, no. 11 [November 1935], p. 8.)
8. *Papers Relating to the Foreign Relations of the United States,* 1912, pp. 1043–44.
9. Argüello wrote: "Nicaragua is a free, sovereign, and independent nation. Sovereignty is one, inalienable, and inviolable and resides essentially in the people from whom the officials established by Constitution and laws derive their power. Consequently, pacts and treaties cannot be made which are contrary to the nation's independence and integrity or in any way affect its sovereignty. (Art. 2.) In conformity with these principles the intervention of U.S. forces in our affairs damages our sovereignty and is an outrage imposed by force upon the rights of a weak people. The argument is without validity that U.S. forces landed to protect the railroad because it is contractually pledged to North American bankers . . . the national railroad was put up as security, remaining the nation's property . . . but even were it the exclusive property of a U.S. company, this would give the U.S. government no right to intervene directly. . . . In conclusion . . . I will hardly surprise you by asking whether the relations between the United States and Nicaragua are those of peace or of war. . . ."
10. *Papers Relating to the Foreign Relations of the United States,* 1912, pp. 1093–1100.
11. Nearing and Freeman, *Dollar Diplomacy,* pp. 159–60.
12. El Salvador proposed that Taft should insinuate to Nicaragua the necessity of seeking a peaceful solution, and Taft replied that the United States government had no intention of leaving its citizens in Nicaragua at the mercy of a rebellion

that had committed the flagrant violations of the principles of honor, of humanity, of order, and of civilization, but that it did intend, in conformity with the request of the Nicaraguan government, to protect its interests and the securing of peace.

13. Charles P. Howland, ed., *Survey of American Foreign Relations* (New Haven: Yale University Press, 1929), p. 181.

14. Nearing and Freeman, *Dollar Diplomacy*, p. 167. (Translator's note.)

15. John Kenneth Turner noted in *Shall It Be Again?* (New York: B. W. Huebsch, 1922): "The fact that a portion of our naval force was enacting the role of an alien army of occupation in a Central American republic was briefly mentioned at long intervals in the press. At such times a phrase or two, such as 'protecting American lives and property,' or 'a legation guard,' was all the explanation deemed necessary. During Wilson's eight years in the Presidential chair, no serious criticism of our occupation of Nicaragua was seen in any of our leading newspapers or magazines. Nor did the national law-making body make any demand upon the Executive for an accounting of his acts. Of the so-called Canal Convention Senator Borah remarked: 'If the American people had known all the circumstances of its making it would never have been made.' That was about all. Evidently the press as a whole, and the leaders of both great political parties, approved of the Wilson policy in Nicaragua. When Wilson's successor continued it, no protest was heard. The policy had, in fact, been initiated by Wilson's predecessor in office.

"For authentic details we may turn to the hearings on the Nicaraguan convention, conducted by the Senate Foreign Relations Committee early in 1916. These hearings were printed 'in confidence,' for the use of the committee only, one copy going to each member under an injunction of secrecy. The writer has had access to one of these committee copies.

"An examination of this secret government document shows the hearings to have been in the nature of a 'frame-up.' That is to say, neither Nicaraguans nor Americans who opposed the convention were given an opportunity to testify. Only one witness was heard who was not either interested in putting the convention through, or in some way connected with the interested parties. In spite of the suppression of illuminating details inevitable from such an arrangement, the document discloses the following essential facts:

"1. That the permanent occupation of Nicaragua was undertaken by the Taft Administration for the purpose of sustaining in power a 'president' opposed by an overwhelming majority of the voters of the country.

"2. That said president, Adolfo Díaz, was raised to power neither by the votes of Nicaraguans, nor the arms of Nicaraguans, but by the armed forces of the United States under the direction of the President of the United States.

"3. That, as a means to raising Adolfo Díaz to the presidency and maintaining him there, we conducted a series of unlawful military campaigns, killed scores of Nicaraguans, overturned three successive governments, seized public and private property, and prosecuted an actual war of conquest until in complete possession of the country.

"4. That Adolfo Díaz, on becoming president, found that he could do nothing of his own volition, but was required to take orders like a butler.

"5. That American domination of Nicaragua did not bring a single 'American benefit' to the Nicaraguan people; that what liberties Nicaraguan citizens had were permanently taken away; that a free press, free speech and free suffrage are unknown; that the government of Nicaragua under the American protectorate is a pure autocracy, administered by aliens, which is forced to hold the Nicaraguan people under a reign of terror in order to perpetuate itself in power.

"6. That the sole purpose of the American war on that little republic was to compel Nicaragua to submit to a general looting of her rich resources by American financiers.

"7. That Woodrow Wilson carried out in every essential the purpose of the conquest begun under Taft; that the looting of Nicaragua under American guns was given a color of legality only under the Wilson regime, by the ratification of the Nicaraguan convention on the recommendation of Wilson.

"8. That the feature of this convention, relating to the 'purchase' of a canal concession and the 'lease' of naval bases, was an after-thought, conceived and put through primarily as a blind, to hide the purely financial features of the protectorate.

"9. That the actual arbiter of Nicaraguan destinies under the protectorate is none other than the local representative of the syndicate of New York bankers for whose benefit the conquest was undertaken and the convention put through."

16. David R. Moore, *A History of Latin America* (New York: Prentice-Hall, 1938), pp. 703–04.

17. U.S., Congress, Senate, *Congressional Record,* 67th Cong., 2nd sess., 1922, 62, pt. 9: 8941.

18. Ramón de Belausteguigoitia, *Con Sandino en Nicaragua* (Madrid: Espasa-Calpe, 1934), p. 51.

Chapter 4: "A Short-lived Benevolent Imperialism"

1. Samuel Flagg Bemis, *The Latin American Policy of the United States* (New York: Harcourt, Brace, 1943), p. x.

2. Charles Evans Hughes, from a speech delivered in Brazil on the 100th anniversary of Brazilian independence, in *Bulletin of the Pan American Union* 55 (November 1922), 435.

3. Sofonías Salvatierra, *Azul y blanco* (Managua: Tipografía Progreso, 1919), pp. 114–15.

4. Hildebrando A. Castellón, *Historia patria elemental para las escuelas de Nicaragua* (Managua: Talleres Gráficos Pérez, 1940), p. 105: "With the Lansing Plan the government of Nicaragua approved the contracts with the holders of external bonds in London, with the New York bankers and with the National Bank of Nicaragua, and the High Commission was set up as fiscal agent. The internal debt was recognized by this commission, which thus won the same reputation as the Mixed Commission of previous years. Careful analysis of the government's contracts and negotiations during 1917 shows extremely harsh conditions, inflated interest, and large capital as security for very little money."

5. Laudelino Moreno, *Historia de las relaciones interstaduales de Centroamérica* (Madrid: Monografías Hispano-Americanas, Editorial CIAP), pp. 330ff, contains such juicy details of the San José conference as:

"The third and fourth clauses—'the Federation guarantees in all the states freedom of suffrage and alternation of power' and 'henceforth no state may enter into contracts that could in any way compromise its sovereignty or territorial integrity'—were rejected by Nicaraguan delegate Castillo . . . stating that his government had contracts with Brown Brothers and Company and J. and W. Seligman Company which, like the Bryan-Chamorro Treaty, should not be subject to the Federation's jurisdiction. This deepened the belief that Nicaragua would not come into the Federal Pact. . . .

"In the next session . . . Sr. Castillo produced a telegram from his government demanding express recognition of the validity of the Bryan-Chamorro Treaty. . . . This was rejected. . . .

"The day before the pact was to be signed, the conference chairman received an exposition from Nicaraguan delegate Dr. Pasos Arana (replacement for Castillo) which upset all the work that had been done. It said that Union was desired by Nicaragua, and by its government, which, despite all that has been said, 'truly represents its people's will'; that the chief Nicaraguan delegate was so strongly pro-Union that he had imperturbably remained at his post despite being sick, and had remained serene in the face of attacks from a press inspired by error and injustice. . . . But 'the government of Nicaragua, with full reason, finds it impossible to sign the pact as presently drawn up because it is contrary to the honor and dignity of the Republic to admit for one moment the inference that Nicaragua could have been beyond its rights in signing the Bryan-Chamorro Treaty, or that the treaty could have been damaging to the interests of Central America.'" Having previously agreed to sign the unity pact on the following day, the delegate concluded his statement: "The time has come to announce our delegation's departure."

6. Curious to find missing from so many proscriptions the fact of having been a minister, ambassador, or military attaché in Washington, a characteristic to become frequent in the biographies of Latin American dictators.

7. James Truslow Adams, *The March of Democracy: A History of the United States* (New York: Charles Scribner's Sons, 1965 [1933]), vol. 4, p. 293.

8. Alfredo L. Palacios, *Nuestra América y el imperialismo yanqui* (Madrid: Editorial Historia Nueva, 1930), p. 70.

9. In a dispatch from New York published by *La Nación* (Buenos Aires) on July 18, 1925, the Associated Press reported: "Chairman Borah of the Senate Foreign Relations Committee has published an article in *Forum* magazine calling for the future Pan-American policy of the United States to be based on reason and not on force. The article, 'The Fetish of Force,' stresses the need to spread throughout the Western hemisphere an atmosphere 'of demonstration of good faith and moral force' in accordance with the spirit of the U.S. Constitution, since this would be the United States' greatest contribution to world peace. . . . He calls recent U.S. treatment of Central American republics 'a very sad chapter in our

international relations . . . we have been consistently unjust. . . . The invasion of Nicaragua was not necessary and hence immoral. . . . While we resort with such facility to force, our talk of replacing force and violence with law and order is nothing but hypocrisy. . . . When will we begin to act honestly? . . .'"

10. Quoted in Máximo Soto Hall, *Nicaragua y el imperialismo norteamericano* (Buenos Aires: Editorial Artes y Letras, 1928), p. 94.

11. Salvador Mendieta, "Sinopsis para Nicaragua y el imperialismo norteamericano," in ibid., p. 80: "To what extent Coolidge and Kellogg really believed in the bolshevism, Mexicanism, and anti-Americanism which Chamorro, Díaz, and the Jewish bankers attributed to Sacasa, one cannot precisely know; but it is certain that both have acted in bad faith, coldly calculating how best to serve the New York bankers, using for the purpose Adolfo Díaz, the most contemptible political pimp so far produced by Central America. Aiding this pimp with recognition of military legitimacy, with air support and the landing of strong U.S. army contingents . . . Washington has cruelly, coldly, and implacably prolonged the horrors of civil war in Nicaragua, with the deliberate object . . . of compromising our finances . . . and assuring for the immediate future the vilest degradation of our poliical parties and public men. Liberals and Conservatives assert that Dennis advised recognition of Díaz after Díaz paid him $120,000—$60,000 in cash and the rest when the secretary of state would confirm recognition."

In *Sandino o la tragedia de un pueblo* (Madrid: Europa, 1934), p. 39, Sofonías Salvatierra writes: When General Chamorro took the Tiscapa fortress on October 25, 1925, it is unclear whether this was by agreement with the U.S. minister on the understanding that the Conservative *caudillo* would replace don Carlos, or whether after aliminating Solórzano the presidency would immediately be given to Adolfo Díaz. . . . In any case, while the State Department did not recognize Chamorro, officials of the economic intervention put no obstacle in his path either in the customs, the bank, or the railroad."

A final pearl about Lawrence Dennis, from George Seldes' *One Thousand Americans* (New York: Boni & Gaer, 1948), pp. 93–94: "An investigation of the contents of the *American Mercury* during the Palmer-Spivak regime discloses the important fact that the first printing in favor of an American fascist party and movement appeared in this magazine. The writer was Lawrence Dennis, who used some of the same material for his book *The Coming American Fascism* (Harper & Bros., 1936), and who was later among the group indicted on the charges of conspiracy to commit sedition—the only 'intellectual' in the lot, as the newspapers reported. . . . Mr. DeWitt Wallace, editor of *Reader's Digest*, indignantly denied all charges that he himself was in favor of some of the things Hitler and Mussolini had done, as *In Fact* charged in 1942, and said statements attributed to him were 'unadulterated lies.' . . .

"In 1947, following a statement by Mr. O. John Rogge, the government's prosecutor in the trial of alleged seditionists, Mr. Wallace was forced to admit that after Dennis had published his overt fascist articles in the *American Mercury* he had been hired for editorial work on the *Reader's Digest*."

12. *La Nación,* December 29, 1925.

13. *La Nación,* December 28, 1926.
14. For more details of this campaign and a more complete explanation of U.S. intervention in Nicaragua, see Gregorio Selser, *El pequeño ejército loco (Operación México-Nicaragua)* (Buenos Aires: Editorial Triangulo, 1958).
15. U.S., Congress, Senate, *Congressional Record,* 69th Cong., 2nd sess., 1927, 68, pt. 2: 1326.
16. *Sandino o la tragedia de un pueblo,* p. 40.
17. Vicente Sáenz, *Rompiendo cadenas,* 2nd ed., (Mexico: Unión Democrática Centroamericana, 1951), p. 36. Sáenz adds: "The little republic was obligated to liquidate to the last centavo the debt it contracted for rifles, machine guns, and millions of cartridges that the regime imposed by the White House received from the United States in token of cordial friendship; amortization and interest on loans contracted by the so-called President Díaz; all the inflated sums spent by Colonel Stimson and his aides on those arms, almost all of which had fallen into the rebels' hands; and of course indemnities to U.S. citizens for 'damages suffered in the revolution.' Washington so stirred up and prolonged the revolutionary movement that, in strict justice, the U.S. Treasury had to meet the claims of its citizens. These claims amounted by May 1927 to $8 million, and it was mixed tribunals, composed as usual of two North Americans to one Nicaraguan, that had to resolve them."

Chapter 5: Sandino, Hero of Las Segovias

1. Samuel Flagg Bemis, *The Latin American Policy of the United States* (New York: Harcourt, Brace, 1943), p. 212.
2. Since his father and mother were unmarried, he had no right to the name Sandino till he was fifteen, after which he signed his name "Augusto C. [for Calderón] Sandino." It was probably the people themselves who dubbed him "Augusto César," as he became known.
3. George Seldes notes in *Lords of the Press* (New York: Julian Messner, 1938), p. 136: "In 1927 Mr. Charles Merz, who had collaborated with Walter Lippmann seven years earlier in exposing the perverted news and downright lies about the Russian Soviets in their first three years, made a survey of the news from Mexico. He showed that the [New York] *Times* story, 'Spread of Disorders Alarms Mexico,' was nothing but a murder and two holdups in three days, a record far below Chicago's. When the oil laws were put into effect the *Times* headline was 'Mexico Is Pictured on Brink of Revolt.' January 24, 1927, the *Times* had a story of a big effort to overthrow the regime which was nothing but a statement from Adolfo de la Huerta who was in exile in the United States."
4. In this connection Nemesio García Naranjo's article published by *La Nación* (Buenos Aires) in June 1928 deserves reprinting here: "U.S. policy in Nicaragua and in Mexico," he wrote, "plainly shows that economic measures are much more effective than warlike ones to make weak peoples capitulate. When he had Sandino to deal with, Mr. Calvin Coolidge lost his cool and ordered his troops to crush the man by force. With Calles, who seemed to be set on defying U.S. rights,

the U.S. president proposed an economic blockade. The result: General Calles has been completely subjugated by the White House, General Sandino continues making war upon the U.S. soldiery.

"This experience will profoundly influence the future international procedures of the Anglo-Saxon colossus. The North Americans are characterized by their practical spirit and lack of conquistadorial pride. Why crush the rebels by highly scandalous and costly military operations, when better results are obtainable by not using armed force?

"A year and a half ago Mexico was reportedly about to bring into force laws that would damage the oil companies operating there. Secretary of State Kellogg had sent two protest notes to which Mexico's foreign secretary had sent vigorous replies. The U.S. government seemed to be resigned, but the oil companies halted their operations; no new wells were drilled, thousands of workers became idle, and Mexican oil production dropped from second place in the world (1926) to fourth. The treasury saw its income shrinking month by month by many millions and a grim economic crisis loomed on the horizon. Faced with this prospect, Calles reformed the laws or, to speak more frankly, annulled them, since everything went back to the way it was before the controversy. Without the United States having to send a single soldier to Mexico, nor even to send another note, an apparently ungovernable rebellion was completely crushed.

"With Sandino it has been just the reverse. Two batallions were sent against him, then two more; countless protests have rung out around the world; many have fallen on the battlefield, but the rebellion continues and looks as threatening as ever. Unquestionably Sandino will lose in the end, but the victory, apart from being very costly, will bring in its train lowered moral and material prestige for the United States. While Calles' submission equips Mr. Coolidge with the halo of being astute, practical, and cool, the campaign against Sandino has left the president with an unenviable reputation for stupidity, opportunism, and violence.

"The comparative results suffice to condemn military interventions, not only as unjust but because they are counterproductive. Defenders of the interventionist principle at the Cuba Conference said with abundant reason that all countries must respect the interests of foreigners; but where they departed from reason and justice was in tacitly admitting that countries ignoring that obligation could be subdued by arms.

"This process of reasoning against peoples that cannot or will not fulfill their international duties is like the logic of those sages of the past century who defended prison for civil debt. They said with total justice that all debts must be paid, but with total iniquity that prison should be used to coerce debtors into paying.

"How then is the observance of law to be enforced? Ah, but law has infinite ways to make itself respected without having to resort to crime. At the beginning of the nineteenth century most people believed in good faith (probably even the debtors believed it) that abolition of prison for debt would undermine society. Yet today we see clearly that with the disappearance of such prisons, credit operations instead of disappearing have multiplied fantastically. Creditors lend more money than ever, and credit is much more protected than formerly. Brutality has never been an effective sanction.

"Lack of protection of the law carries with it the worst of punishments. Individuals and peoples alike who ignore its obligations close upon themselves the doors to wealth and success. And when they realize that the wrong road leads to penury, they turn back to law because they understand that it is the only road to prosperity.

"If Mr. Coolidge had proceeded with Calles as he did in Nicaragua; if he had sent an army to Tampico to stop the announced laws from coming into force; if he had dishonored law by enforcing it with violence; then apart from not obtaining a satisfactorily practical result, he would have stirred throughout the world, and especially in Latin America, a storm of curses and protests.

"Of course Calles' admirers must feel embittered by the submission of the man who seemed to symbolize his nation, to be the sentinel of Latin Americanism: a man apparently worthy of all the sonorous and empty titles showered on those to whom a valiantly rebellious spirit against the United States is attributed. It would have been sad if Calles had fallen as Sandino is going to fall one of these days, riddled with U.S. machine gun bullets. But from a romantic point of view it is sadder to see him crawling to White House orders.

"A passionate fellow with whom I discussed this sad business said it was preferable to see U.S. imperialism armed, with medieval finery and shamelessly hoisting the conquistador's banner. Romantically speaking, yes. But romanticism is something that is felt by the human community only exceptionally, and for that reason we cannot take it as a norm for daily life. Although an acute sentimentalism makes the suave manner of the usurer abhorrent to us, it is always better to deal with Shylocks than with sergeants.

"Let Calles and Sandino bear witness! While Sandino will soon repose in a humble cemetery or an anonymous hero's ditch for continuing to fight General Lejeune, Calles is enchanted with Mr. Dwight Morrow, partner in the banking house of John Pierpont Morgan. Sandino will have been conquered; Calles has been convinced."

5. As U.S. liberal historian David R. Moore describes it in *A History of Latin America* (New York: Prentice-Hall, 1938), p. 705:

"An American army in Nicaragua would maintain order, protect concessions, and promote material welfare. Without it there would be, temporarily at least, civil conflict, probably great loss of life, diminished returns from investments; but also a chance for rule by the majority, not by a minority. Foreign domination meant suppression of freedom and, in certain cases at least, of justice. A criticism that was made of President Coolidge was that he played the lone hand: he set up the United States as the sole guardian of law, order, and justice instead of associating himself with other nations and cooperatively intervening in cases such as these. The Pan American Union, the World Court, the League of Nations were ignored. As the Honorable Elihu Root on December 28 of that same year, 1926, said, 'We have stood out of the League, and we are going on in the old ways, by the old methods—by ourselves.' This single-handed procedure gave occasion for

Latin American suspicion that the United States was too selfishly interested to play the game cooperatively or even justly."

6. From *palmar*, a popular word for "to die" and by extension for to "give death" (kill). Gustavo Alemán Bolaños in his *Sandino!* (Mexico: La República, 1932), p. 9, describes how Sandino entrusted these fourteen- and fifteen-year-olds, numbering about thirty, with guarding some U.S. prisoners—"not without first admonishing them to take good care and making them promise 'that the prisoners would be secure under their vigilance.' But two or three hours later, when the general returned to camp, he found that the prisoners had been dispatched to a better life. . . . The boys explained that 'as these gringos were so big, and the general had told us to take good care. . . .'"

7. Moncada's defeat at Matiguás was thus reported in an Associated Press cable: "General Víquez has informed President Díaz that after a fierce encounter with the Liberals his troops succeeded in capturing the hill positions around Matiguás, Tierra Azul, and Muy Muy. The general adds that the enemy used up almost all of his ammunition and left behind some hundreds of dead and many wounded. He also states that complete and final victory will be won before Holy Week, and that yesterday by his express order his men received the sacrament of communion in a solemn open-air mass and paid homage to the Almighty for the Conservative cause's triumph. Before the news was officially recieved in this city, concrete reports of the bloody action had already been brought by U.S. airmen in Díaz' service who took an active part in the three battles. The good news was celebrated here with rifle salvos, rockets and fireworks, and pealing of church and monastery bells." (*La Nación* [Buenos Aires], April 7, 1927.)

Vicente Sáenz notes that Monsignor Reyes y Valladares, bishop of Granada, excommunicated the Constitutionalists from the pulpit, blessed the arms of the Conservatives, and distributed indulgences, scapularies, and medals among Conservative officers and men.

8. When Moncada had to explain his behavior during the emergency to his officers, he said: "We are 3,000 men with short supplies of ammunition and machine guns. They now have 5,000 with modern arms. I don't doubt that we can achieve initial successes. I know your courage; but I cannot bring myself to lead you into sacrifice, because behind these 5,000 marines thousands more will come as they did in 1912. I would lead you to sure victory as I have always done, but in any case to sure death. However, as your commander I have the obligation to consult the troops, and for this I have come. If it is your wish to fight, I will not abandon you, I will go with you to the sacrifice."

9. Bemis, *Latin American Policy*, p. 213.

10. Henry L. Stimson, *American Policy in Nicaragua* (New York: Arno, 1970 [1927]), pp. 78–79. See also José María Moncada, *Estados Unidos en Nicaragua* (Managua: Tipografía Atenas, 1942), pp. 9–10, where Moncada seeks to justify his surrender, alleging that he was taken under custody to Managua. Later, however, his aide Heberto Correa would describe Moncada as having said to him: "I have no desire for immortality. . . . I don't want to be another Zeledón. I am getting old and if I can live a few more years, so much the better. . . . I say this in connection with the U.S. imposition. . . ."

11. The text of the electoral law was as follows: "(1) With the aid of an expert named by the President of the United States, the Nicaraguan Congress will pass an electoral law approving the points hereunder, *inter alia:* (a) a national electoral commission will be formed to supervise the election and appoint members of departmental councils; (b) this commission will consist of three members: a chairman to be named by the President of the United States, one Conservative, and one Liberal. No action or resolution of this commission will be valid or effective without the approval of the commission's chairman. (2) There will be in each province an electoral commission composed of three members, a Conservative, a Liberal, and a chairman to be named by the national commission. (3) In each polling place there will be an electoral council composed of three members, a Conservative, a Liberal, and a chairman to be named by the national commission. (4) The Liberal and Conservative members of said commissions and councils will be named by the national commission on recommendations from committees of the respective parties. (5) No action or resolution of the provincial commissions and local councils will be valid or effective without the agreement of the [North] American chairman of such commissions and councils respectively. (6) The national armed forces will be dissolved and put out of service simultaneously with disbandment of the opposition forces, and the maintenance of order will be assumed by the National Constabulary to be organized under the instruction, and to the extent possible the direction, of [North] American officers on active service. (7) The National Electoral Commission, provincial commissions, and various local councils will each and all have the right to call on the services of the National Constabulary and give it orders to the end of preventing intimidation and fraud in the election, and of maintaining law and order during the various processes of registration and voting. (8) It is also contemplated that a sufficient force of U.S. marines will remain in the country during organization and instruction of the constabulary and during the election, to reinforce the work of assuring an absolutely impartial election between the two parties."

Chapter 6: The Ant Confronts the Elephant

1. William Krehm, *Democracia y tiranías en el Caribe* (Mexico: Unión Democrática Centroamericana, 1951).
2. Quoted in Alberto Ghiraldo, *Yanquilandia bárbara* (Madrid: Editorial Historia Nueva, 1929).
3. Even a history purportedly on the doctoral level like Samuel Flagg Bemis' *The Latin American Policy of the United States* (New York: Harcourt, Brace, 1943), had to flow with the current (p. 213): "All this [the Blackthorn Peace] took place with general satisfaction, except for the followers of one subaltern *insurrecto* who refused to lay down his arms in the truce of 1927: 'General' Sandino kept on fighting even after his own commander, General Moncada, had been elected President in the Liberal triumph of 1928. Denounced by the leaders of both sides, this partisan took to jungle resistance and was finally killed, treacherously, by the Nicaraguan constabulary in 1934, as he was negotiating with the President near Managua to complete arrangements for surrender. Sandino, a curse to the

common man of Nicaragua, became a mythical hero to anti-Yankee polemicists in Latin America and Europe, and even to some anti-imperialist writers in the United States."

4. The Dunne and Knowles letters are retranslated from *La Nación* (Buenos Aires). (Translator's note).

5. Borah wrote: "Díaz attained the presidency of Nicaragua by intrigues, and retains it by the complacency of the United States. Not only could he not continue as president for an hour if the U.S. Marines departed, but without the aid of the 'neutral zones' and of the United States' extremely partial and conspiratorial neutrality he could not suppress the rebellion of the people against his imposed authority. The people of Nicaragua were and are overwhelmingly opposed to Díaz and his regime. That has been demonstrated more than once in Nicaragua. To recognize him was in my opinion to feed revolution in Central America and to challenge the most basic principles of independence and free government. Nicaragua was weak and we were strong, and when a weak power is near a strong one the fascination of domination seems irresistible.

"But what is done is done. Now the problem is this: How to bring order out of chaos and, at least to an extent, do justice to the people of Nicaragua? How to restore to that people their own government, with the privilege of determining who will be their officials and who will not? It is probable that in any case the plan proposed by Mr. Stimson is the best. Now it is being put into execution.

"There would seem to be two roads to follow. One, withdraw recognition from Díaz, yield to the almost unanimous sentiment of the Nicaraguan people and recognize Sacasa, who in my judgment was the legal president after Solórzano's resignation. But this road was not the most practical or admissible in the eyes of our government, for reasons that can be understood if not approved.

"The other road was to make peace, if possible, and give the Nicaraguan people the opportunity to elect their president. This is the procedure that was adopted. This is one of those cases where it is necessary to do harm to obtain something good. In the normal order of things we would have no business in Nicaragua in the matter of elections. Normally that would be intolerable for Central America and indefensible for us. Normally, it would be another form of imperialism, albeit masked and subtle. But we supported Díaz and now we have fallen into the fact that the people don't recognize or want him as president, and we have reached the conclusion that the Nicaraguan people must be consulted, so that the only road back to a state of order is that the people should have a just opportunity to express their will.

". . . As I see it, some compensatory factors have finally emerged in this unhappy question. The people have given evidence of real national spirit and devotion, and with that a courage worthy of the noblest cause. Many no doubt thought that the opposition to Díaz and his system of government would quickly melt and disappear; that it was simply one faction at war with another because of cravings for benefits and sinecures. But for weeks and months, under the most adverse circumstances and with the most discouraging prospects, the people of Nicaragua have fought, and without any doubt would have won a victory but for the naval forces of the United States. This national spirit has won the recognition and determined policy of the United States, in the sense that the people of Nicaragua are given the opportunity to be heard in an election; and today thousands feel respect for that people. It will be a factor of great weight in the task of channeling present and future matters into an order of normalcy.

"Now it seems evident that our government was on the wrong track from the outset in certain areas. Neither lives nor property of Americans were in any real danger from the Nicaraguan people. Whatever our government's view of this may have been, in all truth what we did was to send forces to defend a weak, unpopular, and illegal government, not to protect U.S. lives and property. Apart from the disturbances and infelicities necessarily accompanying war, I could never find any evidence that any U.S. citizen's life or property was endangered. As for the canal, all we have is a title on paper, and who rejects that title? Who has tried to throw doubt on it? When we consider the circumstances under which that title was acquired, we must admit that its nonrejection is a nice tribute to the Nicaraguan people's patience and friendliness toward the United States.

"The Nicaraguan affair has exposed a well-defined and lamentable aspect of our relations with all Latin America. What of the future? Every day I receive letters from the far corners of the continent expressing the deep disgust of the peoples of Latin America and the deep resentment with which this affair has filled them. But I am full of hope, and it is bolstered by reasons to believe that things will be managed differently in the future and that relations will not deteriorate but get better. . . ."

6. See also Henry L. Stimson, *American Policy in Nicaragua* (New York: Arno, 1970 [1927]). In this book Stimson was at pains to explain that all his country wanted was for peace and stability to reign in "those Central American nations whose territory lies adjacent to and in a naval sense commands the great sea route from our Eastern to our Western states via the Caribbean Sea and the Panama Canal," so that "the vital interest of the United States in its seagoing route through the Panama Canal" should not be imperiled (pp. 104, 109). (Translator's note.)

7. Palacios wrote from Argentina and signed on behalf of the Latin American Union a "message of adhesion to your noble cause. . . . When the North American troops landed in Nicaragua, this institution launched an intense campaign against the northern colossus' new imperialist move—a campaign that is indeed no more than a continuation of that Latin American crusade in which we have been involved since the times of our founder José Ingenieros, denouncing the danger to Latin America of Yanqui imperialist greed and the negative or co-conspiratorial position of our governments. The recent outrages, accelerating the historical process, have ended the period of protests and merely verbal accusations and opened an era in which continuous and resolute action is demanded. . . ."

8. A visitor to Sandino's camp toward the end of his campaign gave these impressions: ". . . The camp was in a clearing beneath bushy trees through which the sun didn't penetrate, and one reached it suddenly without any warning. It had two huts and one bigger one where Sandino was, dressed in khaki riding pants, white shirt and neckerchief, fine calfskin riding boots, and a wide-brimmed straw hat.

Not wearing a pistol or any other weapon, and always in good humor. There were only six men in the camp and a few women whose names I didn't discover, as all called each other 'brother' or 'sister.' Nothing to suggest an army; somewhere a victrola was being played, also a guitar and a trumpet, from which I deduced that this couldn't be Sandino's real headquarters, that there must be another one. I also deduced that there must be more people, and this was confirmed by the fact that each day of my stay I saw an average of three steers cut up. There were also plentiful provisions such as rice, beans, potatoes, and even flour. Also cows, so they didn't lack milk either. And a lot more animals."

And according to General Carlos N. Quezada, "the first thing General Sandino did when he made camp was to open a little path on which he could take a stroll, which he did with his hands linked behind him. It was generally those brief strolls that inspired his sudden and surprising decisions."

9. See Carleton Beals, *America South* (Philadelphia: J. B. Lippincott, 1937), pp. 483–84: ". . . after the World War, with the extension of our cable and news empire to the whole of two continents avowedly with the purpose, along with profit, to promote good-will and commerce, those very agencies, ironically enough, now had to give wide publicity to the battle of Sandino against American marines in Nicaragua. And through the representatives of the United Press and Associated Press there were respectively the American collector of customs, Mr. Clifford D. Ham, and his assistant, Mr. Charles Lindbergh; though most news dispatches from the scene distorted the truth, belittled Sandino, called his followers 'bandits,' glorified the American marines, and said nothing about the aeroplane bombardment of defenseless villages, the marine murder of civilians, the theft and abuses, nevertheless a wave of pride for the man who fought almost single handed so valiantly in the jungle against the might of the greatest nation on earth, swept all of Latin America."

10. General Rafael Riego, liberal revolutionary leader in Spain, executed 1820. (Translator's note.)

Chapter 7: "In Nicaragua, Señores, the Mouse Catches the Cat"

1. Carleton Beals, *The Coming Struggle for Latin America* (Philadelphia: Lippincott, 1938), pp. 217–18.
2. Henry L. Stimson, *American Policy in Nicaragua* (New York: Arno, 1970 [1927]), p. 33, maintains that the *Concón* was not a wreck but one of four ships (along with the *Foam,* the *Tropical,* and the *Superior*) that brought arms and ammunition from Mexico to Nicaragua between August and December 1926. The fact that at this time the United States was trying to incite war against Mexico may help explain this assertion. It may also be noted that when Coolidge referred to these ships, he was careful not to mention whether the proofs obtained to bolster the assertion showed that the cargoes were part of what the United States government had recently sold to Obrégon's government in Mexico "to enable it to suppress a revolution."
3. Emigdio Maraboto, *Sandino ante el coloso* (Mexico: Editorial Vera Cruz, 1929).

1. *Excelsior* (Mexico City), October 17, 1929.
2. Gustavo Alemán Bolaños wrote the following in a courageous *El Heraldo* (Cuba) article while the conference was on: "Each time a speaker opens his mouth and some platitude emerges, Sandino's shadow appears. Each time some honorable delegate's aspirations vaporize into pure brotherly love and he sees . . . 'not one grey cloud in the limpid skies of America,' there enters the shadow of Sandino. And when the hymn to the strong rings out most sonorously . . here's Sandino, coming to perturb the delegates from the heights of the isthmus. Sandino doesn't let us enjoy our Pan-American soup. Comes to the rostrum a member of the 'Nicaraguan' delegation, and Sandino enters simultaneously, a shadow that must produce *some* guilt feelings in the honorable delegates when his name happens precisely to be Augusto—and august he must be, if only for his determined blow for liberty. Yet this presence doesn't scare them, no—hardly disconcerts them. He comes to remind them that there is something around here of what a certain Danish prince sniffed in the air." (*Sandino!* [Mexico: La República, 1932], p. 31.)
3. Samuel Flagg Bemis, *The Latin American Policy of the United States* (New York: Harcourt, Brace, 1943), pp. 251–52. Bemis adds: "The Havana Conference thus presented a diplomatic battleground between the rights and duties of states. Despite the opposition to his program, led by Argentina, El Salvador, Chile, and Mexico, Mr. Hughes succeeded in holding the discussions to the topics on the prepared agenda, including the Rio projects, and in blocking the two objectionable conventions, including notably the doctrine of unqualified nonintervention."
4. A manifesto by Manuel Ugarte and Latin American students, published in *Amauta* (Lima), no. 16 (July 1928), p. 34, and widely circulated in Europe and America, said: "After the Pan-American Conference in Havana, which revealed the incompetence of most of our leaders, a mock election has been announced for Nicaragua which implies further disrepute for Spanish America. In certain circles, patriotism has often consisted of denying realities. If you say that foreign intervention doesn't mean limitation of sovereignty, you are a patriot. If you say nationality remains intact when another country controls the customs, you are a patriot. If you nourish the boastful confidence of weak countries, you are a patriot. Thus some have thought to abolish the dangers by pretending not to see them; thus defeats have been dissembled by refusing to face them; thus we have been brought to this situation of economic and political vassalage which the molders of opinion in our republics never noticed or denounced, and which today puts the autonomous existence of Central and South America on the edge of the abyss.

"We repudiate the politicking that has undermined our future and the dissimulation, not always disinterested, that has poisoned our atmosphere. We want to confront realities, however painful, with the Great Fatherland of the future as our fixed horizon.

"The Nicaraguan crisis stems from three obvious factors. First, the ambitions of the U.S. plutocracy who want to widen their imperialist penetration. Second, the indifference of our America's oligarchic governments, incapable of understanding the problems of the continent. Third, the narrow vision of Nicaraguan politicians, hungry for power even if it is to their country's detriment. Merely stating these phenomena is enough to suggest an attitude toward the problem of Nicaragua.

"Since most of its territory is invaded by foreign troops, and since there is no possibility of voting for the patriots who join the guerrillas in their country's defense, an electoral project is an insult to the people's dignity. The uncontaminated masses of our republics should not let themselves be deceived by the rival cupidities of two cliques traditionally subject to U.S. influence. We are not confused by the sophistry of elections that are a triple travesty: first, because of the presence of invading troops; second, because of these two cliques' submission to the interests of the invader; third, because the elements most deserving respect are condemned to be unheard. Even to discuss such elections would be to lend them an appearance of legality and concede leadership to submissive minorities scrambling for power under the shield of the national enemy.

"The case of Nicaragua cannot be resolved electorally. There are only two parties in the country: *on the one hand, those who accept foreign domination; on the other, those who reject it.* Since the latter cannot vote, public opinion cannot be deceived with empty shams. We cannot then accept that there is any difference between Liberals and Conservatives, and we must stand in solidarity against all the incarnations assumed in our republics by the contemptible egotism of inflated underlings.

"The only leader deserving our enthusiastic support is General Sandino, because he represents with his heroic guerrillas Our America's popular response to Anglo-Saxon imperialism. The comedy of Nicaraguan elections only reveals the collapse beyond recovery of those who had to choose between their own and their country's interests and chose their own. The future will bring down on their heads the condemnation they have earned. And that same future will know, too, how to appraise the altruistic figure of Sandino.

"Our blood has hitherto been shed in sterile civil conflicts that only served to buoy up tyrants and oligarchies. Our peoples' will to fight, their courage and spirit of sacrifice—all the grandeur that lies in Latin American hearts—has been wasted in suicidal agitations, which achieved either confrontations between two factions in the same country or devastation of two or more neighboring republics. If it were possible to unite all these futile immolations in a single lump of heroism, there would be power enough to level the Andes. But instead of applying this popular treasure to the common good, those who held it in their hands have squandered it to serve their personal conceits.

"Now for the first time in decades that blood is flowing for the benefit not of petty ambitions but of us all. That is why we are for Sandino who, in defending his people's freedom, heralds the redemption of our continent.

"(Signed) Manual Ugarte, Latin American University Federation (Madrid); General Association of Latin American Students (Paris); General Association of Latin American Students (Berlin)."

5. Emigdio Maraboto, *Sandino ante el coloso* (Mexico: Editorial Vera Cruz, 1929).
6. *La Tribuna* (San José, Costa Rica), on July 1, 1928, published the views of both banana companies. United said it "respected any decision or arrangement that may be reached, temporary or permanent, with full confidence that in the future as in the past it will continue enjoying the confidence of the governments of the countries where it operates." Cuyamel was "disposed to and desires to cooperate with and help by all means in its power the government of Honduras, in whatever situation it may face, with respect to the border dispute with Guatemala, to the end that, as the company desires, the result of the controversy may be a deserved Honduran victory; and that Honduras may not lose an inch of land, not only in the strip under dispute but also in any Honduran area not in dispute."
7. Charles D. Kepner Jr. and J. H. Soothill, *Banana Empire: A Case Study of Economic Imperialism* (New York: Vanguard, 1935), p. 122: "In answer to attacks in the Honduran press, Zemurray declared that this action had been taken because, due to the new discussion in Nicaragua questioning the arbitrated settlement, the [U.S.] bankers insisted upon a revalidation of the concession."
8. Cited in *Amauta*, no. 19 (November–December 1928), p. 92.

Chapter 9: Fatherland and Freedom

1. Samuel Guy Inman, *Prólogo para América revolucionaria* (Madrid: Editorial Javier Morata, 1933), pp. 17–18.
2. *La Correspondencia Sudamericana* (Buenos Aires), 2nd series, no. 7, January 19, 1929, pp. 17–18.
3. César Falcón would write: "I met him when he was returning to Nicaragua from Mexico. When U.S. imperialist interests were filling the press with the filthy calumny that he had sold out. When after spending his last cartridge and his last man, convinced of the revolutionary futility of letting himself be killed in the mountains, he had left his camp at Las Segovias and we all thought he had stopped making war in order to start making revolution. But Sandino is a man of honor, a fact well known to the Yanqui inventors of the calumnies when he left Nicaragua. He saw himself as in duty bound to show America—an America already convinced of the fact—that he was incapable of selling out for Northern gold.

    "But America was not convinced of the opposite. All the American peoples not merely justified but celebrated his departure from Nicaragua; for in Las Segovias he was fighting for Nicaragua, but outside he could fight for America. For justification, the extent of his army's effectiveness was more than enough. With 300 men, a $1,000 check sent by brothers outside Nicaragua, and a lot of silk flags sent by a grateful America, Sandino could not prolong his action indefinitely."
4. *La Correspondencia Sudamericana*, 2nd series, no. 10 (April 30, 1929), p. 3ff.
5. From the *Diario del Salvador*, July 22: "It was Sandino! A wide-brimmed felt sombrero covered his head. He wore an elegant black and red kerchief tied jauntily around his neck, a checked wool jacket, and high, dark yellow riding boots. A humble lady in the Cisneros barrio, finding herself close to General

Sandino, wanted to embrace him and blessed him in a very moving tone. Dr. Gómez Zarate, the minister of war, and General Antonio Claramount came to pay their respects. Daniel Montalvo, top official of the War Ministry, said after shaking Sandino's hand: 'I won't wash it, so as not to wipe off the hero's imprint!'"

6. Jaime Suárez Silva commented in the Havana *Diario de la Marina:* "A moment's thought about the long duration of Sandino's revolution suffices to throw doubt on the Yanqui marines' chances of success in that country. Sandino has the whole continent behind him. Nicaraguan women have demonstrated their wrath against the foreign intervention by killing marines in brothels. Children have refused to learn English in school, and at a U.S. military parade which they were forced to attend they refused to sing the Yanqui anthem and fearlessly and defiantly intoned Sandino's war cry: 'Death to the traitors!' Inmates of old people's homes decline to use Yanqui products given them as presents. At the time of the last earthquake in Managua, people preferred to sleep outdoors rather than in a shelter imported from the United States. This is the expression, the feeling of the common people."

Chapter 10: General of Free Men

1. In *The Nation* (New York), February 22, 1928, p. 204.
2. The anti-imperialist Argentine magazine *Renovación,* in an editorial commenting on electioneering aspects of the junket, said: "Mr. Hoover, whether he wanted to or not, has beaten all speed records by crossing a mere trio of countries in less than 200 hours since he landed. This would seem enough to show that his purpose is not serious. . . . The Pacific dictatorships put out for him a carpet of official applause, and Mr. Hoover has walked it without tripping. Then he arrived at the Rio de la Plata and ran into popular demonstrations *viva*-ing Sandino. Mr. Hoover cannot have felt very comfortable, for after that he canceled his visits to Mexico, Venezuela, Cuba, and some Caribbean countries."
3. Cited in *La Correspondencia Sudamericana* (Buenos Aires), 2nd series, no. 23 (December 31, 1929), pp. 6–7.
4. Moncada unhesitatingly ordered massacres of his own countrymen to win merit points, as Colonel Celso Morales N. of his own bodyguard attested: "While I was still doing his dirty work I saw these civilians killed: Cruz Chavarría and Antonio Aráuz of Jucuapa; Jerónimo López of El Paraíso, Brígido Aguinaga of Muy Muy; Francisco Escoria of El Chafernal; Virgilio Ruiz, throat cut at the San Rafael hacienda of Salvador Amador; twenty-five Indians of Matiguás whom I could not identify, shot by General Moncada's direct order for their stubbornness in confessing they were for Chamorro; Eligio Sosa of Matiguás; Melesio Mendoza of Puntazuela, hanged and face skinned for razzing Moncada; an Indian of Samulalí because he was carrying some sugar and seemed to be heading in a Conservative direction; Inés Sánchez of Esquipulas; Leónidas Orozco from my own town Jaumaguí; Avelino Salgado of Malpaso; Basilio Torres, young son of Toribio Espinosa, a Liberal of Maisana, because they found him playing with some Springfield cartridges. Another boy of eleven, son of a Malpaso Valley lady,

was shot because he didn't want to say where his father was, and many others whose names I don't recall."

5. In his *Orígen, auge y crisis de una dictadura* (Guatemala: Imprenta Iberia, p. 9), Armando Amador writes: "There was in the Moncada government's foreign relations subsecretariat an individual who, making the best of his position and of his Creole shrewdness, became the lover of Yankee ambassador Hanna's wife. This undersecretary was Anastasio Somoza, who was later nominated to head the National Guard, not only because what education he had was obtained in the United States, but mainly for the political insurance he offered to imperialism and through the influence of his mistress Mrs. Hanna."

Ex-*Time* correspondent William Krehm in *Democracias y tiranías en el Caribe* (Mexico: Unión Democrática Centroamericana, 1951), concurs with this view: "The American Minister, Hanna, and his wife were bewitched by Tacho's effervescent personality. Mrs. Hanna, considerably her husband's junior, adored dancing and Tacho danced so very, very well. Shortly before his death Moncada related to me how Hanna had urged him to groom Somoza for the presidential succession. Moncada demurred; the Liberal Party had nominated Dr. J. B. Sacasa, who did not get along with Moncada. But to please the doting Hannas, the foxy old Moncada did name Somoza commander of the National Guard when the time came to replace the American commander with a native son."

6. *La Nación* (Buenos Aires).

Chapter 11: The Yanquis Went Home!

1. Sofonías Salvatierra, *Sandino o la tragedia de un pueblo* (Madrid: Europa, 1934), p. 104. Most of the documents cited here about the peace negotiations are from this source.

2. Salvatierra's version (ibid., pp. 173–74) is the following: "Very early next morning, February 1, we were ready to go when a lady, one of the owners of the place, said: 'What's the matter with the general? He hardly slept all night.' Moments later Sandino emerged and said, pacing up and down as he always did: 'I got up in a romantic-tragic mood; I think we've got to make peace in these five days or I'll kill myself; and the way to do it is for me to go and seek a direct understanding with Dr. Sacasa.' I realized this news would cause a big sensation in the presidential palace, becuase if the offered guarantees were not forthcoming it would aggravate things for the president's policy and for the peace of the country. All these fears stemmed from the disturbing mistrust which the Guard had aroused by ignoring the orders of the high command. That whole night there was no sleep in government house in Managua. . . ."

Ramón de Belausteguigoitia cites General Portocarrero in a similar version (*Con Sandino en Nicaragua* [Madrid: Espasa-Calpe, 1934], p. 38): "'All partisans of Sandino,' General Portocarrero tells me, 'above all Dr. Zepeda and myself, have believed that with the Americans gone, no reason exists for continuing the war. We were in the camp discussing the possible bases for peace, when General Sandino came up to me and said: "I got up feeling romantic and tragic. I'm going to Managua to make peace, and if I don't make it my life is over." "Don't do that," I said, inferring what he had in mind in case he failed. "Your life doesn't belong to you." "No," he said, "I've thought it out well." . . . We all know the general's stubbornness. That same day I called together his lieutenants and troops and told them what he was planning: he was going himself to Managua to see the president, and if his mission didn't succeed he wouldn't live a moment longer—he wasn't a man to sit in jail, I said. I'll tell you, we were dumbfounded. Sandino's top lieutenants surrounded him trying to convince him, and tears came to the eyes of all of them. He was inexorable. We went to Jinotega, and you know the rest.'"

3. Salvatierra (*Sandino*, p. 180), notes: "Between Sandino and his lieutenants there was a very close bond: that is why they stuck with him through all the privations. The nature of that bond left the opposing camp with no expectation except death—a conviction instilled in them by sad experience. The closeness of the bond was evident when Sandino called all his generals to a separate room and we saw them emerge a while later wiping away tears. Those rough-hewn types, whom nothing could faze, wept at the prospect of Sandino's unexpected and dangerous journey."

Chapter 12: "A Free Country or Death!"

1. José Vasconcelos, *Bolivarismo y monroísmo* (Santiago de Chile; Ercilla, 1937), p. 190.

2. Confirmation that strategic and political factors were the heart of the intervention is provided by a conversation between Vicente Sáenz and President Sacasa on February 6, 1933, revealed by Sáenz in his *Rompiendo cadenas,* 2nd ed., (Mexico: Unión Democrática Centroamericana, 1951), pp. 239ff., from which we cite the following:

"*Sáenz:* It seems to me, doctor, that the economic question has never been paramount in the U.S. interventions in Nicaragua. The big power has no large capital invested here in trade, in agriculture, in cattle-raising, or in industry to justify the arrival of warships and landing of marines. Except for the La Luz and Los Angeles mine of which Secretary of State Knox and the Fletcher family controlled the shares and Adolfo Díaz was bookkeeper at $35 a week, a few concessionaires who form ad hoc companies to exploit national forests, and a few banana plantations on the Atlantic coast, one doesn't know of any other U.S. interests in our territory.

"*Sacasa:* But there are contracts with U.S. banks resulting from the loans we've received. That is, an intimate relationship with the foreign capital investments that constitute our external debt.

"*Sáenz:* If I'm not misinformed, Nicaragua's external debt is only $2.3 million, most of it to British bankers and the rest, a much smaller part, to Wall Street lenders who in fact never lent anything because they used the Republic's own funds to simulate loans. We all know they appropriated the $3 million produced by the 1914 canal treaty. Well, the cost of an intervention such as the country has suffered for so long exceeds in one year the $2.3 million that is Nicaragua's total debt to the United States and Britain.

"*Sacasa:* Sure, in round numbers that's all we owe abroad.

"*Sáenz:* So one can deduce, doctor, that the essence of the intervention here is political, military, strategic, as that devout Methodist Frank B. Kellogg said it was in 1926. Concretely, the misfortune of Nicaragua, which is the misfortune of Central America, lies in what ought to be one of its surest sources of wealth and progress, the interocean canal. And good has been converted into bad by the Bryan-Chamorro Treaty, the treaty of treason, the treaty of imperialism. . . .

"If with respect to the Bryan-Chamorro Treaty, the basic pretext of foreign intervention, you leave it as it is; and if you don't denounce the 1923 treaty which Washington uses as a pretext to impose its will on us, how can we have autonomy as stipulated in the peace conditions signed by you and Sandino four days ago?

"*Sacasa:* You can't change these things without provoking contrary moves by the Conservatives who signed them and accepted them as good. Regarding the 1923 treaties, I sincerely think they're necessary. Furthermore, it's incorrect to spurn the goodwill of the U.S. government which wants to help us. I find the thesis of El Salvador and Costa Rica too radical. What in my view should be done is a simple revision of those agreements, correcting what is wrong and leaving what is right. . . ."

3. According to William Krehm, *Democracias y tiranías en el Caribe* (Mexico: Unión Democrática Centroamericana, 1951), "Sacasa was by no means eager to liquidate Sandino as a political factor, for that would leave him alone to face his disquietingly ambitious National Guard commander. Somoza was not happy about the arrangement. He tried playing off both ends against the middle. Though his guards were worrying and occasionally assassinating the *sandinistas,* he went out of his way to win Sandino's confidence. When the guerrilla leader arrived at Managua in rags, Somoza graciously had a pair of old britches sent up to him from the National Guard barracks, and then the two were photographed together in a friendly embrace. In December 1933 he proposed an alliance to a lieutenant of Sandino's against Sacasa. 'The old imbecile is ruining the country. He opposes me only because he knows that Sandino is behind him. Together we could force a new cabinet on him with Sandino as war minister.'

"When Sandino refused to fall in with the plan, Somoza filled Sacasa's ears with stories of an imminent *sandinista* coup. To offset his bumptious relative, Sacasa put a Sandino lieutenant in charge of four northern departments. It was throwing down the gauntlet to Somoza."

4. Sofonías Salvatierra, *Sandino o la tragedia de un pueblo* (Madrid: Europa, 1934), pp. 244ff.

5. Abelardo Cuadra, *Bohemia* (Havana) no. 7 (February 13, 1949). Cited in *Revolución* (San José, Costa Rica), organ of the Nicaraguan Revolutionary Party, May 1954.

6. Cuadra, ibid.

7. Salvatierra, *Sandino,* p. 246.

8. Among the many versions of these events is Krehm's, which adds interesting details about Somoza's later antics: ". . . Sandino came to Managua with a sack of rock samples under his arm. He was convinced that he had struck gold near his Wiwilí colony, and was breathless with plans for a cooperative mine. That

evening he dined with Sacasa, accompanied by his brother and two aides. As Sandino and his comrades left the presidential palace, they were seized by the National Guard and informed that they must face the firing squad. Remembering the enthusiastic back-thumping of his good friend Somoza a few months earlier, Sandino asked to speak to the commander. Over the telephone Somoza was his usual genial self. He was awfully put out to hear about Sandino's plight, but he just couldn't countermand the orders of his subordinate. Sandino and his companions were executed near the American Embassy. That same evening, with slick timing, the National Guard surrounded the *sandinista* camp at Wiwilí and turned machine guns on the occupants. Three hundred men, women, and children fell under the bullets. . . .

". . . Sacasa did not raise his voice in protest against this carnage. With Sandino gone, he felt himself a guest in the presidential palace.

"To justify the deed, Somoza played up the earlier atrocities of the *sandinistas*. He burst into authorship and produced a book which, carefully read, bears more damning witness against the writer than against the villain. He even had himself triply decorated for his bloody feat with the Cross of Bravery, Medal of Distinction, and Presidential Medal of Merit."

9. In the magazine *Sábado* (Havana), no. 132, (1946).

10. This same policeman was the author of the editorial published by *El Centro-americano* of León on March 8, 1934, which is the frankest admission of responsibility for the crime. These paragraphs help us understand why Somoza ordered the killing of Sandino:

"Sandino was the symbol of patriotism, consecrated by the literature of Latin America and by our race's hatred of the United States. His rebelliousness against the interventionist forces in 1926 gave him the character of a patriot. But the world did not want to see the germ of perfidy that was growing in this man. The hero of one day became a bandit and the patriot unleashed his bloodthirsty hordes to impoverish the Republic and bring fire and death to the largest and richest part of the country. He instilled terror and made Las Segovias a place of fear, if not a desert. He invented torture and the 'waistcoat cut' [chopping off arms to the shoulder] in those once tranquil and blooming regions, and the soil became sterile wherever this barbarian set his feet.

"When Jinotega heard of Sandino's death, joyful bells rang out, and the homes of Estelí burst forth with flowers. Those departments were the chief theater of this plundering vandal who in other lands, too distant to know, appears as the Bolívar of our century.

"When his unjustifiable crimes and the anguished cry of Las Segovias had categorized him as an evildoer, he let his ambition fly and succeeded in becoming a true peril to the state. Protected by the well-known good faith of the president of the Republic, he got control of four departments, thus forming a real state within the state of Nicaragua. His goal was to smash national sovereignty, discredit the existing government by making it appear weak and without support, and lay the foundations for a plan of despoliation disastrous for the country's future, for the institutions which now prevail in Central America.

"This being so, the army, the backbone of constituted government, did its duty of safeguarding national decorum and public tranquility. And the Guard cut off a rotting branch to avoid a hecatomb. It used its legitimate right of defense and saved Nicaragua from a bloody civil war, demonstrating its loyalty to the president of the Republic, albeit at the cost of sacrifice.

"Since Sandino was a danger to peace, it was the army's duty to remove that danger, as it is to be the robust pillar supporting the live faith of Nicaraguans in peace and in their sovereignty. Furthermore, Sandino was outside the law. In the last statement he made to the press he said Nicaragua had only three powers: the president of the Republic, the National Guard, and himself. That was to declare himself in rebellion against the majesty of the State, naming himself as a power in conflict with the constituted powers. The Guard has never made such a claim, it could not do so without striking a note of rebellion. The National Guard is, if you please, the robust force of public power organized under our Fundamental Charter, but never power itself—for such a claim would impair its lofty mission of being the pillar of institutions and the guarantee of peace. From the moment when Sandino called himself Power, then, he declared war on the government and put himself outside the law."

Chapter 13: The Assassin at His Banquet

1. Hubert Herring, *Good Neighbors* (New Haven: Yale University Press, 1941), p. 301.
2. Krehm says that Somoza inspected "whether the citizens had poured kerosene into their outhouses to keep the mosquitoes down. His friends dubbed him 'The Marshal' because the flashlight he carried, to take a good look below deck, did resemble a marshal's baton."

    The data about counterfeiting money were given to the Mexican magazine *Hoy* by no less than Emiliano Chamorro, who had many reasons to know the man he was talking about and many more to envy him.
3. John Gunther, *Inside Latin America* (New York: Harper, 1941), p. 139.
4. "As the time for the next presidential elections drew near, General Anastasio Somoza announced that he would represent the Liberal Party for the office of President. In January, 1936, Sacasa advised Somoza not to appear as a candidate. For two reasons Somoza would be constitutionally ineligible for the presidency. First, he was a nephew of Sacasa, the President who would be administering the affairs of the country at the time of the elections; and second, he was Commander of the National Guard. Vice President Rodolfo Espinosa declared that he would wage war against Somoza if he persisted in trying to be elected. But Somoza would not withdraw. He was supported by the National Guard, by former President Moncada, and by a newly organized Fascist group, the Blue Shirts.

    "Sacasa met the challenge of his nephew by persuading the Sacasa Liberals to join with the Conservatives headed by former President Emiliano Chamorro, form a new united party, and nominate for the Presidency the Liberal Foreign Minister, Leonardo Argüello. This united party had hardly been organized when, late in May, Somoza began an armed revolt. To avoid war Sacasa resigned on June 6, and Congress appointed a provisional president. By resigning Sacasa removed one of the constitutional barriers against his nephew. On June 15 Somoza received a formal nomination from a convention of Liberals, and this nomination was approved by some of the Conservatives. Then, to remove another constitutional impediment, Somoza resigned as head of the National Guard, but he did not do this until a month previous to the date of the elections." (David R. Moore, *A History of Latin America* [New York: Prentice-Hall, 1938], p. 707.)

5. ". . . Wolf fattens them on his ranch at Chomes near Puntarenas. These exports do not exist as far as Nicaraguan statistics are concerned, but turn up in Costa Rican records. The Costa Rican Statistical Report for 1943 gives cattle imports from Nicaragua as 8,562 head. But the Nicaraguan Year Book for 1942 places the total exports from Nicaragua for the same year (not only to Costa Rica, but to Panama and Peru) as 1,467. The 7,185 head that entered Costa Rica from Nicaragua, but didn't leave Nicaragua for Costa Rica, are one of the many miracles of the Somoza regime." (William Krehm, *Democracia y tiranía en el Caribe* [Mexico: Unión Democrática Centroamericana, 1951], p. 164.)

6. Ibid., p. 172.

7. Gunther, *Inside Latin America,* pp. 137–40. On page 141 he tells us: "Economically as well as politically, Nicaragua is closely dependent on the United States. The collector-general of customs is an American, Irving Lindberg; so is General Mullins, director of the military academy of which Somoza is very proud. The United States takes a full 95 percent of Nicaraguan exports (chiefly bananas, tropical produce, mahogany, gold), and furnishes 85 percent of its imports. The Export-Import Bank recently lent the country $2,000,000 for work on a highway from Managua to the east coast, which will assist its lagging internal development. Teaching of English is to be made compulsory in the local schools."

8. On the negotiations about this project, see Gregorio Selser, "Canales y diplomacia," in *Diplomacia, garrote y dólares en América Latina* (Buenos Aires: Palestra, 1962), pp. 199–220.

9. "The game played with foreign exchange is for big stakes by any standard. When the Marines were in Nicaragua, it was brutal imperialism and all that, but they helped keep the *córdoba* firm at parity with the dollar by spending a lot of Uncle Sam's money. There were many speeches and much rejoicing when they left: but before anybody realized it, the *córdoba* got the bends. It was not only that the blue-uniformed tourists had gone, but coffee prices tumbled, and disease put an end to banana exports. Budgetary inflation also played its part; in 1932 an earthquake flattened the capital and the government overworked the printing presses to pay for the expenses incurred. Though parity with the dollar officially continued as a beloved and lingering fairy tale, *córdobas* were being offered for quarters and dimes. Somoza, born under a lucky star, reached the presidency when the world was pulling out of the depression. Gold mining boomed and put coffee in a back seat. In 1939 a Chilean economist was brought in to see about putting the *córdoba* into shape. It became a managed currency backed by a dollar and gold stabilization fund, and instead of maintaining the pretense of parity, it was allowed to drop to five to one.

"Nevertheless the black market in dollars continued and continues to this day. Somoza's friends buy the dollars to pay for their imports at the National Bank at five to one, but most merchants must get them on the black market for six, and six and a fraction, and sometimes more than seven *córdobas* apiece. At the same time they are required to surrender the dollar credits arising from their exports at the rate of five to one. By this process businessmen are mulcted some 20 percent on all their transactions with the outside world. . . .

"The wonder of it all is that from the official figures, there is apparently no reason for the *córdoba* sagging so. On March 31, 1945, the stabilization fund supporting the *córdoba* amounted to 33.8 million *córdobas* or 72 percent of the country's entire circulation. The budget is reported balanced. The commercial balance was broadly favorable—$15,412,444 in exports for 1944 against $10,279,951 in imports—quite apart from the nonrecorded shipments of cattle. . . . By all known norms of economics the *córdoba* should be sturdy. The key to the mystery seems to be the huge quantities of money that Somoza has been sending outside the country against a stormy day. Most of his properties are mortgaged with the National Bank at inflated figures, and the money sent abroad. He does not wish to be caught by a revolution with the bulk of his worldly goods in Nicaragua." (Krehm, *Democracia y tiranía*, p. 169.)

10. According to *La Nación* (Buenos Aires), November 20, 1928, Nicaragua's legation in Washington had said the country had a debt of $6,089,000. And according to Mr. Cumberland this broke down as follows: 1909 debt, $3,297,000 at 5 percent, guaranteed with customs due; merchandise bought from El Salvador without guarantees, $55,000; U.S. loan in merchandise at 6 percent, $265,000 due in 1933; internal bonds at 5 percent, $2,372,000; other unspecified debts, $100,000.

11. Nicaraguan city blocks.

12. "In 1942 the Bank of London and South America put to auction the farm 'Alemania' belonging to Julio Bahlke, who had hidden Somoza on his plantation after his 1926 defeat at San Marcos. At the announced hour, Somoza's chief of staff, Colonel Camilo González, arrived with an entourage of machine guns to discourage competitive bidders. Somoza bought the farm for $60,000, about a tenth of its real value.

"When the Airfields Development Project (the U.S. government and Pan-American Airways) began planning their new airfield at Las Mercedes, near Managua, Somoza embarked upon energetic land purchases in the vicinity. One citizen called Murillo who was unfortunate enough to have a strategic holding was beaten up by the National Guard, and informed through his lawyer that the drubbings would continue until he sold his land. He sold to Somoza, and Somoza passed the property on to the Americans at a good-neighborly profit.

". . . In approximate terms Somoza is the proud possessor of fifty-one cattle ranches and forty-six coffee estates within Nicaragua, and is by far the largest coffee producer. Some of this real estate he came by legitimately through shrewd buying ('My father taught me that it is wiser to buy from heirs')." (Krehm, *Democracia y tiranía*, p. 166.)

13. "Somoza levies $20 per 1,000 board feet of mahogany and other precious woods embarked on the Atlantic coast. . . . Somoza's brother-in-law, Colonel Luis Manuel Debayle, when minister of health, ran the government quinine monopoly to fine purpose; quinine generously mixed with flour sold at outrageous prices in a fever-ridden land." (Ibid.)

14. "After Pearl Harbor, when Nicaragua blossomed forth as an important source of rubber, Somoza waded in and organized his take. He divided the rubber territory amongst a group of favorites who, with money advanced by the National Bank, commenced buying up rubber from the gatherers at 60 *córdobas* and reselling it to the United States at 130. But toward the end of 1942 the Rubber Reserve Corporation warned him off and sent their own men into the rubber region to buy directly from the producers. Somoza, sensing that Washington had a vital concern here, did not persist in his attempt to 'organize' the industry." (Ibid., pp. 167–68.)

15. The chapter of Dávila's book beginning on p. 52, "When Rubber Dropped and Didn't Bounce," provides a microcosm of our peoples' whole drama of colonial dependency.

"In 1912 rubber production reached a new high of 45,000 tons in Brazil, and in 1913 Asian production topped Latin American for the first time. In the early twenties Latin America contributed only 19,000 tons to a world consumption of 317,000; in 1927, hardly 6 percent of a 567,000-ton total. By the eve of World War II in 1938, Latin America had surrendered to Asia 98 percent of the world market, then consuming 895,000 tons. Thus in 1934, 98 percent of the producers were in a situation to organize a closed cartel and impose the price on world buyers.

"The United States then bought two-thirds of that rubber, paying $275 million a year for it. U.S. consumers paid high prices for rubber products, and Latin America, producer of the raw material, bought expensive U.S. tires made of Asian material. Then came the war to cut the vital Pacific supply line, and the United States had none of the material that headed the army's strategic products list.

"What happened then is history: with U.S. direction and financing, the race began to restore production at any price, in Brazil, Mexico, Haiti, Colombia, Ecuador, Venezuela, Honduras, Nicaragua, Panama, Guatemala, and Costa Rica; and the United States improvised a synthetic rubber industry valued at $750 million. As a result of all this, Latin American rubber production rose from a prewar 15,000 tons to 32,164 in 1945. Today it is again sinking rapidly." (Dávila, *Nosotros, los de las Américas* [Santiago de Chile: Editorial Pacífico, 1950].)

16. Greatly depreciated (see note 9): originally the *córdoba* was approximately $1.

17. "War scarcities to Somoza were what Prohibition had been to Al Capone. Nails, tires, machetes were sold through friends at anywhere from 200 to 600 percent over cost. It was a field day, but the scandal grew to such proportions that he felt compelled to hand over price control to the American Sub-administrator of Customs, Major T. G. Downing." (Krehm, *Democracia y tiranía*, p. 168.)

18. Krehm arrived in Managua just at the time of these events, which cost prison and exile to hundreds of opponents. He relates in his lively style:

"In a resplendent limousine bearing an official license plate arrived Nicolasa Sevilla, working madam of one of Managua's cut-rate brothels. Flourishing a knife, she threatened the wives and daughters of the capital's fancier families, and spewed spirited obscenities at them. Her eloquence was backed up by swarms of screeching strumpets, who jostled and insulted the demonstrators. The 'loyal' forces carried the day by surprise. Afterward Somoza received 'La Nicolasa' in the presidential palace and thanked 'his good friend' in hearty language proper to her trade. Nicolasa, indeed, became quite a pillar of the regime, and even invaded the Assembly to buffet oppositionist deputies. Several months later the cause was deprived of her services when she was wounded in a brothel brawl and confined to bed nonprofessionally."

Krehm later interviewed Somoza for *Time:* "I began by asking him whether he wasn't sore at *Time* for allusions recently published. No, it was still his favorite magazine. Only there were a lot of people going around Managua spreading slanders about him. I told him I had three notebooks and a bellyful of Somoza's businesses and I didn't wish to discuss them. But discuss them we somehow did. On cattle he flushed a little when I mentioned the names of his chief purchasing agents. He finally suggested that I see X, a leading cattleman who had been allowed to export to Costa Rica, as proof that he didn't hog the trade for himself. Since X had been my principal informant on cattle, I felt that I was on the right track. . . . As we continued on his enterprises, his voice became plaintive. 'Goddamit, I wanta make sure my family has enough to live on when I die.' He admitted that he obtains credits from the Central Bank that he could never hope to get if he were a private citizen. But he does it for the country's good. He had worked hard ever since he was a kid. . . . 'Goddamit, I'm tired of the presidency. I work like a dog.'" (Ibid, p. 175.)

19. International Labor Office, *Salarios mínimos en América Latina* (Geneva, 1954), p. 141, where the character of recent labor legislation in America may be studied *in extenso*.

20. Krehm, *Democracia y tiranía,* p. 177, notes concerning Decree 336: "In April 1945 a Labor Code was actually passed. Without a doubt it was the most extravagant in Latin America, and perhaps in the world. The workers were promised the moon . . . on paper: four weeks paid vacations annually; six weeks paid leave for pregnant women workers before delivery and six afterward. But none of this was ever implemented. As the country's principal capitalist, passionately attached to pennies, Somoza's interests lay elsewhere. His foreign minister was attorney for La Luz Mining Company that exploits the Mosquito Indians in iniquitous fashion. When a couple of gold mines were shut down by strikes in June 1945, the government was anything but encouraging to the unions, and Somoza's flirtation with labor came to an abrupt close. Shortly afterward he expelled from the country the chief *lombardista* leaders [Vicente Lombardo Toledano, Mexican labor leader then trying to form an all–Latin America labor confederation]."

21. At a Fourth of July banquet in the U.S. embassy in 1948, Somoza declared: "The problem of most concern to my government is compulsory unemployment. Never have we felt so dangerous a crisis as that we are going through." He went on to offer the panacea: "a war against the communists, against the USSR, could save democracy from the crisis."

Chapter 14: Sandino's Glory and Renown

1. Greek youths who killed the tyrant Hippias (514 B.C.). (Notes in this chapter are the translator's.)
2. Fortress in which Spaniards held out for fifteen months against Roman invaders (134–133 B.C.).
3. Portuguese rebel leader against Romans, executed (140 B.C.).
4. Spanish heretic burned at the stake (1553).
5. Indian rebels against Spanish conquistadors in Peru and Alto Peru.

Afterword

1. Most of the force that took up arms against the Somoza tyranny were young folk—adolescents and even children—and *los muchachos* (the lads) was the term by which Nicaraguans spoke of them. To talk about the *sandinistas* was to invite prison or death at the hands of the National Guard.
2. A. C. Sandino, *Manifiesto a los pueblos de la tierra y en especial al de Nicaragua,* March 13, 1933 (Managua: Tipografía La Prensa, 1933).

Bryce, James Lord, 27
Bucareli treaties, 64
Buchanan, James, 17, 23
Buitrago Díaz, Salvador, 155, 159
Butler, Maj. Smedley, 35, 205, 212n

Cabañas, Trinidad, 14
Cabezas, Gen. Rigoberto, 24
Cabrerita (guitarist), 86
Caldera, Augusto, 76, 109
Caldera, Octavio A., 186
Calderón Guardia, 184
Calderón Ramírez, Salvador, 158, 164, 175
Calles, Plutarco Elías, 53, 64, 217n–19n
Calvo, Joaquín Bernardo, 27
Canal construction: in Colombia, 22
———: in Nicaragua, 21–23; Peace Protocol and, 162; Sandino on U.S. rights over, 77; temporary agreement for (1850), 10; Vanderbilt and, 11; Zelaya opposes U.S. for, 26; *See also* Bryan-Chamorro Treaty
Canales, Sgt. Emilío, 175
Cañas-Jerez Treaty (1857), 21, 23
Cannon, Lee Roy, 29, 31, 33, 36
Caperton, Admiral, 46
Carazo, Evaristo, 24
Cárdenas, Adán, 24
Cárdenas, Zoila Rosa, 176
Carranza, Venustiano, 86
Carranza Doctrine, 124
Carrera, Rafael, 13
Cass, Gen. Lewis, 22
Cass-Irissari Treaty (1857), 22–23
Castellano, Lic. Francisco, 14, 15, 35
Castellón, Cayetano, 101
Castrillo, Salvador, 34

Castro, José N., 178
Centeno, Col. Dionisio, 132
Central American Court of Justice, 25, 43, 103
Central American Federal Congress, 22
Chacón, Lázaro, 107, 109, 136
Chamorro, Diego Manuel, 37, 38, 49
Chamorro, Frutos, 14, 15
Chamorro, Gen. Emiliano, 34, 41, 49, 51, 76, 149; and all-out effort to destroy Sandino (1929), 112; background of, 44; on behavior of National Guard (1933), 169; becomes president, 45–46; Bryan-Chamorro Treaty and, 44; coups led by, 28–29, 32–33, 49–50; and Mena War, 35, 38; 1927 visit to Washington by, 93; in 1932 elections, 140, 146, 147; and Patriotic Group, 155; Sandino on, 144; Somoza and, 180, 181, 193; supports coup against Argüello, 194
Chamorro, Pedro Joaquín, 24, 148, 155
Chávarri, Gen. Manuel, 94
Chavarría, Col. Perfecto, 153
Chiang Kaishek, 83
Church (Catholic): opposes Sandino, 120
Clarence, Henry, 24
Clayton-Bulwer Treaty (1850), 10, 23, 209n
Cole, Bundy, 40
Cole, Byron, 14, 15
Colindres, Gen. Juan Gregorio, 80, 94, 143; death of, 195; as head of provisional government, 152, 153
Colindres, Mejía, 106

Intervention: British, 24–25; end of European, 25; Honduran, in Nicaragua (1854), 14; U.S., in Dominican Republic, 81; U.S., in Guatemala (1954), 102, 105, 205
————: U.S., in Nicaragua: Root on need for, 28; Seventh Pan-American Conference and putting an end to, 184; Sixth Pan-American Conference and, 103–4; Walker and first, 14–20, 22, 23, 32, 35, 131, 205; *see also: Sandinista* army; Sandino, Augusto Nicolás Calderón; United States Marines; *and specific presidents and treaties*
————: U.S., threat of, against Mexico (1922), 63
Investments, *see* Economy
Irías, Gen. Alfonso, 132, 157
Irías, Julián, 46, 156
Irissari, Dr., 22

Jackson, Andrew, 22
Jarquín, Lt. Tranquilino, 129
Jefferson (U.S. minister to Nicaragua), 46
Jefferson, Thomas, 11
Jerez, Gen. Máximo, 14, 15, 19, 21–22
Jiménez, Sebastian, 152
Jiméncz Prado, Rito, 195
Juárez, Benito, 123

Kellogg, Frank B., 55–58, 60, 62, 64, 93, 103, 144, 205
Kirkland, Samuel, 11
Knowles, H. H., 81
Knox, Philander C., 25, 27–33, 37, 40, 100
Knox-Castrillo Treaty, 35

Krehm, William, 72, 74, 178, 181, 183

Labor Confederation (Nicaraguan), 194
Labor force, *see* Economy
Labor movement, *see* Left, the
Lacayo, Federico J., 155, 159
Lacayo Sacasa, Benjamin, 194
Ladd, Edwin, 51
Lane, Arthur Bliss, 174, 177
Lansing Plan, 46, 214*n*
Lara, Gen. Escolástico, 158, 163, 164
Latimer, Adm. Julian, 53, 54, 57, 66, 71, 102
Law, George, 12
Lay, Julius, 149
Layrac, Louis, 32
League of Campesinos (Nicaraguan), 186
League against Imperialism, 97
Lebowasky, Lt. Charles, 151–52
Lee, Lieutenant, 154
Left, the: Mexican, 63; in Guatemala and El Salvador, 193;
————: in Nicaragua: Argüello and, 194; Somoza opposed by, 185–88, 191–94; and victory of National Liberation Front, 205
Liberal Party (Nicaraguan), *see* Liberals
Liberals:
————: Nicaraguan, 24, 70, 156, 164, 171–73, 192; under F. Chamorro, 14; and Dawson accords, 34; joining *sandinista* army, 69; Martínez tries to unify Conservatives with, 49; in Mena War, 35; in 1916 elections, 46; and 1926 intervention, 54–56 (*see*

Sandino

by Gregorio Selser
Translated by Cedric Belfrage

This is a compelling and dramatic account of a struggle in Nicaraguan history which is well-known throughout Latin America, but which has never received the attention in the United States which it so richly merits: in 1927 a guerrilla war was unleashed in the jungles and mountains of Nicaragua by a ragged and hungry group of compatriots who grew in number from 26 to 3,000 — against 6,000 well-fed, well-trained, and well-equipped U.S. Marines. For seven years the invaders were held at bay.

The leader of this remarkable guerrilla band was Augusto César Sandino. A mechanic and miner of peasant and Indian stock, he never lost sight of his prime objective: to rid Nicaragua of the U.S. army of occupation and the business interests it was protecting: "Seeing that the United States of North America, lacking any right except that with which brute force endows it, would deprive us of our country and our liberty, I have accepted its unjust challenge, leaving to History the responsibility for my actions."

And indeed, history has more than vindicated Sandino. The seeds he and his followers planted have come to fruition a little more than fifty years later; the Frente Sandinista de Liberación Nacional has not only